"Pastors minister; theologians seek—and minister—understanding. Ministering understanding of how the Bible addresses real-world issues is the great privilege and responsibility of the pastor theologian. Gerald Hiestand and Todd Wilson have put together a whole ministry team that ministers understanding worth its weight in gold on one of the most socially complicated, politically fraught, yet existentially unavoidable issues of our day or any: human sexuality. In an age where the male/female duality is in danger of becoming extinct, these essays serve as salient reminders of the beauty and mystery of God's created order: 'Male and female he created them' (Gen 1:27)."

Kevin J. Vanhoozer, research professor of systematic theology, Trinity Evangelical Divinity School

"For Gerald Hiestand and Todd Wilson, the ideal of the pastor-scholar is not merely theoretical but intensely practical. The example they set through their Center for Pastor Theologians is an invitation to practice ecclesial theology. So is their new volume of thoughtful essays on God's beautiful, well-ordered, and yet mysterious purposes for human sexuality—a book that demonstrates the value and relevance of having a community of wise scholars 'do' theology in the service of the church."

Philip Ryken, president, Wheaton College

"There's a public conversation about human sexuality happening nearly everywhere today, but this book helpfully locates it right at the intersection of the pastoral and the theological. *Beauty, Order, and Mystery* provides a remarkably easy introduction to a vexed set of issues because the chapters are approachable and accessible even as they display deep reflection and up-to-date learning. In this particular multitude of counselors there is much wisdom."

Fred Sanders, Torrey Honors Institute, Biola University

BEAUTY, ORDER, AND MYSTERY

A CHRISTIAN VISION *of* HUMAN SEXUALITY

EDITED BY GERALD HIESTAND & TODD WILSON

IVP Academic
An imprint of InterVarsity Press
Downers Grove, Illinois

InterVarsity Press
P.O. Box 1400, Downers Grove, IL 60515-1426
ivpress.com
email@ivpress.com

InterVarsity Press® is the book-publishing division of InterVarsity Christian Fellowship/USA®, a movement of students and faculty active on campus at hundreds of universities, colleges, and schools of nursing in the United States of America, and a member movement of the International Fellowship of Evangelical Students. For information about local and regional activities, visit intervarsity.org.

All Scripture quotations, unless otherwise indicated, are taken from The Holy Bible, New International Version®, NIV®. Copyright © 1973, 1978, 1984, 2011 by Biblica, Inc.™ Used by permission of Zondervan. All rights reserved worldwide. www.zondervan.com. The "NIV" and "New International Version" are trademarks registered in the United States Patent and Trademark Office by Biblica, Inc.™

While any stories in this book are true, some names and identifying information may have been changed to protect the privacy of individuals.

Cover design: David Fassett
Interior design: Beth McGill
Image: Scene from Dante's Paolo: Francesca da Rimini and Paolo Malatesta by Jean Auguste Dominique Ingres at Musee des Beaux-Arts, Angers, France / Bridgeman Images

ISBN 978-0-8308-5385-4 (print)
ISBN 978-0-8308-8988-4 (digital)

Printed in the United States of America ♻

Library of Congress Cataloging-in-Publication Data
Names: Hiestand, Gerald, 1974- editor. | Wilson, Todd A., 1976- editor.
Title: Beauty, order, and mystery : a Christian vision of human sexuality /
  edited by Gerald L. Hiestand and Todd Wilson.
Description: Downers Grove, IL : InterVarsity Press, [2017] | Includes index.
Identifiers: LCCN 2017033989 (print) | LCCN 2017035976 (ebook) | ISBN
  9780830889884 (eBook) | ISBN 9780830853854 (pbk. : alk. paper) | ISBN
  9780830889884 (digital)
Subjects: LCSH: Sex—Religious aspects—Christianity—Congresses.
Classification: LCC BT708 (ebook) | LCC BT708 .B434 2017 (print) | DDC
  233/.5—dc23
LC record available at https://lccn.loc.gov/2017033989

P	23	22	21	20	19	18	17	16	15	14	13	12	11	10	9	8	7	6	5	4
Y	36	35	34	33	32	31	30	29	28	27	26	25	24	23	22	21	20			

To Jill and Katie

Contents

Acknowledgments

N
O BOOK COMES INTO BEING without the help of many hands. This is perhaps especially true with an edited volume. As such, the contributors to this volume have justly earned pride of place in our acknowledgments. The topics of sexuality and gender are fraught with difficulty on the left and the right. Our contributors are to be commended for having managed to communicate the wisdom of the church in the spirit of Aristotle's golden mean. The essays in this volume are both gracious and clear, winsome and firm, pastoral and theological. We are grateful to partner with such an excellent group of ecclesial theologians.

We owe a debt of gratitude to the Center for Pastor Theologians, the organizer of the conference from which the papers of this book are drawn. The Center has served as a catalyst for our work and has been a repository of wisdom and counsel on all things pastoral and theological. The theological leadership of the Center—John Yates, Michael LeFebvre, John Isch, Jeremy Mann, and Zach Wagner—deserves our gratitude and bear a measure of responsibility for any blessing this book brings to the church. Special thanks are owed to Zach especially for his labor in indexing this volume.

Likewise, we are profoundly grateful for Calvary Memorial Church in Oak Park, Illinois, the congregation where we are privileged to minister. Calvary has graciously served as the host home for the CPT for the better part of a decade, and it is not an understatement to say that the CPT would not be what it is without Calvary's partnership and support.

We are thankful for IVP Academic and their commitment to the ecclesial theology project and the CPT's vision of the pastor theologian. We are especially thankful for our editor David McNutt whose enthusiastic participation in the production of this book has gone a long way toward making it a reality.

We are deeply grateful for the partnership of the CPT's four senior theological mentors: Scott Haffemann, Doug Sweeney, Paul House, and Kevin Vanhoozer. Their commitment to the CPT's mission, contribution to the Fellowships, and friendship and encouragement to the two of us has been an important catalyst for the CPT project and its associated publications.

And finally, to our families, and most especially our wives (to whom this book is dedicated), we remain ever grateful. Their patient endurance in the midst of our already busy schedules is a gift that we do not take lightly. May the Lord pay them back tenfold what they have given to us!

Introduction

The Need for a Christian Vision
of Human Sexuality

TODD WILSON AND

GERALD HIESTAND

THE CENTER FOR PASTOR THEOLOGIANS is an organization dedicated to assisting pastor theologians in the study and written production of biblical and theological scholarship for the ecclesial renewal of theology and the theological renewal of the church. In other words, we're committed to the audacious task of trying to resurrect the vision of the pastor theologian in our day.[1]

Why? Because we believe passionately, as we like to say, in a "third way"—a way of being a pastor and doing ministry that stands in between the important work of the academic theologian, on the one hand, and the indispensable work of the local church pastor, on the other hand. Our hope, and indeed our prayer, is for the recovery of the ecclesial theologian, one who combines great theological learning with deep spiritual urgency and a care for souls—all for the good of the church.

The Center has a number of exciting initiatives that enable us to promote this vision and pursue our calling.[2] One of our key program elements is

---

[1]For our attempt at a fuller-scale articulation of this vision, see Gerald Hiestand and Todd Wilson, *The Pastor Theologian: Resurrecting an Ancient Vision* (Grand Rapids: Zondervan, 2015).
[2]For more on the Center for Pastor Theologians, see pastortheologians.com.

an annual conference held in late autumn each year at the historic Calvary
Memorial Church in Chicago, Illinois, where we have the privilege of
serving as pastors.

This annual conference gathers together pastors, scholars, students, and lay
people to reflect on themes that are both theologically substantive and ecclesially significant—that is, they're issues of real import to the life and ministry
of the church. It's our effort to do what we call "ecclesial theology" together
in community.

The 2015 conference theme was, naturally, very near and dear to our
hearts: the identity and possibility of the pastor theologian.[3] The theme of
the 2016 conference was no less exciting since it is surely one of the most
pressing issues of our time: human sexuality.

Sadly, in our culture, sex has become so commercialized as to be an
embarrassment to us all. Add to that the sordid underworld and mass
consumption of pornography—which mars the imagination and turns the
beauty of sexuality into the brutality of exploitation—and collectively, we
find ourselves a long way from the primordial, Edenic vision of "naked
and unashamed."

But we've also lost sight of human sexuality as graciously ordered by a good
Creator. The definition of marriage, the purpose of sex, the meaning of being
male and female—these are far less obvious today than they were even a generation ago. Lines once clear have become blurred, and we're left as "unscripted
anxious stutterers," to borrow a phrase from Alasdair MacIntyre.[4]

What makes this doubly tragic is that we the church, as well as the
culture, lose out on the mystery of the Christian vision of human sexuality.
God the Son took on human flesh and became man. Jesus was born of a
virgin, traveled a vaginal canal, nursed at his mother's breast, went through
puberty, grew armpit hair, and all the rest that is essential to him being born
with an XY chromosome. There is something mysterious indeed about all
of this—not to mention God's climactic sixth-day declaration that "male
and female he created them" (Gen 1:27). But this profound mystery has

---

[3]The addresses from this conference are brought together in Todd Wilson and Gerald Hiestand,
 eds., *Becoming a Pastor Theologian: New Possibilities for Church Leadership* (Downers Grove, IL:
 InterVarsity Press, 2016).
[4]Alasdair MacIntyre, *After Virtue: A Study in Moral Theory*, 3rd ed. (South Bend, IN: University of
 Notre Dame Press, 2007), 216.

been exchanged for a constructivist and reductionist vision of sexuality, where these gloriously sexed bodies are viewed as little more than cultural products or biological necessities.

For centuries the earliest Christians catechized in an effort to expose new believers to the beauty, order, and mystery of the Christian faith—to the glory of God incarnate, a bloody and redemptive sacrifice, the promise of bodily resurrection, the hope of a new heavens and new earth. In some respects, the contributors to this volume desire to do the same. These essays, each of which was first delivered at the conference, share in this aim to commend to the church and to those outside the church a Christian vision of human sexuality—one that celebrates the beauty, order, and mystery of human sexuality.

The essays are diverse, as was our intention. Not all the contributors would agree on each and every point at issue in debates over human sexuality or sexual ethics. But this group of contributors would all share a belief in the historic Christian consensus on sexuality, something that Todd Wilson, in the opening talk of the conference (chapter one of this volume) referred to as "mere sexuality": what most Christians at most times have believed about human sexuality. While differences have always been present, there has at the same time been a consensus—centered around the significance of biological sexuality—that the distinction between male and female matters to God and ought to matter to us.

In this increasingly post-Christian and neopagan world in which we find ourselves, the church needs to rediscover this Christian vision of human sexuality—but more than that, to commend it as beautiful, profound, and good. Nothing less will be compelling to those outside the faith or do justice to the reality of which we speak.

Part One

A THEOLOGICAL
VISION *for* SEXUALITY

1

Mere Sexuality

TODD WILSON

W E HAVE SEVEN CHILDREN and, as a matter of practical necessity, own a twelve-passenger van—the awkward kind you piled into for youth group ski trips. You can imagine, then, that I was interested to hear Ed Stetzer, executive director of the Billy Graham Center for Evangelism at Wheaton College, share with the *New York Times* back in June of 2015 that the number of evangelicals who had come out in favor of same-sex marriage was so minimal "you could fit them all in an SUV."[1]

Several years on, I'm sure Ed Stetzer would state things differently. Now you would need at least our twelve-passenger van, if not a bus. And I suspect in a few years, there won't be any elbow room in a small city. Over the last few decades, there has been a sea change of opinion on same-sex practice and gay marriage not only in the culture but also in the church.

I think back to when I was an undergraduate at Wheaton College in the mid-nineties, before the invention of the iPhone or even the regular use of email. At that time students didn't talk about same-sex practice; it was simply off our radar. Who, then, would have thought that just over a decade later, a large group of Wheaton students would assemble on the steps of

---

The content of this chapter is drawn from my book-length treatment of this same topic, *Mere Sexuality: Rediscovering the Christian Vision of Sexuality* (Grand Rapids: Zondervan, 2017).

[1]Michael Paulson, "With Same-Sex Decision, Evangelical Churches Address New Reality," *New York Times*, June 18, 2015, www.nytimes.com/2015/06/29/us/with-same-sex-decision-evangelical-churches-address-new-reality.html.

Edman Chapel to protest as a well-known Christian author shared her story of how she came to Christ and renounced her lesbian past?[2]

Speaking of Wheaton, as I was writing this chapter I learned of the news that one of Christianity's leading philosophers and public intellectuals, Nicholas Wolterstorff, had just come out in support of same-sex marriage—not only civil marriage, but ecclesial marriage. Back in October of 2016, at an event in Grand Rapids, Michigan, Wolterstorff said, "When those with homosexual orientation act on their desires in a loving, committed relationship, [they] are not, as far as I can see, violating the love command."[3] As a philosophy major during my undergraduate days at Wheaton, Wolterstorff was one of my heroes. His books helped root me in my newfound faith and orient me to the life of the mind. Needless to say this bit of news was not only surprising but, if I'm honest, disappointing.

My wife, Katie, recently had a similar experience. Like many across the country, she has been challenged by popular Christian author Glennon Doyle Melton's *New York Times*–bestselling book *Love Warrior*. It's a gritty and insightful look at marriage, the life of recovery, and the path toward greater self-understanding. Doyle's book has touched the lives of tens of thousands, even entering the inner sanctum of Oprah's Book Club, a coveted privilege for any writer interested in expanding their book's reach. Many were of course saddened when Doyle announced in August of 2016 that she was separating from her husband, the father of their three children. But the bombshell came three months later when she revealed to six hundred thousand Facebook followers that there was a new love in her life—soccer star Abby Wambach: "Oh my God, she is so good to me. She

---

[2]Kate Tracy, "Wheaton Students Protest 'Train Wreck Conversion' Speaker's Ex-Gay Testimony," *Christianity Today*, February 21, 2014, www.christianitytoday.com/gleanings/2014/february/wheaton-students-protest-exgay-chapel-rosaria-butterfield.html.

[3]See Gayla R. Postma, "Wolterstorff: Biblical Justice and Same-Sex Marriage," *Banner*, October 24, 2016. For critical interaction with Wolterstorff, see Matthew Tuininga, "Sexuality and the Gospel: My Response to Nicholas Wolterstorff," *Perspectives: A Journal of Reformed Thought*, December 4, 2016, https://perspectivesjournal.org/blog/2016/12/04/sexuality-gospel-response-nicholas-wolterstorff. (Though see Nicholas Wolterstorff, "Response to Matthew Tuininga on Sexuality and Scripture," *Perspectives: A Journal of Reformed Thought*, February 28, 2017, https://perspectivesjournal.org/blog/2017/02/28/response-matthew-tuininga-sexuality-scripture-2.) Also see especially Wesley Hill, "Nicholas Wolterstorff's Cheap Shots," *First Things*, web exclusive, November 1, 2016, www.firstthings.com/web-exclusives/2016/11/nicholas-wolterstorffs-cheap-shots.

loves me for all the things I've always wanted to be loved for. She's just my favorite. My person."[4]

These cultural snapshots hit close to home for my immediate family. Casting a wider net to friends and extended family, I would gather many more, all demonstrating the great change both our culture and the church have undergone in opinions on same-sex practice. What was unimaginable even a decade ago when President Bill Clinton signed into law the Defense of Marriage Act (DOMA) has now become the law of the land with the recent United States Supreme Court ruling in *Obergefell v. Hodges* to legalize same-sex marriage in all fifty states—surely one of the most rapid and profound shifts of opinion in American history. But more remarkable still is the fact that evangelicals have kept pace with this sea change of opinion.

Ed, we're going to need more than an SUV.

How Can a God Boy Think Gay Is Okay?

All of this forces us to pause and ask, What has happened? Why has there been such a dramatic change in the way evangelicals view same-sex practice and gay marriage?[5] To put a finer point on it, How could something so obviously problematic to believers living just a generation ago become so widely embraced today, not least by Bible-carrying, conservative evangelicals? Or to put it more simply, as has been done effectively in a recent book, how can a God boy come to think gay is okay?[6]

The reasons for this revolution in understanding are complex.[7] There have been significant intellectual and cultural trends at work under the surface of our society for decades, if not longer, like tectonic plates imperceptibly shifting until they collide and cause us all to shake. But at the risk of oversimplifying, let me suggest that two factors go a long way to help

---

[4]Kate Shellnutt, "A Christian Mom Blogger Announces She's Dating Soccer Star Abby Wambach," *Washington Post*, November 14, 2016, www.washingtonpost.com/news/acts-of-faith/wp/2016/11/14/a-christian-mom-blogger-announces-shes-dating-soccer-star-abby-wambach. As of February 19, 2017, this story was updated to include the news that the two are engaged.

[5]See "Changing Attitudes on Gay Marriage," Pew Research Center, May 12, 2016, www.pewforum.org/2016/05/12/changing-attitudes-on-gay-marriage.

[6]See Justin Lee, "God Boy," in *Torn: Rescuing the Gospel from the Gays-vs.-Christians Debate* (New York: Jericho Books, 2012), 12-18; similarly, Matthew Vines, *God and the Gay Christian: The Biblical Case in Support of Same-Sex Relationships* (New York: Convergent Books, 2014).

[7]See Robert Putnam, *American Grace* (New York: Simon & Schuster, 2010), 127-29, 402-6.

explain why many evangelicals find it easy or even necessary to affirm the sanctity of same-sex practice or gay marriage.

First, evangelicals have experienced a profound loss of functional biblical authority. This rising generation of Christians has come of age in a world marked by "pervasive interpretive pluralism." The phrase was coined by sociologist Christian Smith and forcefully presented in his 2011 book *The Bible Made Impossible*.[8] This is what it means: your average evangelical Christian knows that the Bible can be used to support a number of different views on a host of important issues. Take any passage of Scripture and you'll find sincere Christians who hold one view—and a similar number of equally devout believers who hold an opposing view.

What does pervasive interpretive pluralism look like in real life? Let me give you one example. Back in March of 2014, popular Christian speaker, blogger, and author Jen Hatmaker took issue with Christian relief organization World Vision's decision to no longer refuse to hire people in same-sex marriages (a decision they later reversed). She took to her blog to express her dismay at both World Vision's seeming naiveté and the overconfident, vitriolic responses of their critics. I want to draw your attention to a few lines that reveal the presence of pervasive interpretive pluralism: "Thousands of churches and millions of Christ-followers faithfully read the Scriptures and with thoughtful and academic work come to different conclusions on homosexuality (and countless others). *Godly, respectable leaders have exegeted the Bible and there is absolutely not unanimity on its interpretation. There never has been.*"[9]

Neither Jen Hatmaker nor any other evangelical Christian would suggest that the Bible is a wax nose to be shaped however you choose. I don't know any Bible-loving believer who would make such a radical claim about Scripture. Jen Hatmaker surely wouldn't. But I do know plenty of Christians, perhaps you do as well, who have concluded that we can't reach a consensus

---

[8]Christian Smith, *The Bible Made Impossible: Why Biblicism Is Not a Truly Evangelical Reading of Scripture* (Grand Rapids: Brazos, 2011). I should note that one need not come to all the same conclusions as Smith to grant the saliency of his point about the problem of pervasive interpretive pluralism.

[9]Jen Hatmaker, "World Vision, Gay Marriage, and a Different Way Through," March 25, 2014, http://jenhatmaker.com/blog/2014/03/25/world-vision-gay-marriage-and-a-different-way-through (emphasis original).

on what the Bible really teaches. So they have resigned themselves to the idea that there isn't enough biblical material to make an open-and-shut case for much of anything—not least same-sex practice. And so, the reality of pervasive interpretive pluralism undercuts the functional authority of the Bible in the lives of these Christians. It's not that they dispense with the Bible. It's just that Scripture no longer speaks decisively on many issues, at least not on the issue of same-sex practice.

A second factor influencing the opinion of evangelicals on same-sex practice is the refashioning of moral intuitions. Our moral intuitions are those pretheoretical responses we have to particular actions, those gut-level responses that tell us whether something is right or wrong before we even think about it.[10] In his book *The Righteous Mind*, moral psychologist Jonathan Haidt gives several examples of our moral intuitions at work. How do we know that it's wrong to urinate on the American flag? Or why are we so confident that it's not right to eat your dead pet for dinner rather than bury it in the backyard? Did we logically reason our way to these conclusions? No, probably not. In fact, most of us do not need an intellectual reason that justifies why either of these actions is wrong. We just know in our gut that they are.

For many in previous generations, same-sex intimacy struck them as odd if not offensive, not because they reasoned their way to that conclusion but because they felt it was wrong somewhere in their gut. They had a moral intuition, or an intuitive sense, that something was wrong with same-sex intimacy. It didn't need to be explained; it just was. (Sadly, this same moral intuition has been the driver behind an untold amount of harm done to gays and lesbians. When people see same-sex practice as gross or disgusting, they will have a hard time not acting in ways that are callous, bigoted, homophobic, and ultimately dehumanizing.) By contrast, for many in this present generation, displays of same-sex intimacy are not met with those same sorts of feelings—not because they have reasoned their way to approving the moral status of same-sex practice but because their moral intuitions have been fashioned (or refashioned) in a way that causes them to see same-sex intimacy as perfectly normal and unobjectionable.

---

[10]For a fascinating discussion of the origins of morality and moral intuition, see Jonathan Haidt, *The Righteous Mind: Why Good People Are Divided by Politics and Religion* (New York: Vintage, 2013), 3-31.

How did this happen? No doubt the normalization of same-sex relationships in popular culture has done much to shape moral intuitions about
same-sex intimacy. But the key factor is not the media but relationships.
Unlike their parents, most younger evangelicals know gays and lesbians as
classmates and teammates or colleagues and friends. Because of this, they
see their lives and relationships, know their stories and struggles, and appreciate, in many cases, the dignity and sanctity of who they are as people—
even in their same-sex relationships. Swiss theologian Karl Barth pointed
this out years ago when he said that Christians need to reckon with the fact
that many same-sex relationships are "redolent of sanctity."[11] In other words,
they're hard to dismiss as entirely sinful and wrong—regardless of what the
Bible says or the church teaches.

What, then, has been the upshot of these two factors coming together in
the hearts and minds of many evangelical Christians? To borrow a concept
from the sociologists, it has undermined the "plausibility structure" of historic Christian sexual ethics.[12] For an increasing number of Christians, the
Bible's teaching about human sexuality in general, and homosexuality in
particular, no longer makes sense. At best, it seems quaint, like an antique
that no longer serves any good purpose; more to the point, it strikes many
as offensive, like a pre–Civil Rights view of blacks as less than human. Either
way, what centuries of Christians have always believed has nowadays become
a point of stumbling, while same-sex relationships and other departures
from historic Christian sexual ethics seem normal, even laudable.

A Truncated Vision of Human Sexuality

But underlying both of these factors is an even more decisive issue: a trun-
cated vision of human sexuality. We've lost sight of a positive Christian
vision for why God made us as sexual beings in the first place. We've lost our
grasp on the deep logic that connects our created nature as male and female
with how we ought to live relationally and sexually with one another. What

---

[11]Karl Barth, *Church Dogmatics*, III/4, §54 (Edinburgh: T&T Clark, 1976), 166. I'm indebted to
Christopher C. Roberts for alerting me to this reference; Christopher C. Roberts, *Creation and
Covenant: The Significance of Sexual Difference in the Moral Theology of Marriage* (New York: T&T
Clark, 2007), 161.
[12]See Peter L. Berger, *The Sacred Canopy: Elements of a Sociological Theory of Religion* (New York:
Random House, 1967), 45.

used to be assumed by Christians of all denominational stripes has been lost in the confusion of our post-Christian culture. Listen to what *New York Times* columnist Ross Douthat says about the impact of the 1960s sexual revolution: "Over the course of a decade or so, a large swath of America decided that two millennia of Christian teaching on marriage and sexuality were simply out of date."[13] We are suffering from a loss of vision.

This is why the challenge we face is not one but many. We confront dozens of challenges in matters of sexuality, each of which are an expression of this underlying loss of vision—alarmingly high rates of premarital sex, increasing cohabitation, adultery, divorce, out-of-wedlock births, dysfunctional sexual relations between spouses, the hook-up culture on college campuses, sexual abuse, and, of course, pornography. As biblical scholar Luke Timothy Johnson wryly points out, "There is more than enough sexual disorder among heterosexuals to fuel moral outrage."[14]

If we're going to live into the fullness of the gospel and pursue sexual wholeness and holiness, we need to rediscover the Christian vision of human sexuality I call "mere sexuality."

So what is it? What is mere sexuality?

I'm using the word *sexuality* in a more general sense than we normally might use it. We tend to use the word to refer to a person's sexual activities, habits, or desires. In other words, sexuality almost always connotes sexual activity. But I'm using the word in a more general way to refer to the state or condition of being biologically sexed as either male or female. Philosophers will use the word *sexuate* to refer to the state or condition of being biologically sexed, and *sexuality* to refer to sexual activity or desire.[15] That's a nice terminological move, but since it is uncommon and sounds a bit unusual I've chosen not to use *sexuate* in this chapter, even though it captures the way in which I will use *sexuality*.

On this understanding of the word *sexuality*, it would make sense to talk of a child's sexuality because that child is biologically sexed, even though he or she has not experienced sexual activity or sexual desire. It would also

[13]Ross Douthat, *Bad Religion: How We Became a Nation of Heretics* (New York: Free Press, 2013), 70.
[14]Luke Timothy Johnson, "Homosexuality & the Church," *Commonweal*, June 11, 2007, www.commonwealmagazine.org/homosexuality-church-0.
[15]I would like to thank Matthew Mason for pointing out this terminological distinction.

make sense to talk about Jesus' sexuality—even though Jesus never engaged in sexual activity and was free from illicit sexual desire.

But what about that little four letter word *mere* in the phrase "mere sexuality"? You might be familiar with a famous book that has a similar sounding title, C. S. Lewis's classic *Mere Christianity*. For Lewis, "mere Christianity" was a shorthand way to refer to the basic themes that have characterized the Christian faith through the ages. It's not Baptist Christianity, or Anglican Christianity, or Presbyterian Christianity, or Roman Catholic Christianity, but mere Christianity—the convictions they share in common, in other words, what virtually all Christians everywhere have always believed.

By using the phrase "mere sexuality," I have something similar in mind. I use it as a shorthand way to refer to the themes that have characterized the Christian vision of sexuality down through the ages. By calling it *mere* sexuality, I'm saying this is what most Christians at most times in most places have believed about human sexuality—the historic consensus.

Does such a consensus exist? Yes, there is an historic consensus about human sexuality that has been part of the church in each of its major expressions—Orthodox, Catholic, and Protestant. It's been around for centuries, from roughly the fourth to the middle of the twentieth century. And it has only seriously been called into question within the last forty to fifty years, with the liberalization of Christian sexual ethics in the foment of the 1960s sexual revolution.

This does not mean that there has been complete unanimity on every issue in the Christian tradition. For example, Gregory of Nyssa, the fourth-century Cappadocian father, believed that human beings would reproduce asexually in heaven, while Thomas Aquinas, the thirteenth-century Dominican priest, strongly disagreed. Yet Aquinas was of the opinion, following his esteemed philosophical master Aristotle, that women were misbegotten males, a rather dubious view that subsequent Christian tradition rightly and roundly rejected. Augustine, Bishop of Hippo and author of *Confessions* and *City of God*, doubted whether sexual desire could ever rise above the level of lust. Luther, however, thankfully begged to differ—as did Calvin and others following in their Protestant wake. Or in his massive study of human sexuality, Pope John Paul II offers rather specific proposals about femininity and feminine values that, say, the famed Swiss theologian Karl

Barth would have found deeply problematic on both methodological and christological grounds.

So there is real diversity and even divergence within the church's tradition, and we don't want to paper over those differences. Yet despite these disagreements, the consensus I'm calling mere sexuality has been surprisingly robust through the centuries, and we can identify its basic contours. They include a number of interrelated beliefs and convictions, but at the heart of mere sexuality and the church's historic teaching on human sexuality is the belief that sexual difference, being male or female, is both theologically and morally significant—it matters to God and it ought to matter to us.[16]

On the very first page of the Bible we read that "male and female [God] created them" (Gen 1:27).[17] Immediately, then, we're confronted with both the canonical and theological priority of sexual difference in Christian thinking. It is essential to who we are, not accidental or peripheral, flexible or negotiable. Sexual difference is part of our nature as creatures. It is not something we create, like iPhones or automobiles. God has woven sexual difference into the fabric of creation. And because of this, our being male and female is integral to our calling as image-bearers, not least in that most basic of all human communities—the one known as marriage. As a result, we can't ignore or minimize the fact of our being either male or female without undermining our ability to flourish and find fulfillment.

And since our sexual difference is core to who we are, it will not be eradicated at the resurrection but persist for eternity, though in a fully glorified expression. Our resurrection bodies will be sexed bodies, just as Jesus' risen body is a sexed body. He is, and always will be, a crucified, circumcised Jewish male.

---

[16]In his carefully researched book on the significance of sexual difference for the moral theology of marriage, *Creation and Covenant*, Christopher C. Roberts shows that for centuries there has been a Christian consensus on sexuality. He explains, "After an initial patristic period in which Christian beliefs about sexual difference were fluctuating and diverse, a more or less rough consensus on sexual difference existed from the fourth to the twentieth centuries." Roberts, *Creation and Covenant*, 185-86. He summarizes, "There is an ancient Christian tradition, from Augustine to John Paul II, which has believed and argued that sexual difference is significant." Ibid., 236.

[17]All scriptural quotations in this chapter are from the English Standard Version unless otherwise noted.

These, then, are the basic contours of what has been a time-honored and widespread Christian consensus on sexual difference, with implications that touch virtually every dimension of our lives. This is what I'm calling mere sexuality, what most Christians at most times in most places have believed about human sexuality.

A MORE ROBUST APPROACH

By calling this vision "mere sexuality," I tap into what Christians of the past have consistently taught, and what the vast majority of ordinary believers have always thought. In other words, I appeal to church tradition and make no apologies for that. Mere sexuality is what celebrated philosopher Alasdair MacIntyre calls a living tradition—"an historically extended, socially embodied argument."[18] For Christians, their views on sexuality go back nearly two millennia and have been embodied in the lives of ordinary believers the world over. This is itself a strong, albeit not a decisive, argument in support of mere sexuality—and, incidentally, a strong word of caution to those who depart from it. The problem is that this living tradition is now on life support as it drifts inexorably toward death, at least in the minds of many Christians. The church has forgotten what it has always believed.

In an age of rampant postmodern uncertainty where sincere Christians disagree about a growing number of things they used to take for granted, it's important for evangelicals to retrieve this historic consensus. Many evangelicals have been weaned on a way of reading the Bible that is superficial and has proven itself largely unable to withstand the destabilizing effect of competing interpretations. Far too many good Bible-believers are committed to Scripture but skeptical of tradition. As a result they operate with a bastardized view of the classic Protestant doctrine of Scripture—not *sola Scriptura* ("Scripture alone") but *nuda Scriptura* ("Scripture in isolation"). But this emaciated approach can't stand its ground in the face of the twin challenges of pervasive interpretive pluralism, on the one hand, and the widespread refashioning of moral intuitions, on the other.

This is why I'm convinced that redoubled efforts to lay out what the Bible really teaches about homosexuality, or any other aspect of Christian sexual

---

[18]See Alasdair MacIntyre, *After Virtue*, 3rd ed. (Notre Dame, IN: University of Notre Dame Press, 2007), 222.

ethics for that matter, will only take us so far—or only keep us tethered to orthopraxy for so long. Serious engagement with what the Bible says on these matters is necessary and I applaud these efforts. But they aren't sufficient in themselves to withstand the cultural and philosophical challenges we face. Such efforts may convert a choir member or two, but we'll be preaching to the choir. It will do little to stop those disaffected with historic Christian sexual ethics.

My point is that our strategy needs to be more robust. It is time for evangelicals to rediscover the historic Christian vision of human sexuality. Now, more than at any time since the first centuries of the church, we need a countercultural Christian sexual ethic and, at an even deeper level, a distinctively Christian view of human sexuality. We need a fresh encounter with what has been called the "jarring gospel of Christian sexuality" that transformed the pagan world.[19] We need to recover the moral logic behind Christian sexuality: how babies relate to marriage, and marriage to sex, and sex to identity, and identity to being male and female—and how all of this relates to the person of Christ.

CASTING VISION WITH JOY, TEARS, AND HOPE

But our task must go beyond recovering a lost vision. If we're going to avert the slide of evangelical Christianity into a neopagan sexuality, then we need to cast vision for mere sexuality. We need to recover this vision for our own sake, and then advocate for it for the sake of others—as an exercise in pastoral persuasion, speaking convincingly into our contemporary context.

But this goes beyond the work of scholarship and touches on the need for winsome communication. We need more than sound exegesis and good theology—we need compelling Christian rhetoric and prose and poetry. Our challenge is not only to convince minds but to capture imaginations. We want people to see the truth of God's design for human sexuality but also to see its goodness and its beauty. Taking a cue from theologian and cultural critic Carl Trueman, we need to win the aesthetic, not just the argument. As he puts it, "Arguments can be true or false, good or bad. But today who cares? We live in an age where the primary moral binary is between the

---

[19]See Kyle Harper, *From Shame to Sin: The Christian Transformation of Sexual Morality in Late Antiquity* (Cambridge, MA: Harvard University Press, 2013), 3.

tasteful and distasteful. Control of aesthetics is where the real power to change people lies."[20]

How do we do that? Well, I don't presume to have all the answers or a silver bullet. But if our vision-casting for God's design for human sexuality is going to be effective, it must be done with joy, with tears, and with hope.

It must be done with joy, as those who are ravished by the beauty of mere sexuality—not just convinced of the truth of it. The rising generation of evangelicals needs to encounter both the rational coherence of the Christian vision of sexuality and its moral and aesthetic beauty. Here we can take a cue from C. S. Lewis, who early in his career saw that rational argument would only take a person so far. What was ultimately needed, he insisted, was a baptized imagination. This is why Lewis not only wrote the *Abolition of Man* but followed it with his Space Trilogy, fleshing out some of the very same points. He later explained that "by casting these things into an imaginary world, stripping them of their stained-glass and Sunday School associations, one could make them for the first time appear in their real potency."[21] That's a wonderful description of what is required for us to commend the beauty of mere sexuality: to make it appear for the first time in its real potency, whether in our preaching or in our Tweets or in our songs, or better yet, as an embodied reality in our own lives.

But our vision-casting also needs to be done with tears, as those who share with others in the heartbreaking complexity of these issues. There is a lovely gentleman in our congregation, a godly man in his early sixties, who wakes up most mornings wishing he were a woman. He has had these desires for most of his life, starting when he was just five years old. I weep with him in his struggle.

Or consider the email I recently received from a young couple who was thinking about moving to Chicago and attending our church. Their dreams and plans were interrupted with the birth of their first child who was born with female genitals but an XY chromosome—a rare medical condition known as intersex. This precious young couple didn't even know what intersex was until they had a child born with the condition.

---

[20]Carl R. Trueman, "We Need to Win the Aesthetic, Not the Argument," *First Things*, October 12, 2016, www.firstthings.com/blogs/firstthoughts/2016/10/we-need-to-win-the-aesthetic-not-the-argument.

[21]C. S. Lewis, "Sometimes Fairy Stories May Say Best What's to Be Said," in *Of Other Worlds: Essays and Stories* (New York: Harcourt, Brace, Jovanovich, 1982), 42.

These are the stunningly complex and often heartbreaking situations of people in our world and in our churches. They're not "issues" to be solved but people to be loved, even to the point of weeping with those who weep, shedding tears of grief and sadness with them. We will not communicate a faithful and compelling vision for mere sexuality if our posture is overly muscular and not sufficiently brokenhearted.

Finally, if our efforts are going to be effective, then we need to cast this vision with hope, as those who believe in the future promise of the gospel—that while we experience a measure of healing in this life, complete transformation will occur in the life to come. This promise is not grounded in the righteousness of our sexual propriety, but in the death and resurrection of Jesus Christ—and it is true for even the chief of sinners.

Ultimately, each of us needs to know in the depth of our soul that "no one is righteous, no, not one. . . . All have turned aside; together they have become worthless; no one does good, not even one" (Rom 3:10, 12); that "a person is not justified by works of the law," nor by his heterosexuality, but only "through faith in Christ Jesus" (Gal 2:16); that we all deal with sexual struggles of one kind or another; that we all need forgiveness and healing for our sexual sin; and that we all need to know, in the depth of our souls, that Jesus is more than willing to meet us there—in our brokenness, in our shame, in our sin.

"Behold," Jesus says, "I stand at the door and knock. If anyone hears my voice and opens the door, I will come in to him and eat with him, and he with me" (Rev 3:20). As we combine our joy in God's beautiful creation of people with our tears at the fallen state of our bodies and souls, we cling to and proclaim the hope that Jesus continues to love us, to seek us, and to send us the Holy Spirit. We need to know that as we open the door of our lives to Christ Jesus our Savior, he will indeed humbly enter in—bringing with him all of his grace and beauty and power—washing us, sanctifying us, and justifying us in his own glorious name!

2

Embodied from Creation Through Redemption

Placing Gender and Sexuality in Theological Context

BETH FELKER JONES

THE PURPOSE OF THIS ESSAY is to place gender and sexuality in theological context by thinking about them in relationship to the big-picture biblical arch from creation through redemption. There will always be more to be said, and these topics require an important aspect of humble reservation and acknowledgment of mystery, but it's also important to claim theological resources for helping us think well about gender and sexuality. We're not just left in the lurch, for God has chosen to reveal his goodness to us. We're after a biblically shaped imagination, one trained in Scripture-shaped instincts for the work of living our embodied, sexed, and gendered lives together. Thinking about sex in gender in light of creation, fall, and redemption points us toward a hopeful vision of our bodies as witnesses to the God who is love.

CREATION

There are basic truths of the doctrine of creation that should shape our theology of gender and sexuality: humans are created in the image of God. God's work of creating humans as embodied creatures is good work.

God's good creative work calls us to good creative work, to relational and vocational work.

Rejection of Gnostic hierarchical dualism is fundamental to the Christian doctrine of creation. Gnosticism would divide humans into two, splitting material from spiritual and teaching the superiority of the spiritual. For the Gnostic, flesh is bad and sex is impure. Simply to be a sexual person is to be unredeemed.[1]

But against those who "forbid marriage and demand abstinence from foods" (1 Tim 4:3), Paul insists that "everything created by God is good, and nothing is to be rejected, provided it is received with thanksgiving" (1 Tim 4:4).[2] Genesis teaches us about created goodness and so should shape for us a theological vision of human relationship and bodies as created goodness. The very existence of human relationship is good. Embodied difference is good.

God gives good work—dominion and fruitfulness—to embodied human beings, human beings who are male and female, human beings who are supposed to witness, to the world at large and to one another, to the goodness of God.

Dominion and fruitfulness are embodied work, and dominion and fruitfulness are, in a certain way at least, work that has to do with sex. Human work is to garden, to be put in "Eden to till it and keep it" (Gen 2:15). Human work is done in community, and that community includes sexual differentiation—the fact that we are created male and female.

Creation gives us something to work with as we think about gender and sexuality. We're all bearers of the divine image, and we bear that image in the diversity of male and female flesh. Our bodies are good, and we have good work—the work of dominion and fruitfulness—to do with our bodies. But all of this—image bearing, embodiment, and work—has been vitiated under the condition of sin, and so there's only so far the doctrine of creation can take us if we are to be vigilant about the existence, power, and scope of sin. Many Christian theologies have tried to run a full theology of bodies, sex, and gender from creation alone, downplaying the ways that sin infects our created nature.

---

[1]Peter Brown, *The Body and Society: Men, Women, and Sexual Renunciation in Early Christianity* (New York: Columbia University Press, 1988), 116.
[2]All scriptural quotations in this chapter are from the New Revised Standard Version unless otherwise noted.

FALL

I'm more and more aware of how hard it is becoming to say that maleness and femaleness are created goods. And it should be hard. It should be hard because sin is real, because nature as we know it is fallen nature. And outside of redemption, we lack the tools we need to tell the difference between created goodness, which is still real even under the condition of sin, and sinful disruption of that created goodness, which makes our image bearing and our bodies and our work something different than what they ought to be. Thorns, those many consequences of sin written onto creation itself, seem natural to us. And so we're tempted to baptize those thorns and pretend they belong to the goodness of creation. We're tempted, even, to demand that bushes grow thorns and to call that unnatural demand the will of God.

We must ask whether our theologies are willing to name the effects of sin—noetic, spiritual, and somatic—on the way we exist as fallen male and female creatures. When we affirm that God created human beings, male and female, we have to ask how much access we have to God's original, good creative intentions for us as such. When we attribute something to human nature, male nature, or female nature, Christians always need to ask which nature we're talking about. Nature as God created it to be? Or fallen nature, twisted by sin?

Protestant theology rightly tends to insist that the effects of the fall be taken with utmost seriousness, but, in a painful irony, those strands in the Protestant tradition that are most insistent on this point are often the same strands that would adopt a theology of gender that seems unable to recognize that gender roles are contingent and constructed. The roles or norms that would confidently call one list of attributes masculine and another list feminine are contingencies of geography, history, race, and class. More important, those roles and norms are contingencies that we know only under the condition of sin.

Our eyes also need to be opened to ways our cultural assumptions about femininity and masculinity may interfere with Christian discipleship. If we allow ourselves to be bound by false assumptions about what maleness and femaleness must look like, vocation and sanctification may be hindered. Mistaken, even sinful, rules and false ideals about what it means to be male and female have done incalculable damage to real men and women. While other aspects of the social construction of masculinity and femininity may not be sinful in themselves, it's still a good idea to recognize they don't come from our bodies or nature or God, because that recognition keeps us from marginalizing men and women who don't follow those conventions.

We learn from Scripture that we must be suspicious of the ways we tend to see things. We live in a sinful world, under a condition of sin, and sin influences our perspectives. It affects our ability to see what is true and what is false. It affects our ability to distinguish between what is natural—as God intends it to be—and what is sinful, or the way selfish human beings want it to be. We need to be suspicious of ourselves when we're convinced we know exactly how things ought to be. We need God to heal our abilities to see and know the world. The long, sad history of violence and oppression based on gender and sexuality should spur us to ask these questions especially as we seek theologies of gender and sexuality. Because being male and female belongs to created nature, we tend to think we get it, but when we're overly confident, we're likely to be deceived.

REDEMPTION

But all of this suspicion of our abilities to understand nature is not the end of theological reasoning, for God does not abandon us to our broken and sinful perspectives. God heals and transforms us and reveals divine intention to us in the redemption made available in Jesus Christ. We must continue to seek God's good intentions for the sanctification of our sexed and gendered bodies.

Broadly speaking, the Christian tradition has imagined two different ways that God might redeem embodied gender and sexuality: either gendered bodies are a problem to be wiped away in redemption or they are an intrinsic part of that nature which God, in making all things new, will take up into grace.[3]

Understanding the materiality of gender difference as an obstacle to be removed has been a live option in the Christian East. Historian Peter Brown describes Origen as having "conveyed, above all, a profound sense of the

---

[3]Portions of this section are adapted from my *Marks of His Wounds: Gender Politics and Bodily Resurrection* (New York: Oxford University Press, 2007).

fluidity of the body. Basic aspects of human beings, such as sexuality, sexual differences, and the seemingly indestructible attributes of the person associated with the physical body, struck Origen as no more than provisional."[4] Gregory of Nyssa followed in that stream, abandoning Origen's most problematic speculations but nonetheless spiritualizing redemption when faced with the messy materiality of male and female bodies. Nyssa "had no doubt whatsoever that the present division of the sexes into male and female formed part of the present anomalous condition of human beings."[5] If we read the gendered body in this way, it becomes part of the tradition of the "garments of skin," those things added by God to humanity only after the fall, meant to ensure survival. The garments of skin are gifts of grace, to be sure, but they are nevertheless outside of both God's creative and final intentions for humanity.

But redemption of the sinful ways we experience gendered bodies does not necessarily mean that those bodies themselves are outside of God's redemptive intention.

Augustine paints a strikingly different portrait of our embodied hope. For Augustine, materiality itself, while disordered under the condition of sin, is not a problem to be overcome. It is itself God's grace for humanity. When Augustine considered gender and the resurrection, he asked whether the bodies of women would retain their sex. He gave a simple and radical answer:

> Both sexes are to rise . . . for then there will be no lust, which is now the cause of confusion [that of those who suppose there will be no female bodies at the end]. . . . Vice will be taken away from those bodies, therefore, and nature preserved. And the sex of a woman is not a vice, but nature. They will then be exempt from sexual intercourse and childbearing, but the female parts will nonetheless remain in being, accommodated not to the old uses, but to a new beauty, which, so far from inciting lust, which no longer exists, will move us to praise the wisdom and clemency of God, Who both made what was not and redeemed from corruption what He made.[6]

---

[4]Brown, *Body and Society*, 167.
[5]Ibid., 294.
[6]Augustine, *The City of God*, trans. R. Dyson (Cambridge: Cambridge University Press, 1998), 22.17.1144-45.

Several things are happening in this passage. First, Augustine denies the fear of the Nyssan tradition that, if gendered bodies are to persist, disordered sexuality will persist as well. Second, Augustine insists that resurrection means that vice will be removed but nature preserved. Sexed bodies, male and female, are the stuff of nature, and God does not make us new by destroying nature. God saves us rather than some other creatures altogether. Part of who we are is written on our materially different bodies. They incarnate the histories of lives together and our lives before God. Finally, Augustine imagines a way of being embodied in which material gender difference reflects particular beauty, beauty that orders the saints to God. Here, rather than material difference being an obstacle to the unity of the body, it displays for that body the glory of God. Because a woman's sex is not a defect, because it is natural, sexed bodies will persist (even as they are radically transformed) at the resurrection.

If we are to incline this way, we must be insistent about our tendency as sinners to misunderstand the nature of our bodies. We must name the dangers lurking behind any assumption that we have straightforward access to redeemed bodies. We have shaped dreadfully distorted sinful caricatures of "male" and "female," and then called them God's intention. But if materiality matters for the life of the fully redeemed, it matters for those on the way. What is more, God does not leave the wayfarers entirely without access to the body redeemed.

The fact that we get it wrong does not stop maleness and femaleness from being created goods. Male bodies are good. Female bodies are good. God made them and God loves them. Dangerous stereotypes are instruments of sin, but difference itself is a good thing. God made us to be different from each other and to love and be there for each other through our differences.

Whenever humans have denied this, the result has been bad for female bodies, for girls and women. Some ancient Gnostics, for instance, taught that sexed bodies would be erased in our salvation. This might sound like liberation, especially to, for instance, a woman who has been hurt because of being a woman, but if we take a closer look, we see that these Gnostics see female bodies—far more than male ones—as the special problem that redemption needs to get rid of. We find texts suggesting that a woman may be saved by becoming male, and we have records of extreme ascetic practice among women—hardcore fasting—being celebrated because it erased the femaleness of their bodies as starvation shrunk breasts and ended menstruation.[7]

We must recoil from a vision of holiness that equates it with masculinity. This way of thinking assumes that the female body is an aberration, a problem to be solved, while it gravely underestimates the sinfulness and disorder of male bodies, as we know them. Here, we must unequivocally reject the seductive and popular lie that hope for women lies within Gnosticism.[8] Liberation bought at the price of the erasure of women is no freedom. This is the fundamental reason I don't buy arguments that would do away with so-called "binary sexuality"—the understanding that humans exist in two sexes, male and female. A sinful world may hate and despise female bodies (and lots of other bodies too), but God made them and loves them and is redeeming them.

Moves to ignore maleness and femaleness as created goods are so often moves to denigrate the female. How can we refuse to do so? Part of the answer is that Christians need to emphasize redemption. Maleness and femaleness are created goods, but—more—they are redeemed goods.

God heals our brokenness and gives us the power of the Holy Spirit to help us live lives that stretch toward those good intentions. God redeems what we have forfeited. God makes the broken whole. In God's redeeming power, our very bodies become temples of God the Holy Spirit (1 Cor 6:19), and Christ's life becomes visible in our bodies. Paul is full of confidence about this: "If the Spirit of him who raised Jesus from the dead dwells in you, he who raised Christ from the dead will give life to your mortal bodies also through his Spirit that dwells in you" (Rom 8:11).

Augustine's embrace of material continuity as the primary continuity of resurrection encourages us to value our sexually differentiated bodies and to realize that our bodies are being taken up into and for the work of redemption. "Therefore, my beloved, be steadfast, immovable, always excelling in the work of the Lord, because you know that in the Lord your labor is not in vain" (1 Cor 15:58).

---

[7]Teresa M. Shaw, *The Burden of the Flesh* (Minneapolis: Fortress, 1998), 235.
[8]Popularized by Elaine Pagels, *The Gnostic Gospels* (New York: Vintage Random House, 1979), and lucratively appropriated in Dan Brown, *The Da Vinci Code* (New York: Doubleday, 2003).

And we labor in embodied difference. In that same embodied difference, God gives us grace for Jesus to be made visible in our flesh.

> Do you not know that your bodies are members of Christ? Should I therefore take the members of Christ and make them members of a prostitute? Never! Do you not know that whoever is united to a prostitute becomes one body with her? For it is said, "The two shall be one flesh." But anyone united to the Lord becomes one spirit with him. Shun fornication! Every sin that a person commits is outside the body; but the fornicator sins against the body itself. Or do you not know that your body is a temple of the Holy Spirit within you, which you have from God, and that you are not your own? For you were bought with a price; therefore glorify God in your body. (1 Cor 6:15-20)

Here, Paul insists that our bodies have meaning and purpose. Our flesh is for mission, for witness, for giving glory to the God who saves. And sexually differentiated bodies have something important to do with all this. With those bodies, we're supposed to be witnessing to who God is and what he has done.

Conclusion

Because of the resurrection, we are not free to imagine redemption apart from our very particular bodies.[9] Salvation, both on the way and in glory, is embodied. In their material life together, embodied creatures are redeemed in a way impossible for disembodied. Our embodied hope, which the Spirit grants to our embodied desire, must transform our present bodily practices.

Redemption happens through the body, not only through gender difference but also through the physical continuance of the material difference and specificity that makes us who we are. Finally, our bodies are for praise, praise of the One who is Victor over death, who will shape us into witnesses to beauty, to goodness, to holiness, and to peace.

Embodied sexuality is not incidental, something that we can shake off as though it doesn't really touch the core of our existence. Paul, writing to the church in Corinth, names sexual sin four times in a list of ten types of sin

---

[9]Parts of the section are adapted from my book *Faithful: A Theology of Sex* (Grand Rapids: Zondervan, 2015).

(1 Cor 6:9-10). He takes sexual sin seriously because it is so intimate, so personal, and so bodily. Other sins are "outside the body; but the fornicator sins against the body itself" (1 Cor 6:18). These are not the words of prude or of someone who has a problem with bodies. These are the words of someone who understands that our bodies are good and that what happens in the body is intimate and personal. Sex matters because it goes to the very heart of what it means to be human.

We can reclaim the goodness of our sexed and gendered bodies, and we can testify to what God has done by being gendered and sexual in ways that are mutual, that treasure difference, and that reflect God's own faithfulness.

We see a vision of this way of being embodied in the Song of Songs, a story of the natural goodness of sexually differentiated bodies being reclaimed and redeemed. The work of God, which began in creation, has not been wiped out by sin, and God is working to bring healing and wholeness and delight.

Phyllis Trible illuminates the Song of Solomon as an explicit redemption of the brokenness of Genesis chapters two and three. In sin, the garden of delight was lost. In the Song, that garden is rediscovered and reclaimed in the love between the man and the woman. Trible writes,

> Using Genesis 2-3 as a key for understanding the Song of Songs, we have participated in a symphony of love. Born to mutuality and harmony, a man and a woman live in a garden where nature and history unite to celebrate the one flesh of sexuality. Naked without fear or shame (cf. Gen. 2:25; 3:10), this couple treat each other with tenderness and respect. Neither escaping nor exploiting sex, they embrace and enjoy it. Their love is truly bone of bone and flesh of flesh, and this image of God male and female is indeed very good (cf. Gen. 1:37, 31).[10]

In God's redeeming power, desire is reclaimed from the fall. Instead of disordered desire we catch a glimpse of happy delight in the loved one. That delight is free to be happy and secure because it happens in a context of friendship and mutuality. The Song gives us a portrait of love and of good sex in which the lover is also a "friend" (Song 5:16). The Song repeats a refrain of mutuality. "My beloved is mine and I am his" (Song 2:16). "I am my

---

[10]Phyllis Trible, *God and the Rhetoric of Sexuality* (Minneapolis: Fortress, 1978), 161.

beloved's and my beloved is mine" (Song 6:3). God redeems us, and so makes space for true fidelity. In the garden of delight, complete faithfulness between husband and wife testifies to God's complete faithfulness to us.

The words of the Song testify to a love that cannot be destroyed, that is faithful no matter what may come. "Set me as a seal upon your heart," says the lover,

> as a seal upon your arm;
> for love is strong as death,
>   passion fierce as the grave.
> Its flashes are flashes of fire,
>   a raging flame.
> Many waters cannot quench love,
>   neither can floods drown it.
> If one offered for love
>   all the wealth of one's house,
>   it would be utterly scorned. (Song 8:6-7)

Gendered and sexed embodiment is meant to be a witness to the God who is faithful to Israel and to us. Sex matters to God because bodies matter to God, because God created our bodies and has good plans for us as embodied people. Sex is a witness to what God does in our lives, the same God who says to Israel, "I will take you for my wife forever; I will take you for my wife in righteousness and in justice, in steadfast love, and in mercy. I will take you for my wife in faithfulness; and you shall know the LORD" (Hos 2:19-20). Our bodies, all our bodies, are both very good and terribly disordered. The right ordering of people toward God will be accomplished in the resurrection body when our bodies will give unmitigated witness to the Creator, when, "just as we have borne the image of the man of dust, we will also bear the image of the man of heaven" (1 Cor 15:49).

3

How Should
Gay Christians Love?

WESLEY HILL

SEVERAL YEARS AGO, IN RESPONSE to the St. Andrew's Day
Statement—a theological proposal put forward by several prominent
members of the Church of England—Rowan Williams, then Archbishop of
Canterbury, invited Christians to imagine a certain sort of homosexual
person. This person, Williams implied, is not just hypothetical: he was (and
presumably is) acquainted with many such persons. And Williams in his
essay invites readers to imagine them saying something along these lines:

> I am not asking just for fulfillment. I want to know how my [life] may become
> transparent to Jesus, a sign of the kingdom. I do not seek to avoid cost. . . . I
> want to live in obedience to God; I truly, prayerfully and conscientiously do
> not recognise Romans 1 as describing what I am or what I want. I am not
> rejecting something I knew in the depths of my being. . . . [But] I do not be-
> lieve my identity as a desiring being is a complicated and embarrassing extra
> in my humanity as created by God. And it is hard to hear good news from the
> Church if it insists that my condition is in itself spiritually compromised.[1]

The sort of person Williams is asking us to imagine is a person I know quite
well. In my speaking and writing on the topic of homosexuality and the

---

[1]Rowan Williams, "Knowing Myself in Christ," in *The Way Forward? Christian Voices on Homosexuality and the Church*, ed. Timothy Bradshaw, 2nd ed. (Grand Rapids: Eerdmans, 2004), 18, 17
(order slightly altered).

Christian pastoral care of LGBTQ persons, I have met many such persons.
And in most ways, I am one myself.[2]

It can be easy for heterosexual Christians who are not acquainted with
many LGBTQ people to traffic in stereotypes. Straight believers often betray
a narrow vision when they casually use phrases like "the gay lifestyle" as if
there were only one! It is all too easy for churches and individual Christians,
with their immersion in family life, to consider gay people as one more it-
eration of irresponsible single people, as though gay life were all about
clubbing and hooking up and always veering right to the edge of unsafe
sexual habits and always standing at the ready for a risqué and bawdy parade.

But many gay people are, in actuality, very interested in Christian discipleship. (It is one of the great untold stories of the LGBTQ community, according to Andrew Marin's recent statistics, that 86 percent of them grew up
going to church, and of those who have left, 76 percent say they would be
open to returning.[3]) Many of us, like me, don't frequent gay clubs. Many of
us have no interest in promiscuity or fleeting hookups. Some of us don't have
sex at all, and some of us are virgins. Almost all of us would tell you that we
don't remember a moment in our childhood or adolescence when we "chose"
to be gay. We didn't sign up for a particular "lifestyle" out of rebellion or de-
fiance. A great proportion of us were confused when we gradually realized
we were attracted to persons of our own sex, and we agonized over when and
how to come out. Many of us have spent years of our lives and vast sums of
money, time, and energy trying to become "ex-gay." And many of us have,
through no activism or belligerence of our own, been offered silence or embarrassment or even outright rejection from our fellow believers. After all
this, our question, still, is how we ought to live lives that are, as Williams says,
"transparent to Jesus." How can we live out our lives as LGBTQ people in such
a way that Jesus is seen through us, that our faith, hope, and love are nour-
ished, and that our lives are a gift to those around us?

Keeping all this in view, I don't want to frame what I have to say as a refu-
tation of the "liberal gays" who are "over there." I write as a self-consciously

---

[2] I have tried to tell some of my own story in two books, *Spiritual Friendship: Finding Love in the Church as a Celibate Gay Christian* (Grand Rapids: Brazos, 2015) and *Washed and Waiting: Reflections on Christian Faithfulness and Homosexuality*, 2nd ed. (Grand Rapids: Zondervan, 2016).
[3] Andrew Marin, *Us Versus Us: The Untold Story of Religion and the LGBT Community* (Colorado Springs: NavPress, 2016).

gay, celibate Christian man, speaking on behalf of other LGBTQ Christian believers (celibate or not), who are already members in our churches and who are asking the question earnestly and prayerfully, "How should I live my life?" Or, more urgently, "How and whom should I *love* with my life?"

Throughout its history, the church has not confronted exactly this question. It has not had a category of "LGBTQ people" with whom to confront this question.[4] It has prohibited, I believe, all forms of same-sex sexual intercourse, but it has not had to face the more poignant question, "How and whom should I, as a gay or lesbian person, love with my life?" until recently.[5] The church is thus, understandably, in turmoil. It is grappling with how to read Scripture and its own tradition in response to a changing culture and a new subcultural community. Making matters more complicated, the church's theologians and pastors are not speaking with one voice in their answers to the cries of LGBTQ believers.

In what follows, I want to describe in some detail two of the most powerful answers that I have encountered in my reading in this whole area. I want to suggest, in the end, that even though I disagree with these answers (and I want to explain why I think we all ought to disagree with them), the questions they pose to us and the wrestling they force us to do is salutary.

GAY SANCTIFICATION?

The first of these answers is found in a book published in 1999 by Eugene Rogers titled *Sexuality and the Christian Body: Their Way into the Triune God.*[6] Rogers is a systematic theologian who works seriously with Scripture and with classic theologians such as St. Thomas Aquinas and Karl Barth. In my corner of the Anglican Communion, Rogers has been highly influential. His writing is often beautiful, and his theological work is born out of his own personal experience. His argument is one that we must take seriously precisely because it draws from the deepest wells of Christian liturgical, spiritual, and moral theology.

---

[4] See David Halperin, *One Hundred Years of Homosexuality* (New York: Rutledge, 1990), 3-40; Holt N. Parker, "The Myth of the Heterosexual: Anthropology and Sexuality for Classicists," *Arethusa* 34 (2001): 313-62.

[5] I have offered arguments for this conclusion about the church's prohibitions in my recent essay "Christ, Scripture, and Spiritual Friendship," in *Two Views on Homosexuality, the Bible, and the Church*, ed. Preston Sprinkle (Grand Rapids: Zondervan, 2016), 124-46.

[6] Eugene Rogers, *Sexuality and the Christian Body: Their Way into the Triune God* (Oxford: Blackwell, 1999).

Rogers's primary claim is that marriage is a Christian practice designed for the *sanctification* of the married couple. It is about God drawing the couple into God's own triune life in such a way that each of the spouses come to know themselves as the object of God's desire. "Marriage," Rogers writes, is a "bodily [practice] through which God enters the soul and disarms it with delight, lightening the load of impediments to love as it, embodied, hurries forward to something more and better for the body to mean."[7]

That sentence offers a taste of Rogers's poetic, deeply spiritual theology. He is concerned to present a theology of Christian marriage oriented toward holiness. He wants Christian marriage to be a practice that directs and purifies sexual desire so that the married couple becomes a participant in God's intratriune love and, thus, a window through which the world can glimpse God's love. As he sketches this theology of marriage, Rogers leans heavily on a lecture that Rowan Williams gave to a group of LGBTQ Christians in the United Kingdom titled "The Body's Grace," and in particular, this key quotation:

> The whole story of creation, incarnation, and our incorporation into the fellowship of Christ's body tells us that God desires us, *as if we were God*, as if we were that unconditional response to God's giving that God's self makes in the life of the Trinity. . . . The life of the Christian community has as its rationale—if not invariably its practical reality—the task of teaching us to so order our relations that human beings may see themselves as desired, as the occasion of joy.[8]

Rogers's question, like Williams's, is, how can that happen for gay Christians? How can they come to see themselves as occasions of joy, as desirable, as (to borrow C. S. Lewis's terminology) ingredients in the divine happiness? Here is how Rogers puts it: "The question for both sides [of the current debate] is this: by what sort of sacramental practices can the Church best teach gay and lesbian Christians to see themselves as occasions of joy, that God desires them as if they were God?"[9] And Rogers's answer to that question is marriage. *Marriage* is the way the church can teach gay and

---

[7]Ibid., 213.
[8]Rowan Williams, "The Body's Grace," in *Our Selves, Our Souls and Our Bodies: Sexuality and the Household of God*, ed. Charles Hefling (Boston: Cowley, 1996), 59 (italics original).
[9]Rogers, *Sexuality*, 27.

lesbian Christians that they are desirable, that they are desired by God in and through their love for, and the love they receive from, their spouse. Rogers says it this way:

> The vows do this: "for better for worse, for richer for poorer, in sickness and in health, till death do us part." Those ascetic vows—which Russian theologians compare to the vows of monastics—commit the couple to carry forward the solidarity of God and God's people. Marriage makes a school for virtue, where God prepares the couple for life with himself by binding them for life to each other.
>
> Marriage, in this view, is for sanctification, a means by which God can bring a couple to himself by turning their limits to their good. And no conservative I know has seriously argued that same-sex couples need sanctification any *less* than opposite-sex couples do.[10]

But how does Rogers make this work scripturally? He is well aware of Paul's claim in Romans 1 that same-sex sexual relations are "contrary to nature" (Rom 1:26).[11] But he notices that later in the same letter, Paul describes *God's own* action as "contrary to nature": God takes wild olive branches, which are a symbol for Gentile believers in Jesus, and grafts them onto the cultivated olive tree, which is a figure of Israel. As Paul says to his Gentile readers, "you were cut from what is by nature a wild olive tree, and grafted, contrary to nature, into a cultivated olive tree" (Rom 11:24). Rogers argues that just as the early church had to grapple with the shocking reality that God was welcoming the Gentiles into Christ's church, so we today must be ready to acknowledge and celebrate the fact that God is welcoming gay and lesbian and transgender people into holy matrimony. Rogers says it this way:

> As God grafts Gentiles, the wild branches, onto the domestic covenant of God's household with Israel, structured by the Torah of the Spirit, so God grafts gay and lesbian couples (whom detractors also associate with sexual license) by a new movement of the Spirit onto the domestic, married covenants of straight women and men.[12]

---

[10]Eugene F. Rogers Jr., "Same-Sex Complementarity," *The Christian Century*, May 11, 2011, www.christiancentury.org/article/2011-04/same-sex-complementarity.

[11]All scriptural quotations in this chapter are from the English Standard Version unless otherwise noted.

[12]Rogers, *Sexuality*, 50.

Rogers's argument is a very powerful and often moving one. I vividly remember exactly where I was—in a small coffee shop in St. Paul, Minnesota—when, at a time in my life when I was desperately searching for what Christianity had to say to me as a gay man, I read Rogers's book for the first time. I was struck by its obvious determination to work seriously with Scripture and the Christian tradition. I thought at that time, and I still think now, that it is one of the very best "affirming" arguments I've encountered.

SEX AFTER CHRIST

Before I respond to Rogers, I want to look briefly at one more "affirming" argument. This one is also by an Anglican ethicist, Robert Song, and it is titled *Covenant and Calling: Towards a Theology of Same-Sex Relationships*.[13] Unlike Rogers, Song does not argue for grafting gays and lesbians onto the covenant of *marriage*. Instead, he argues that the church can recognize heterosexual marriage as a Christian calling, celibacy as a complementary Christian calling, *and* what he calls "covenant partnerships" as a third, additional Christian vocation.

The way he arrives at this conclusion is by attending to the unfolding of the biblical canon. In Genesis, he argues, the meaning of sex is inextricably tied to procreation. God brings male and female together so that they may form a covenant bond that is oriented toward the bearing of children, so that the earth can be populated and so that, specifically, God's elect people Israel can increase. But once Christ comes and rises from the dead and the group designated as God's people is no longer defined by ethnic descent, sex needs no longer to be tied to procreation. Here is how Song himself puts it:

> According to the Christian narrative of the redemption of the world in Christ the Church has no ultimate stake in the propagation of the species or the indefinite continuation of society outside of Christ. . . . Sex BC is not the same as sex AD. . . . Life in the community of the resurrection is life in which the hope of children is no longer intrinsic to the community's identity.[14]

In other words, with the coming of Christ, the axis of history has shifted (Mk 1:14-15; 1 Cor 10:11). The need of the believing community to procreate in the

---

[13]Robert Song, *Covenant and Calling: Towards a Theology of Same-Sex Relationships* (London: SCM Press, 2014).
[14]Ibid., x, 18.

face of death is gone, since Christ has defeated death. In the resurrection, when death is abolished, Jesus says that "they neither marry nor are given in marriage" (Mt 22:30). There would be no need for marriage and childrearing in a world without death. Therefore, since Christians believe that that decisive defeat of death has happened already in the events of Good Friday and Easter Sunday, we are those who can sanction—and indeed celebrate—sexual partnerships that are not oriented to bearing children.

Song's argument is based on rich exegesis of the Genesis creation narratives, Jesus' teaching about marriage (Mt 19, 22; Mk 10), and Paul's teaching on celibacy (1 Cor 7). He seeks to integrate all this material in a theologically coherent synthesis by pointing to the radical, apocalyptic disjuncture between the norms of creation, in which marriage bears an intrinsic relation to childbearing, and the new, eschatological creation, in which celibacy and nonprocreative sexual partnerships can bear witness to a deathless kingdom in which procreation is no longer necessary in the way it formerly was.

When this kind of theologically coherent account is considered alongside the recognition that many gay and lesbian people today experience their sexual orientation as something that enables them to form life-giving bonds with the same sex, then one can begin to feel the powerful tug of the progressive case for the Christian affirmation of LGBTQ partnerships. If certain people are unlikely to be able to love someone of the opposite sex in a way that would make traditional marriage viable for them, and if they *are* likely to be able to love someone of the same sex in a permanent, faithful, stable way, and if the gospel has opened the door to contemplate vocations that do not include bearing children, then it would seem that there is good reason to make space in the church for the celebration and solemnization of same-sex partnerships. That is Robert Song's argument in brief.

MARRIAGE AND SEX ACCORDING TO JESUS

Having sketched these "progressive" proposals, I want now to step back and offer some criticism of them both. The way I want to approach this task is, however, not intuitive. I want to turn to Matthew 19:1-9, in which Jesus is asked about divorce by the Pharisees, and allow that text to set the stage for my criticism of Rogers and Song:

Now when Jesus had finished these sayings, he went away from Galilee and entered the region of Judea beyond the Jordan. And large crowds followed him, and he healed them there. And Pharisees came up to him and tested him by asking, "Is it lawful to divorce one's wife for any cause?" He answered, "Have you not read that he who created them from the beginning made them male and female, and said, 'Therefore a man shall leave his father and his mother and hold fast to his wife, and the two shall become one flesh'? So they are no longer two but one flesh. What therefore God has joined together, let not man separate." They said to him, "Why then did Moses command one to give a certificate of divorce and to send her away?" He said to them, "Because of your hardness of heart Moses allowed you to divorce your wives, but from the beginning it was not so. And I say to you: whoever divorces his wife, except for sexual immorality, and marries another, commits adultery." (Mt 19:1-9)

There are at least three relevant features of this passage for my purposes. Notice first the way Jesus answers the Pharisees when they allude to Deuteronomy 24:1-4, which is the provision in the Mosaic law for a man to divorce his wife. In response to the Pharisees' use of this verse, Jesus quotes another passage from the Pentateuch, from the book of Genesis, and he introduces his quotation with these words: "Have you not read that he who created them from the beginning." Jesus positions the theological moment of creation over against the *later* moment in Deuteronomy the Pharisees appeal to. The question is, why?

The answer lies in Matthew 19:8, in which Jesus says, "Because of your hardness of heart Moses allowed you to divorce your wives, but from the beginning it was not so." The reason Jesus presses the *difference* between the creation in the beginning and the later Mosaic provision for divorce is because something deleterious has occurred *in human beings.* Jesus uses the metaphor of "hardness": the human heart has calcified, grown stony, unresponsive, and cold toward God and neighbor. The Pharisees, Jesus seems to imply, have an underdeveloped doctrine of the human plight. They are inclined to read Moses' provision for divorce as if it represented God's absolute will for his people from the beginning. But for Jesus, that leaves human recalcitrance, evil, and stubbornness unaddressed. As C. E. B. Cranfield has put it,

The Pharisees were inclined to ignore . . . the need to distinguish clearly between those elements of the [Old Testament] law which set forth the perfect
will of God (what we may call—in one sense of the word—His *absolute* will,
that is, His will in itself, not affected by the fact and results of human sin), on
the one hand, and, on the other, those elements which, taking into account
the fact of men's sinfulness, indicate not God's perfect, absolute will, but His
will in response to the circumstances brought about by human sin.[15]

Second, notice the way Jesus fuses together texts from the first and second
chapters of Genesis. "Have you not read that the one who made them at the
beginning 'made them male and female'"—that is a quotation of Genesis
1:27—"and said, 'For this reason a man shall leave his father and mother and
be joined to his wife, and the two shall become one flesh'?"—that is a quotation of Genesis 2:24. "So they are no longer two, but one flesh. Therefore
what God has joined together, let no one separate" (Mt 19:5-6 NRSV). Jesus,
in other words, reads the sexual difference of humanity in Genesis 1:26-27—
the creation of humanity as male and female—alongside the affirmation of a
bond of faithful union in Genesis 2:24. With that fusion of the two texts,
sexual difference and the meaning of marriage are pulled together and inter-
twined. The creation of male and female, in other words, is the basis for the
covenant bond that a man makes with a woman in matrimony.

Third and finally, notice the way that Jesus operates on the assumption
that his followers now are no longer subject to the Mosaic provision for
divorce. Jesus proceeds on the assumption that it is now possible to go back
to "the beginning," to live in light of Genesis and its affirmation of an inseparable bond of marriage. The kingdom of God that Jesus is announcing
and bringing to bear on the world is not something that sanctions the
current status quo. It is not something that simply fits itself into the preex-
isting Mosaic concession to human hardness of heart. On the contrary, the
kingdom is one in which God's promise to Israel through the prophet
Ezekiel is coming true: "A new heart I will give you, and a new spirit I will
put within you; and I will remove from your body the heart of stone and
give you a heart of flesh" (Ezek 36:26 NRSV). The axis of history has shifted.
Because Jesus is bringing God's saving reign into the world, his followers

---

[15]As quoted in W. D. Davies and Dale C. Allison, *Matthew 19–28*, International Critical Commentary 3 (London: T&T Clark, 2004), 14.

do not have to make compromises with human hardness of heart. Rather, we are those who can begin, however haltingly, to live in light of the world God originally intended to make before sin and death ruined it all— because that is the world God is remaking now. As W. D. Davies and Dale Allison have written,

> Jesus, whose followers should have no hearts of stone but hearts of flesh (Ezek 36.26), demands conformity to the will of God as it was expressed in the beginning.... The coming of the kingdom is the beginning of the restoration of paradise, the union of creation and redemption, the final realization of what God intended from the beginning.[16]

In this understanding, Jesus' bearing of the saving reign of God does not set aside or overturn the original creation. Rather, it begins to heal it, reclaim it from sin's clutches, and restore it to what God first had in mind.

CREATION AND KINGDOM: BREAK WITH THE PAST?

All three of these points are relevant when we ponder arguments for Christian same-sex marriage like the ones Rogers and Song have offered. In the first place, Rogers and Song downplay the need to *interrogate* gay experience and same-sex desire. Everywhere in their books it is simply assumed, first, that same-sex sexual desire is more or less fixed, that it gives one an identity in the world, that misery will result if those of us who are lesbian or gay do not find a way to affirm it and express it, and that it is always capable of bearing witness to divine love. But nowhere do they explore the possibility that same-sex sexual desire may in fact be instead a result of the fall. The positive *experience* of lesbian and gay Christians—that our loves are life-enhancing—seems to be self-evident to Rogers and Song: they argue *from* this reality rather than *for* it. As the Catholic moral theologian Christopher Roberts has observed,

> It is as if Augustine's argument against the Pelagians, to the effect that human desires must be subject to theological judgment and cannot simply be trusted for their goodness, had never been made. Augustine wrote persuasively that not all sexually differentiated desires are theologically honorable; desires must be interrogated in relation to the ontology of creation and love of the heavenly

---

[16]Ibid., 14.

city. [Rogers and Song seem] unprepared to do the same and to inspect same-sex desire from perspectives that might problematize it.[17]

In the second place, Rogers (though not Song, who argues instead for sexually active "covenant partnerships") proceeds as if the creation of male and female is inessential to the meaning of marriage. Marriage is an institution whose definition is capable of expansion. Male-and-female is *one* form that marriage can take, numerically the dominant form, but it is not the only form.[18] Recall, however, that Jesus holds Genesis 1, with its emphasis on the sexual difference of male and female and their bearing children, together with the affirmation in Genesis 2 that it is *for this reason* that people marry. The emphasis on the "one-flesh" bond is not, as Brownson has argued, simply about kinship regardless of sexual difference; it is, rather, a unity-in-difference. As the New Testament scholar Ian Paul has written of Genesis, "The twin themes of similarity and difference wind their way through the story like a double helix," and Jesus appears to share this perspective.[19]

Finally, Rogers and Song both see the new creation that God has inaugurated in Jesus Christ as something that breaks with or moves beyond the original creation. God is doing a "new thing" in welcoming and affirming gay and lesbian partnerships. But is this an adequate understanding of the relationship between creation and redemption? If we take Matthew 19 as our starting point, we are given a picture of God's kingdom as something that restores to us the original creation, and it to us. Jesus might well have spoken of God's reign as something that is pressing into new territory, leaving behind the old material of creation as so much rubbish and ushering us into an entirely new way of being human. But that is not the picture in Matthew 19. Instead, to quote Davies and Allison again, Jesus draws our attention to "the *union* of creation and redemption."[20] And the early church, following

---

[17]Christopher C. Roberts, *Creation and Covenant: The Significance of Sexual Difference in the Moral Theology of Marriage* (New York: T&T Clark, 2007), 197.

[18]Megan DeFranza and James Brownson have recently made similar arguments, suggesting that "male and female" in Genesis 1 is an illustrative type but not exhaustive of all the variations of human sexuality that God has made. See James V. Brownson, *Bible, Gender, Sexuality: Reframing the Church's Debate on Same-Sex Relationships* (Grand Rapids: Eerdmans, 2013); Megan K. DeFranza, *Sex Difference in Christian Theology: Male, Female, and Intersex in the Image of God* (Grand Rapids: Eerdmans, 2015).

[19]Ian Paul, *Same-Sex Unions: The Key Biblical Texts* (Cambridge: Grove Books, 2014), 8.

[20]Davies and Allison, *Matthew 19–28*, 14.

the lead of passages like this, rejected as heresy the doctrines of the Man-
ichees (that bodies are something to be redeemed *from*) and the Marcionites
(that the Old Testament is now to be set aside in favor of the New). In the
words of Karl Barth, God's reconciling work in Christ is "the confirmation
and restoration of the order of creation."[21] God intends in Jesus Christ the
reconstitution of marriage, not its redefinition.

Augustine was one of those early Christians who argued strongly that what
God had designed in the beginning—the bodies of male and female creatures—would not be disfigured or erased in the resurrection of the dead, in
the new creation. Rather, as Beth Felker Jones points out in her remarkable
book *Marks of His Wounds*, "Sexed bodies, male and female, are for Augustine
the stuff of nature, and God does not make us new by destroying nature. God
saves *us* rather than some other creatures altogether."[22] And this is, I think,
ultimately the Achilles' heel of arguments like Eugene Rogers's and Robert
Song's: their arguments pull apart rather than hold together the doctrines of
creation and redemption. Bodies, and the sexed difference of those bodies,
matter. And what matters to God will not be cast aside in the kingdom of God.

GAY CHRISTIANS ARE CALLED TO LOVE

In conclusion, I want to return to something I said above. I have devoted
much space to criticizing what I think are fairly disastrous theological moves
in the arguments of Rogers and Song. But I want to come back to what I
think they get right: Rogers and Song, better than any theologians I have
read, urge us to grapple seriously with the question of what gay and lesbian
sanctification—which is the same thing as gay and lesbian *love*—looks like.

For far too long in evangelical churches, many Christian leaders have
operated on the assumption that sanctification looks like a therapeutic
regimen in which gay Christians are promised that they can be delivered
and healed from their same-sex attractions. I have sat in a counselor's office
and been *promised* categorically that I could become heterosexual. When
these promises have failed to come to fruition, gay and lesbian believers have
been harmed.

---

[21]Karl Barth, *Church Dogmatics* IV/3, §69 (Edinburgh: T&T Clark, 1961), 43.
[22]Beth Felker Jones, *Marks of His Wounds: Gender Politics and Bodily Resurrection* (Oxford: Oxford
    University Press, 2007), 95-96.

What, then, is our answer to Rogers and Song's question? How can our gay experience, in the words of Oliver O'Donovan, "be clothed in an appropriate pattern of life for the service of God and discipleship of Christ"?[23] This is the question I wish to leave with pastor theologians. What does it look like for someone who is same-sex attracted, or who experiences gender dysphoria or any of the myriad other nonheterosexual sexualities, to see themselves as wanted, as occasions of joy, as ingredients in the divine happiness? By what sort of practices will our churches teach gay and lesbian believers this? How will our fellow Christians help us to see that we all have callings, positive vocations, and not just mandates of self-denial?

I have a gay Catholic friend named Eve Tushnet, a celibate woman who is devoting her life to Christ and the church. She writes this:

> We are often told, including by many Christians, that the church asks gay people to lead an empty life devoid of love, or forces us to choose between human love in this life and God's love in the afterlife. These false choices break hearts and spirits. Gay [Christians] . . . can love and be loved, both by Christ who loves everyone and by the particular humans on whose shoulders we lean. Not only faith but hope and love are open to us, too.[24]

Amen.

---

[23]Oliver O'Donovan, *Church in Crisis: The Gay Controversy and the Anglican Communion* (Eugene, OR: Cascade Books, 2008), 117.

[24]Eve Tushnet, "Gay and Catholic: What the Church Gets Right and Wrong About Being Gay," *On Faith*, October 8, 2010, www.onfaith.co/onfaith/2010/10/08/gay-and-catholic-what-the -church-gets-right-and-wrong-about-being-gay/7950.

4

Sexuality and the Church

How Pastoral Ministry Shapes
a Theology of Sexuality

JEREMY TREAT

O N JANUARY 1, 2013, MY FAMILY AND I moved from Wheaton, Illinois, to Los Angeles, California. It was a journey across the country that also represented my own vocational path, going from a PhD program in theology to pastoring a young, urban church in the heart of Hollywood. I knew the cultural changes would be intense, but I had no idea how much it would shape my life and ministry. The first neighbor we met was a single mom with a transgender daughter, Daniela, who used to be Daniel. My first day driving into work I immediately noticed on the streets an unusual amount of muscular, African American men wearing dresses (I later learned that particular strip of Santa Monica Blvd. is the highest concentration of transgender prostitution in the city). When my oldest daughter started kindergarten, she quickly met kids with two moms or two dads, especially since one of their first class projects was titled "All Families Are Different." And all of this was just setting me up for the day-to-day ministry of discipling, counseling, and preaching in a hypersexualized and extremely broken city. The church I pastor is filled with many men and women who experience same-sex attraction, and hardly a day goes by that I do not deal explicitly with real-life questions and situations regarding gender, sexuality, and marriage.

In this essay I want to answer the question of how my ecclesial and cultural context has shaped my theology of sexuality. On the one hand, it has not changed at all. I believe as firmly as ever that God created two distinct genders—male and female—and that sex is reserved for a covenant marriage between a man and a woman. And yet, on the other hand, my context has completely changed my theology of sexuality; not necessarily *what* I believe about sexuality but certainly *how* I approach it and *why* it is such an important matter. In short, I have learned that sex is never just about sex. Rather, one's beliefs about sex, gender, and marriage mediate their broader views of life. The meaning we attribute to sexuality is inseparable from the stories we live by, the wounds we have received, and the relationships we have (or do not have). The contemporary debates over sexuality, therefore, are not ultimately conflicts about what happens under the covers but are a collision of worldviews.

What the church needs is not primarily to attack opposing views or even merely to restate our position; we need a positive and captivating counterproposal. As Christopher Roberts says, "Mere opposition to same-sex marriage is not the same thing as a positive theological and evangelical account of sexual difference."[1] The church must show how sexuality is part of a grander vision of life that includes a more compelling narrative, a more authentic community, and a more profound ethic.

A MORE COMPELLING NARRATIVE

The story of Caitlyn Jenner was more than another tabloid headline or Hollywood gossip story; it felt like a cultural tipping point. Bruce Jenner was by American terms a man's man: muscular, athletic, successful, wealthy, and always with a beautiful woman at his side. And with the declaration of his word, in what was lauded as an act of courage and honor, Bruce became Caitlyn. The fact that it happened at all demonstrates how quickly our culture has changed; the fact that it was celebrated shows where we are headed.

The media frenzy around Jenner made it difficult to know what to believe, but the moment it all made sense to me was when Bruce Jenner was

---

[1] Christopher C. Roberts, *Creation and Covenant: The Significance of Sexual Difference in and for the Moral Theology of Marriage* (New York: T&T Clark, 2007), 3.

interviewed by Diane Sawyer just before he changed his identity to Caitlyn. The conversation eventually came to the point where Jenner reflected on why, after years of internal tension, he had decided to make the change. The defining words of wisdom, he said, came from his son-in-law Kanye West: "Look . . . I can be married to the most beautiful woman in the world, and I am. I can have the most beautiful little daughter in the world. I have that. But I'm nothing, if I can't be me. If I can't be true to myself, they don't mean anything."[2]

This was the key that unlocked Jenner's gender dilemma. "Be true to myself." As Jenner recounted this pivotal moment of his journey, one could almost feel the heads nodding around the country as his words echoed with altruism and morality.

The more I thought about Jenner's comments, the more I was struck that the idea of "being true to yourself" only makes sense in a hyperindividualistic culture. If you told someone in a collectivist society (a culture in which they put the community before the individual) to "be true to yourself," they would probably respond by saying, "Why would I do that? Why not be true to my community? Why not be true to my family?" Jenner's moment of realization showed that he did not merely have a different view of gender, he was operating by a completely different narrative. It is the same narrative that has captivated our culture and, more than we want to admit, our churches.

The secular narrative. The secular narrative is a master story that is grounded in the authority of personal choice and culminates in individual happiness. It is the narrative of the sovereign self. The philosopher Charles Taylor says this "expressive individualism" is the cultural air that we breathe, where "each one of us has his/her own way of realizing our humanity, and that it is important to find and live out one's own, as against surrendering to conformity with a model imposed on us from the outside."[3]

Much has been written on individualism and its pervasive influence on Western culture. Dale Kuehne's *Sex and the iWorld*, however, has demonstrated how individualism has particularly shaped the way our culture

---

[2]"Bruce Jenner—The Interview," by Diane Sawyer, *20/20*, ABC, April 24, 2015, http://abc.go.com /shows/2020/episode-guide/2015-04/24-bruce-jenner-the-interview.
[3]Charles Taylor, *A Secular Age* (Cambridge, MA: The Belknap Press of Harvard University Press, 2007), 486.

thinks about sexuality. Individualism is not merely the context for contemporary sexuality but is, rather, the determining factor. Kuehne argues that "humans are made for relationship and that we find our deepest fulfillment not when seeking self-fulfillment but when living and engaging in the full constellation of healthy human relationships."[4] In a culture of individualism, however, fulfillment is found not in relationships but through unhindered personal choice. Sexuality becomes not a way to relate deeply with another in commitment but to express yourself. Covenant is replaced with consent.

In the secular narrative, it must be acknowledged that the coronation of self is at the same time a revolt against God. Sin is the attempt to dethrone God and replace him with the sovereign self, where individual desire reigns, personal choice is the authority, and independence is considered freedom. Sin is autonomy (self-rule), which is exactly what the secular narrative celebrates. It is Eden all over again.

A practical example of how this plays out in society was in 2016 with President Barack Obama's redefinition of Title IX that mandated opposite-sex use of bathrooms, locker rooms, and showers at all public schools in America. According to the mandate, students are able to determine their own gender and therefore which bathroom they will use accordingly. What is going on here? Is this just a nonreligious decision about civility? Certainly not. This is expressive individualism played out to its logical end. *I* decide who I am. We, as fallen humanity, are kicking against the idea that we have a Creator. No one can impose a gender upon me; *I* choose my gender. In reality, this is not the rejection of the idea of a deity; it is the deification of self. I speak, and it is so. I determine what is right or wrong for myself. Each individual is the great I AM.

Locating ultimate authority in the individual has major implications for our society. For decades if not centuries, secular culture has been touting science as the ultimate authority. Faith-based statements have not been considered to be on the same level as evidence-based claims. But consider what is happening with these rulings on gender. The authority is no longer science; it is self. It can be proven scientifically that someone is a boy or a girl, but the new law demands that self trumps science. If someone is born a male

---

[4]Dale S. Kuehne, *Sex and the iWorld: Rethinking Relationship Beyond an Age of Individualism* (Grand Rapids: Baker Academic, 2009), 25.

and is biologically a male but decides to be a female, his self-determination wins out. Such a decision, on the part of the individual and the government, is only possible within the narrative of the sovereign self.

Right doctrine, wrong narrative. In talking about the secular narrative, the church must acknowledge that this is not an "us versus them" conversation, as if expressive individualism only affects those outside the body of Christ. Far from it. Individualism is the air that we breathe even when we attempt to speak out against it. I believe that many—if not most—Christians in America are attempting to uphold Christian doctrine while unknowingly living by the secular narrative. This is why many Christians believe that homosexuality is a sin but have a hard time explaining why it is a sin, other than God making an arbitrary rule.

This is significant, for at the end of the day, one's master narrative will shape his or her particular beliefs more than the other way around. For example, Charles Taylor makes the case that when people are converted to secularism, they are usually not convinced by the data of science but rather by the story of science.[5] Not many people are getting behind the microscope or reading the scientific literature. They are, however, drawn to a narrative that culminates in a basically good humanity that can make the world a better place through our own ingenuity.

The secular narrative is pervasive, it is shaping cultural views on sexuality, and it is influencing the church more than most could imagine. It is not enough, therefore, for the church merely to restate the historic theological position (though this too is important). The church needs a robust theology of sexuality *and* it needs to place it within a broader narrative of a gracious God restoring his broken creation through his beloved Son.

The beauty of God's design. Before introducing the biblical narrative, I want to share a bit of my own journey to show why it matters that this narrative is compelling. As a preacher, I started recognizing that every time I talked about gender, marriage, or sexuality from the pulpit I had a very defensive and apologizing tone: "Now I know this is difficult to hear, but let me explain." "It's not as bad as it appears." One day, though, I heard someone talking about the beauty of God's design for gender and marriage, and I felt

---

[5]Taylor, *Secular Age*, 362.

convicted about the way I had been thinking and talking about God's Word. That day, I vowed never to be defensive or apologize about what God says is beautiful, even if the world says it is ugly. Biblical marriage is not an old-fashioned or outdated religious moral code, it is a blueprint for human flourishing from the God who never runs out of wisdom and who cares for his creation more than a husband for his bride.

We need a more compelling narrative. We need theology that sings. We need logic on fire. When it comes to sexuality, we need to show not only that God's design is true and good, but also that it is beautiful.

We have seen that the secular view of sex is shaped by a master narrative that places the sovereign self at the center of the universe. This may be the place of sex and romance within the American Dream, but it is far from the teaching of the Jewish Messiah about the kingdom of God. Scripture presents sexuality within the story of a gracious God restoring his broken creation through his beloved Son. The people of God must know this story, for as Christopher Ash says, "It is the proper work of Christian theology (and in particular creation theology) to place sexuality within the metanarrative of God's purpose for human kind."[6]

The biblical narrative. The story of humanity begins in the Garden, but contrary to popular opinion, it was never meant to stay there. Most people assume that God placed Adam and Eve in Eden as a sort of eternal honeymoon. According to Scripture, however, God did not give the first man a vacation; he gave him a task. Adam is placed in Eden and told to work and keep the Garden, and he is given Eve as a partner to fill the earth and cultivate it for human flourishing. Eden was a beautiful garden, but the rest of the world was wild and untamed. Adam and Eve were given the task of expanding the borders of Eden to the ends of the earth. However, they could not do this alone. So not only are Adam and Eve given each other to partner in this mission but they are also called to start a family in order to further the task. Sex is good in and of itself, but sex is not merely an end itself. Christopher Ash, in *Marriage: Sex in the Service of God*, shows how sex and marriage fit into God's greater purposes: "Humankind was made male and female that we might use our sexuality in the service of God;

---

[6]Christopher Ash, *Marriage: Sex in the Service of God* (Vancouver, BC: Regent College Publishing, 2003), 66.

those who marry are to direct their marriages to the stewardship of God's created order."[7]

Sex was God's idea, and he created it as a gift to be enjoyed and as a means to accomplish the greater purpose of his people filling the earth and making it more like Eden. Within this story we can see that male and female are created different not for the sake of competing with one another but for complementing one another. It is this sexual difference and sexual complementarity that is the basis for the comprehensive union of a man and a woman in sex and marriage.

There is, of course, more to the story. Sin twists the goodness of sexuality in all of us and the gospel is the ultimate remedy that renews God's purposes for creation. Briefly unpacking the beginning of the story, however, is sufficient to show how different this narrative framework is than that of the secular narrative. It is not the story of human progress within which we create our own identity and express ourselves. It is the story of a gracious God putting together by grace what has been torn apart by our sin. That is the narrative we need so that we may understand both the beauty and brokenness of our sexuality.

A More Authentic Community

I had a conversation a while ago with a gay man who was considering becoming a Christian. He was drawn to the way and the teachings of Jesus, he acknowledged the wickedness of his own heart, and he saw the abundance of God's grace. He had read the Scriptures enough to know that to follow Jesus was to deny his own flesh and give up many of his own dreams. But there was one thing that was really holding him back: his experience with the church. When he had sought community from the church, he had encountered a hypocritical and hurtful people. He wanted Christ and he even knew that it would require him giving up his lifestyle, but the very people who were supposed to be a welcoming family to him had become a barrier.

This man's experience was not merely shaped by his interactions with a few select individuals. It is bigger than that. There are systemic patterns in American Christianity that have made it nearly impossible for those

---

[7]Ibid., 134.

attracted to the same sex to feel welcome and involved in the body of Christ.[8] For far too long the church has called out certain sexual sins without at the same time offering the grace of Christ and the support of community.

For many of us, our community needs to catch up with our theology. In fact, if our theology does not shape the right kind of community, then our theology is off in the first place. There are three specific areas where I believe the church must grow if it is going to develop more authentic communities.

The dignity of singleness. The white picket fences of American values must come down because they are dividing the family of God. For too long the church has idolized marriage and denigrated singleness. Jesus and Paul dignified singleness with their lives, and their teachings were clear: there are two equally viable options for the Christian—marriage or celibacy (Mt 19:3-12; 1 Cor 7:1-11). Both are gifts from God to be used in service of God's greater mission. They are gifts, not curses. A spouse is never a ball and chain. Singleness is never a life sentence to loneliness. Both have joys and both have challenges. Both are valid options for the Christian.

Vaughn Roberts says,

> Single people . . . too often believe the lie that they are bound to experience miserable, isolated lives unless they can find a spouse. In their commendable desire to protect marriage and the family from contemporary challenges, churches can unwittingly become a part of the problem by giving the impression that romantic love is an essential ingredient to human flourishing.[9]

Single people are not second-class citizens in the kingdom of God, nor are they incomplete if they do not find a spouse. Jesus was fully human and deeply satisfied in God and he was, of course, single.

American culture celebrates singleness but for far different reasons than Scripture; namely, as an expression of independence and the "do whatever I want" definition of freedom. The church does not merely need to celebrate singleness but to dignify it and to learn how to integrate singles and families in the body of Christ. In Christ, we are children of God. That means married

---

[8]According to Andrew Marin, 86 percent of LGBT people spent their childhood in church, with more than half of them leaving those religious communities as adults. Andrew Marin, *Us Versus Us: The Untold Story of Religion and the LGBT Community* (Colorado Springs: NavPress, 2016), xxv.

[9]Vaughn Roberts, *True Friendship: Walking Shoulder to Shoulder* (Leyland, England: 10Publishing, 2013), 35-36.

and single people are part of the one primary family that is more significant than every other family.

The significance of friendship. To proclaim the dignity of singleness, the church must also provide the type of community where single brothers and sisters truly experience the intimacy of the family of God. Our relational needs were never meant to be fulfilled through one romantic relationship. We need a community of friends. Friendship is not an added bonus to the Christian life but is essential for following Jesus as the community of his disciples. What has become a cheap concept in our culture has a rich tradition in the church and deep roots in Scripture. It is time for the church to recover a robust theology of friendship and shepherd its people into deep, meaningful friendships.

In the twelfth century, Aelred of Rievaulx taught that there are three types of friendships, each based on different shared goals. Carnal friendship is based on affinity or amusement. Worldly friendship is based on usefulness. Spiritual friendship is based on a mutual commitment to following Jesus. Spiritual friends have a shared vision of a good and fulfilling human life and help each other in their pursuit of such a life. Aelred proclaimed, "What statement about friendship can be more sublime, more true, more valuable than this: it has been proved that friendship must begin in Christ, continue with Christ, and be perfected by Christ."[10]

Long before Aelred, Augustine also drew from the deep well of friendship, both in his theology and in his life. What is surprising about Augustine is that he converted to Christianity upon hearing the story of a legendary hermit named Anthony. Although Augustine embraced Anthony's ascetic rigor and discipline, he radically redefined Anthony's understanding of monasticism, going the opposite direction from isolation to connection with others. The reason for this great divergence was Augustine's experience and theology of what he called "that most unfathomable of all involvements of the soul—friendship."[11] For Augustine, friendship with God was the source and center of friendship with others.

Augustine provides an example of a man who was sexually promiscuous in his youth and early adulthood and then after becoming a Christian, was

---

[10]Aerlred of Rievaulx, *Spiritual Friendship* (Collegeville, MN: Cistercian Publications, 2010), 57.
[11]Augustine, *The Confessions of Saint Augustine*, trans. John K. Ryan (New York: Doubleday, 1960), 2.9.

celibate and yet experienced profound relational fulfillment. According to Peter Brown, "Augustine . . . hardly ever spen[t] a moment of his life without some friend, even some blood-relative, close by him."[12] For the church to truly function as the body of Christ, it must learn to cultivate deep, meaningful friendships with singles and families.

The power of compassion. As a pastor, most conversations about sexuality that people initiate with me begin with beliefs: "Well, I believe . . ." or "Do you think it is wrong to . . . ?" But although the discussions usually start with theological opinion they almost always end up at personal experiences. Why? Because beneath the theological doubts there are almost always relational wounds. In fact, just about every person that I know who experiences same-sex attraction has wounds from the church, whether they grew up in the church or not.

Most people's stories are defined more by hurt than doubt. When we talk about topics having to do with sexuality, we need to remember that we are not merely talking about "issues"; we are talking about image-bearers of God. We are not talking merely about policies but people. Real people, with wounds, stories, questions, and struggles—all of which matter and ought to shape our interactions. We need to think about people holistically: theologically, psychologically, physically, socially, and so on.

Theology matters, but sound doctrine cannot replace the healing power of compassion, empathy, and love. Compassion does not compromise theology; it enriches it. Although people might come across like they are looking for an argument, what most people need is a safe space to express the tension they feel between their faith in God and what they are experiencing in their lives. While we need sound doctrine, we also need communities of compassion.

There are two particular practices that the church needs to embody to foster communities of compassion. The first is listening. Hagar longed to be heard and seen, and Scripture says, "The LORD has listened to your affliction" (Gen 16:11).[13] We all want to be known and heard, and God does this primarily

---

[12]Peter Brown, *Augustine of Hippo: A Biography*, rev. ed. (Berkeley: University of California Press, 2000), 20. Brown also says, "No thinker in the early church was so preoccupied with the nature of human relationships." Ibid.

[13]All scriptural quotations in this chapter are from the English Standard Version unless otherwise noted.

through the means of community. Dietrich Bonhoeffer, in *Life Together*, calls this "the ministry of listening." According to Bonhoeffer, "The first service that one owes to others in the fellowship consists in listening to them."[14] When someone is hurting, we often assume that they need to hear something from us, but what they truly need is first to be heard and known. To be become communities of empathy and compassion, the church must learn to listen.

We also need to be a people who apologize. We spend so much time defending the Christian view of sexuality that we overlook the need to apologize for our own inconsistencies with it. We are a people of truth, but sometimes the most truthful thing we can do is to acknowledge the failures of our own traditions. When it comes to the LGBTQ community, we need less apologetics and more apologizing. Only this kind of humility and compassion will open the way for the type of relationships necessary for showing God's love to people in sexual brokenness.

A MORE PROFOUND ETHIC

To flourish in an age of sexual confusion, the church needs to recapture the narrative of redemption and cultivate authentic communities of grace. The church also needs a more profound ethic. By "profound" I mean that we need an ethic that is set apart from the mainstream cultural ethic, present within the public square, and grounded in something lasting.

Set apart. Unfortunately, it has taken our nation shifting its views on sexuality to remind the church that we have distinct views on sex, gender, and marriage. There was a time in our country when Christians could talk with anyone about sex, gender, and marriage and assume that they believed the same thing, even if that person was not a Christian. That time is no more. God's people are "strangers and exiles" (Heb 11:13) who have unique beliefs and a distinct ethic that are shaped by the story of Jesus and the authority of Scripture.

According to recent polls, Christianity is in decline in America.[15] A closer look at the research, however, shows that nominal Christianity is in decline while biblical, Christ-centered faith is thriving. Nonetheless, there

---

[14]Dietrich Bonhoeffer, *Life Together* (San Francisco: HarperSanFrancisco, 1993), 97.
[15]"America's Changing Religious Landscape," Pew Research Center, May 12, 2015, www.pewforum
.org/2015/05/12/americas-changing-religious-landscape/.

is certainly a sense that "Christian America" is no more. And to that I say "good riddance" because it never was "Christian America" in the first place. It was a people who had confused the American Dream with the kingdom of God, exchanged biblical doctrine with pop psychology, and replaced devotion to Jesus with vague morality. The end of "Christian America" is not an obstacle for the church; it is an opportunity to rediscover the true nature of the church as exiles in a foreign land. We have become too at home in our culture. America is not the Promised Land. We are not home. We are sojourners. As followers of a Jewish carpenter we should not expect our beliefs and ethic to align with mainstream culture.

We do not live in a culture where Christians are perceived as moral and others as amoral. There is a new morality. The one indisputable law of the new morality is that you cannot deny yourself. Yet the call of Jesus is exactly that: "If anyone would come after me, let him deny himself and take up his cross daily and follow me" (Lk 9:23). Christians have always been different, but while our view of sex, gender, and marriage used to be a point of contact, it is now a point of distinction. And that is fine. We are exiles.

Within. As exiles, followers of Jesus are called to be set apart from within. God calls his people to be in the city yet distinct from the city and for the city. Miroslav Volf calls this "internal difference." According to Volf, "to live as a Christian means to keep inserting a difference into a given culture without ever stepping outside that culture to do so."[16] In this day and age our primary need is not relevance but resilience. The gospel does not need to be updated; it needs to be proclaimed.

The church is called to be within the culture for the sake of seeking the common good. While many Christians have acknowledged the calling to "seek the welfare of the city where I have sent you into exile" (Jer 29:7), we also must recognize that in order to seek the common good we have to help define the common good. Volf says, "A vision of human flourishing—and resources to realize it—is the most important contribution of the Christian faith to the common good."[17] The secular Western narrative defines human flourishing as individual experiential satisfaction. Scripture offers a grander vision: humanity flourishing out of a place of love for God and neighbor.

---

[16]Miroslav Volf, *A Public Faith* (Grand Rapids: Brazos, 2013), 93.
[17]Ibid., 63.

Grounded. The Christian ethic is unique, and it is also substantive. The depth of the Christian ethic is especially powerful when compared to the reigning morality of the day, which often proves rather tenuous. For example, tolerance is the secular culture's highest virtue, and yet it is often enforced in rather intolerant ways. It is not difficult in our culture to see how "tolerance" is often used as a concept for people get their way and look virtuous doing so. We need a more substantive understanding of tolerance, one that is not based on the equality of all ideas but on the equality of people. It is possible to love someone without affirming their actions. One need not agree with another to show them respect.

Another example of how the new morality often lacks substance or grounding is in causes related to human rights. Whether regarding race, gender, or socioeconomic status, many people argue for the equality and dignity of all people. But why? Keep asking questions and one quickly realizes that most people in our culture are building on the distinctly biblical idea that all people have dignity and value because they are made in God's image.[18] It is not a self-evident truth that all people are created equal, which is why Aristotle said some people were born to be slaves and why many cultures today still base a person's value not on their God-given dignity but on how much they contribute to society.[19]

Christianity offers a deep, thoughtful tradition of ethics and morality. In an age of moral confusion and new ethical possibilities (e.g., bioethics), the church more than ever needs to ground itself in the teachings of Christ, whose very throne is founded on righteousness and justice.

Conclusion

For too long, when it comes to sexuality, the church's no has been much bigger than its yes. Of course, we need to say "no" to sin. But people are longing for a greater yes—a positive vision of flourishing under the beauty of God's design and the power of his grace. We need a more compelling narrative, a more authentic community, and a more profound ethic.

---

[18]See Nicholas Wolterstorff, "Is a Secular Grounding of Human Rights Possible?," in *Justice: Rights and Wrongs* (Princeton, NJ: Princeton University Press, 2010), 323-41.
[19]Aristotle, *Politics*, ed. R. F. Stalley, trans. Ernest Barker (Oxford: Oxford University Press, 2009), 1.6.

5

Continuing the Task

RICHARD MOUW

MY ASSIGNMENT AT OUR CONFERENCE on sexuality was to offer some reflections at the final plenary session. I came to the event, then, with some notes for what I might say. But I was mainly prepared to listen carefully to all that was said at the previous sessions. As it turned out, this was an important learning experience for me on both a general level and a specific one.

On the general level, I gained a deeper appreciation for the commitment of the Center for Pastor Theologians to the development of a robust ecclesial theology. As envisioned by those who lead the Center, ecclesial theology ranges more broadly than ecclesiology, the subdiscipline of theology that focuses on the nature and mission of the church. For the work of the Center, ecclesial theology does not just look theologically *at* the church; it examines a wide range of significant theological topics *from* the church. It is an exercise in serious theological reflection conducted by persons who are deeply engaged in pastoral ministry.

I find the case for that kind of ecclesial theology to be compelling. I was trained in the academic guilds and I thank God for everything that I have learned during my decades of participation in scholarly communities. But I am aware of the fact that when it comes to formulating a theology that equips the people of God for active discipleship in the world, the academy's theological contribution has not been adequate. Some of this inadequacy has to be attributed to failure, but much of it is understandable. The academy, even at its best, is at least a step removed from the practical challenges that many Christians experience in their daily lives. We need pastor theologians who are in touch with those challenges, theological thinkers who are standing alongside people who face new questions in our culture. How do we respond to those questions in a way that honors the authority of God's Word and the supreme lordship of Jesus Christ over all of life?

There is a tendency for those of us in the theological academy to assume that the only "real" theology that happens in the Christian community takes place within our academic institutions. We teach theology to those who are preparing to lead the local church, and then we hope that they apply that theology to the lives of church members. One defect in this view, of course, is that it fails to see that the church members themselves have something to contribute to theological thought. I was inspired on this matter by the great John Henry Newman's insistence on—to use the title of one of his important tracts—"consulting the faithful in matters of doctrine." While Catholic teaching had long emphasized the presence of a *sensus fidelium* in the laity, Newman argued that this "sense" was itself theological in nature. While ordinary church members may not be able to articulate theological matters clearly in the technical language employed by theologians, they must be taken seriously, Newman argued, because their convictions are expressive of "a sort of instinct" that resides "deep in the bosom of the mystical body of Christ."[1]

Newman's thoughts on this subject motivated me to write a book setting forth a parallel case for the evangelical context.[2] But in setting forth my own perspective I was still thinking in terms of a relationship between two parties: the academy and the members of local churches. I did not pay much attention to the unique theological role of persons in pastoral leadership positions. For folks like me, then, the Center's insistence on the need for pastor theologians to work actively at developing a robust ecclesial theology has been an important corrective. Pastors should not be thought of as merely facilitating an exchange between the laity and the academic theologies. They

---

[1] John Henry Newman, "On Consulting the Faithful in Matters of Doctrine," in *Conscience, Consensus and the Development of Doctrine: Revolutionary Texts by John Henry Cardinal Newman*, with commentary and notes by James Gaffney (New York: Doubleday, 1992), 406.
[2] Richard J. Mouw, *Consulting the Faithful: What Christian Intellectuals Can Learn from Popular Religion* (Grand Rapids: Eerdmans, 1994).

have their own theological voice: while informed by what they have learned in the academy, they can contribute to a theological perspective that is informed by a direct engagement in specific contexts of ministry.

This unique theological voice can be seen as expressing what Arthur Holmes, long an influential teacher at Wheaton College, pointed to in his 1983 book, *Contours of a World View*. Holmes distinguished between two kinds of philosophy and two kinds of theology.[3] On the one hand, he said, there is academic philosophy and academic theology. This is where scholars pose questions to each other. But there is also, he observed, the need for "worldviewish theology" and "worldviewish philosophy," where we wrestle with questions that emerge out of the daily living—questions having to do with challenges that Christian people face as they attempt to live obediently as disciples of Christ in the cultures where they find themselves. Pastor theologians are crucial contributors to worldviewish theology.

In our days together discussing sexuality topics from the perspective of pastor theologians, we engaged in worldviewish theology as we looked to God's Word and to the Christian tradition for guidance in how the church can faithfully address the complex challenges posed to us in our highly sexualized culture. Not that academic resources were simply ignored. Pastor theologians clearly see the need to draw on those studies while focusing on urgent questions that we face in the day-to-day life and mission of the local church.

Thus the second level of my learning experience at the conference was wrestling specifically with issues of sexuality within the context of an ecclesial theology. This is a mode of theological reflection that cultivates what has been traditionally referred to as *phronesis*, the practical wisdom that looks to the complex realities of our lives while directly engaged in the practices of ministry. Again, the theological contribution of pastor theologians is much needed these days—certainly in facing the challenges of our highly sexualized culture. I have been hearing frequent references recently in evangelical circles to the importance of a theologically informed capacity for "faithful improvisation"—certainly a key to the kind of theology of sexuality we desperately need these days.

---

[3] Arthur F. Holmes, *Contours of a World View* (Grand Rapids: Eerdmans, 1983), 35, 39-40.

Throughout my teaching career I have placed a strong emphasis on the importance of articulating a Christian worldview. And I still see the importance of that. Brian Walsh and Richard Middleton once nicely summarized the basic worldview concerns in the form of four questions: Who am I? Where am I? What's wrong? What is the remedy?[4]

To answer these worldview questions with a specific focus on sexuality is to provide the framework within which our much-needed faithful improvisation must take place. Who are we? We are creatures of the living God, created by him to live serve his purposes for created life in a way that glorifies him. Where are we? We are placed by the Lord in a world—in a cosmos—that he has lovingly fashioned: "The earth is the LORD's, and everything in it, / the world, and all who live in it" (Ps 24:1).[5] What is wrong? We human creatures have rebelled against the living God, and our sin permeates all aspects of our lives—and in very obvious ways, our sexuality. God sent the Son into the world to save us by sovereign grace through the blood of the cross. Through the power of the Holy Spirit, we can begin to be restored to the kinds of faithful beings that God intended us to be in creation. This means, among many other things, a healing of our sexual brokenness. Ministering to that brokenness in our contemporary context requires all the *phronesis* we can muster.

WORLDVIEWING AND SEXUALITY

To walk the path of faithfulness in our present cultural context is to encounter many twists and turns, coming upon phenomena that we had not focused upon before. And this is certainly true as we seek to walk the path of faithfulness in our present sexualized culture. These realities have caused me in recent years to be a little less inclined simply to talk about "having" a worldview, as if our theology was something like a software system that allows us to enter the practical questions with the expectation that our worldview will generate clear answers. More often than not, these days I am inclined to favor the gerund *worldviewing* over the noun *worldview*.

---

[4]Brian J. Walsh and J. Richard Middleton, *The Transforming Vision: Shaping a Christian World View* (Downers Grove: InterVarsity Press, 1984), 35.
[5]Scriptural quotations in this chapter are from the New International Version unless otherwise noted.

In this regard the biblical image of following a "way," particularly as that image looms large in Psalm 119, has become very helpful to me: "I run in the path of your commands, / for you have broadened my understanding" (Ps 119:32). We need to seek that kind of broadening by allowing, in order to do the right kind of worldviewing, God's Word to be "a lamp for my feet, / a light on my path" (Ps 119:105).

Here is a case in point for a recent turn in the path. A pastor called me for advice on how to deal with a challenge posed by a family who had been attending worship services. The parents, the pastor said, were "seekers"—not yet committed to faith in Christ, but attracted to the Christian community— and on the previous Sunday the three children in the family attended Sunday school for the first time. One of those children, a twelve-year-old, is a boy who two years earlier had decided to claim a female identify. This led to problems for some members of the congregation. A few parents had immediately called the pastor to complain, and one had stated the complaint in harsh terms: "If whatever that thing is shows up in Sunday school next week," the parent said to the pastor, "our family will look for another church!"

I must say right off that having to come up with theological-ethical counsel on transgender identities is a new topic for me. To be sure, the reality was there all along, but suddenly the need to think clearly on the subject has become urgent. Not only have those of us in evangelical educational institutions been confronted with cases on our own campuses, but those cases have serious legal ramifications. Our sexual standards policies for our schools were not written with this phenomenon in mind, and our efforts to address the topic with theological clarity are ongoing.

So I do not have a lot of wisdom to offer the pastor who called me. But I do see the angry parent's complaint as pointing to a serious theological issue. To call that twelve-year-old child a thing—"whatever that thing is"—is not only inexcusably cruel, it is a theological heresy. That twelve-year-old is a special creation, fashioned in the very image of the God and Father of Jesus Christ. The pastor who called me has some important theological work to do in that congregation.

Furthermore, this particular case is an instance of a more general defect in contemporary church life. We need to pay much more attention than we do to *catechesis*, in the broad sense of the term: the general teaching ministry of the local church. Recent political events in the United States underscore the importance of education for citizenship. A few "political sermons" are not sufficient in this regard—indeed they may even be counterproductive. Dialogues, panels, lecture series, book clubs, Sunday school materials—all of these can broaden our understanding of what it means to be agents of the kingdom of God in public life.

A *catechesis* for sexuality is a crucial requirement today. The angry parents who called the pastor may have understandably been worried about exposing their children to confusing gender realities in the life of the church. But shielding our children from those realities is only a temporary measure. Even homeschooled children will become aware in many ways of transgender topics—as well as same-sex relationships, promiscuity, and the like. The church would greatly help those parents who are anxious about a transgendered Sunday school student by offering a course in "raising our children in a sexually confusing culture."

Moving to Specifics

The real specifics in the requisite catechesis will have to be addressed by pastor theologians, and our conference moved us nicely in that direction. For some further moves in this regard, I have six recommendations that I hope can prod us along toward more clarity about the specifics.

First, pastor theologians should pressure seminaries to pay careful attention to the practical pastoral challenges of sexuality in our culture. Theological schools have not done well in this area. The failure of *catechesis* in the local congregation is due in good part to the fact that the subject has not been covered well in seminary education.

Every area of the traditional seminary curriculum is relevant in this regard, potentially providing tools that can aid pastor theologians in fulfilling their own unique theological role. The relevance of biblical studies is obvious here. Yet there is much misuse of the biblical materials on the part of seminary graduates—a sign that the questions have not been dealt with adequately in seminary courses. Take, for example, the application of Leviticus 20 to matters relating to present-day same-sex relations. If two men have sexual relations with each other they are to be put to death (Lev 20:13). I have heard this proclaimed by pastors who simply assume that it is a word—

maybe with the mode of punishment lessened—for contemporary life. Just a few verses later, however, a married couple who has sexual intercourse during the woman's menstrual period are to be banished from the community (Lev 20:18). This proscription is clearly not enforced today, which means that some hermeneutical moves must be made before proscriptions in this chapter can be applied to contemporary life.

My own hermeneutical system tells me that what is set forth in the Old Testament has force for today if it is confirmed by the careful study of the New Testament. Wesley Hill's treatment of biblical materials at our conference was greatly illuminating in this regard. The care with which he handled interpretations that departed from the traditional teachings was a model for what we need these days on the local level. It is a fact that what we say in our pulpits about some matters is very likely being heard by Christian brothers and sisters who struggle with same-sex attractions. We owe it to them to show that we handle these matters with pastoral sensitivities.

During my Fuller presidency I received a note from a student who was very upset about a classroom experience. "I had a terrible time in class today," she wrote. A professor said that "same-sex attractions are the result of the devil working in a person's heart—he likened it to demon possession," and then, "as a lesbian student at Fuller Seminary, I was deeply wounded by this."

Since she signed her name, I responded by inviting her to meet with me in my office. When she arrived, I said, "I don't want to talk about your sex life, but I do want to know more about what it's like to be a lesbian student at Fuller Seminary." She told me that in her undergraduate years she had been active in a LGBTQ advocacy group at her university. Then in her junior year at the university, through the ministry of Campus Crusade, she came to a saving faith in Jesus Christ. "I'm in seminary," she said, "because I want to bring the healing power of the gospel to people like me." Then she added, "I do still struggle with my sexuality. I've gone through all those efforts to change and nothing has worked—so my struggle continues." Her tears began to flow down her cheeks, as she said with deep passion, "Please don't make me go to a liberal seminary."

I told her how glad I was that she was studying at Fuller. "The only thing I can ask of you about your sexuality struggles is that you take a vow of celibacy for the time that you are studying here. I do hope that somehow your experience at Fuller will help you go deeper than a temporary vow of celibacy, but that's all I can ask of you."

I have thought much since then about that conversation. The professor whose comments offended her—did he have no sense that there might be same-sex attracted persons hearing his "they're just demon-possessed" comments? And her fellow students who were preparing for pastoral ministries—does the fact that none of them challenged the professor's comments mean that they might say the same thing to their congregations? And what was the seminary doing to encourage and guide the young woman in her desire to lead people in the LGBTQ community to a saving knowledge of Christ? Wouldn't it be wonderful for all of us to pray and think with her about her plans to witness to the power of the gospel?

Seminaries need to be encouraged to wrestle openly with these issues. And pastor theologians are in a strategic place to issue the challenges to theological scholars, from a context of engagement with people for whom such struggles play an important role in their efforts to be faithful.

Second, we need to think deeply together about how we arrived at our present cultural situation in facing these challenges. Our discussions at the conference brought up some important points about recent cultural developments regarding sexuality. There is more to be explored, however.

While evangelicals have always been concerned about their larger culture's departures from biblical standards for sexuality, our efforts took on a more organized form in the early 1980s, particularly with the emergence of the Moral Majority and other manifestations of what journalists came to label "the New Christian Right." Opposing "sex education" in the public schools, we focused primarily on political strategies, attempting to influence school board elections as well as working to enact legislative change.

While activists with opposing views also adopted some of these strategies, many of them also initiated a quiet effort to bring about cultural change. TV dramas began consistently depicting same-sex relationships in a positive light. Openly gay and lesbian persons had daily visibility as news commentators, standup comedians, and hosts on variety shows.

We need to learn from the way that the supporters of the LGBTQ agenda have used the media to bring about change. How can we promote, through compelling portrayals of human relationships, a holistic understanding of

God's will for human flourishing? An evangelical who has done it well in the mainstream media is David MacFadzean, a theologically astute person working in Hollywood. He was a script writer for *Roseanne*, and then he became the producer and primary writer for *Home Improvement*, which was for a couple of years one of the leading situation comedies on television. *Home Improvement* never had any kind of overt expression of religion. The married couple who were the main characters played jokes on each other and argued with each other, but they stayed faithful to each other as they also practiced being good neighbors. The basic theme that was consistently on display, MacFadzean has reported in his presentations at Fuller Seminary, was "covenantal fidelity," a portrayal of what it is like to live in obedience to God's creative purposes for humankind. For us to encourage and support such efforts in the realm of popular culture is to work at promoting a different kind of cultural conversation.

Third—and this recommendation has to do with how we engage those with whom we disagree about these matters—we have to approach discussions of sexuality with humility and honesty. One of the rules that has been helpful for those of us who participate in interfaith dialogues is that is that you don't contrast "your" best case against "their" worst case. In the formal discussions I have been engaged in as a Reformed theologian with my Catholic counterparts, we have been careful to honor this rule. We Reformed types don't compare John Calvin's theology to the practices of village Catholicism in Spain. Nor should Catholics show the superiority of Vatican II documents to the views of snake handlers in Mississippi. We either put our best case against their best case or our worst case against their worst case.

And we evangelicals do have some worst cases to admit to in engaging others on sexuality concerns in contemporary life. There is no denying the fact that evangelical Christians have been inexcusably cruel on occasion to persons in our own churches who have experienced same-sex attractions. Repentance and pleas for forgiveness are good places to start. The Lord honors a contrite spirit.

Fourth, we do well to acknowledge diverse viewpoints among those with whom we disagree. I had an argument with a fellow Presbyterian about eight years ago, a pastor who was very much against my traditional understanding of same-sex relationships. At a certain point I asked him how he interpreted

Romans 1. His response was, "I don't read it. I can't stand Paul. He's wrong on many things, as far as I'm concerned. I never preach from Paul's writings." That is a distressing viewpoint. It is very different, however, from the views of other people who reject the traditional interpretation of Romans 1. I have had several public dialogues about same-sex topics with my good friend Barbara Wheeler, a fellow Presbyterian educator. We have serious disagreements, but when I ask her about Romans 1, her response is, "Let's go through the text together." She obviously has paid close attention to the biblical materials, and while we disagree on how to interpret things, our arguments take place under the authority of God's Word. It is important for us to engage alternative interpretations, not putting everyone with whom we disagree into the same category.

Fifth, we need to think of how to provide "episcopal" guidance for our movement. This recommendation needs some serious discussion, even though the solution does not come easily in the evangelical context. Our Catholic and Anglican friends do not have to put "episcopal" within quotations marks, but we do. There is no office of bishop in the transdenominational evangelical movement. Evangelicalism embraces diverse polities. I celebrate that diversity, but I also yearn on occasion for some kind of guidance from a central authority.

A poignant case in point for me is when an elder in a local congregation told me about a disturbing elders' meeting he had just attended, where the lengthy discussion focused on a married lesbian couple, the parents of two children, who had begun attending worship services and had recently come to faith in Christ. Now this family wanted to be received into the life of the congregation, including having their children presented for baptism. The congregation was Reformed in its theology.

At the end of the elders' meeting, the tentative decision that the majority of the elders agreed to was that they could join the church if they got divorced and separated. He said, "I never thought I would hear in an evangelical conversation the stipulation that people can only join our church if they get divorced!" I don't know exactly how to decide this kind of case, so I am not advocating an answer here. But I do know that simply advocating divorce is much too facile. For those of us who believe, for example, that in the baptizing of children God is signing and sealing the promises of the covenant to them, what are we saying to those children when we say, "You can only come to the font if your parents divorce and they don't live together anymore"?

These are tough issues. What does faithful improvisation mean in a case like this? There is much theological and pastoral work that we need to do here. And my elder friend was right when he went on to express worries about having the case decided by "a group of volunteer elders in a local congregation." He wants pastoral guidelines from a more disciplined, theologically informed source. We don't have an evangelical pope, nor do I want to see us appoint one. But we do need to have something like a consistent "episcopal" guidance on the new challenges that come our way in our local settings.

Sixth and finally, we need to think globally on this topic. It is necessary to draw upon the wisdom of Christians in other times and places. Our presentations at the conference did this well by paying attention to Christian thinkers of the past. The "Great Tradition" has much *phronesis* to offer us. But for evangelicals, an important strand of our tradition is the missionary encounter with other cultures. We have, for examples, at least a century and a half of dealing with polygamy in Africa, and many of the challenges we face today in the West have parallels to those challenges. How have Christian leaders in other cultures addressed the situation of a man with his seven wives who respond positively to the promises of the Gospel? Believers in other cultures have shown some "faithful improvisation" that carries lessons for us in our present cultural context.

No Unnecessary Obstacles

I want to conclude with a brief return to the need for all of us to approach an ecclesial theology of sexuality in a spirit of humility. We have a lot to be humble about in this area of our lives. Our sexual hopes and fears are expressive of impulses and needs that are grounded in the deepest places of our being—places where the dynamics of trust and vulnerability loom large for each of us.

The Scriptures teach us that we are, each of us, created for relationships with others. In insisting that believers who have not been called to a God-honoring marriage relationship commit themselves to celibacy, we should not do so in a way that denies them access to intimate friendships. To be sure, as the Catholic magisterium has insisted, genital intimacy in a committed same-sex relationship is an instance of *disordered friendship*. But the fact of the *disorder* should not keep us from ignoring the value of the intimate *friendship*. To affirm this value is to be willing to explore difficult—but highly significant—pastoral territory.

As we do explore these matters it is crucial that we not pose unnecessary obstacles to persons struggling with various manifestations of sexual disorder. What we have received as good news in our own journeys must also be proclaimed to others. There is nothing that anyone has to do in order to come to the cross of Calvary. The only prayer any human being needs to pray in approaching that cross is this one:

> Just as I am, without one plea,
> but that thy blood was shed for me,
> and that thou bidst me come to thee,
> O Lamb of God, I come.

May we work at developing the kind of pastorally effective ecclesial theology that enables us—with credibility as sinners who have ourselves fled to Jesus for the healing of our own brokenness—to invite many in our confused sexual culture to meet us at the cross of Calvary.

Part Two

The BEAUTY
and **BROKENNESS** of
SEXUALITY

6

Cutting the Fruit While Watering the Root

Selfies, Sexuality, and the Sensibilities of the American Church

DANIEL J. BRENDSEL

Consider the selfie. By now, it's a fairly mundane artistic tradition.

KAREN SWALLOW PRIOR, *"JANE EYRE AND THE INVENTION OF THE SELF"*

W E LIVE IN AN AGE IN WHICH to truly "experience" a great reality we must turn our backs on it, literally. An image gone viral from the wildly entertaining 2016 presidential election campaign captures the contemporary ethos perfectly. It's of a room filled with five hundred supporters of Hilary Clinton. And almost all of them have their backs turned on her—not out of contempt, not out of inattention, not out of protest, but in deep admiration. They are eagerly seeking to capture the moment in a selfie.

The swift rise of the selfie to cultural importance and ubiquity is astonishing. The word *selfie* is difficult to find in use prior to 2002. By 2013, Oxford Dictionaries had chosen *selfie* as their "Word of the Year," citing a 17,000 percent increase in usage in the English language from 2012 to 2013.[1] Word

---

[1] "The Oxford Dictionaries Word of the Year 2013," *Oxford Dictionaries Blog*, November 19, 2013, http://blog.oxforddictionaries.com/press-releases/oxford-dictionaries-word-of-the-year-2013.

usage corresponded to societal saturation with the reality of selfies, a situation that has not changed over the past few years.

Selfies have entered the upper echelons of politics and religion; all current American presidents and Roman Catholic popes have been known to take selfies. They are a chief means by which celebrities build their "brand"; I now expect every few weeks to see a sidebar weblink announcing how Kim Kardashian has "broken" the Internet with her latest provocative selfie. Scores of websites are devoted to selfies, my personal favorite being felfies.com, specializing in self-taken photos of farmers with their livestock. In 2015, twenty-four billion selfies were posted on the Google Photos site alone, which is to say nothing of the number of selfies shared on Facebook and Instagram, or via mobile messaging apps such as Snapchat.

Selfies are everywhere. They are a cultural artifact with which we have to do in some manner most days—whether by way of viewing one, seeing others taking one, or producing one ourselves. They are so pervasive as to be considered "normal," unexceptional to the sensibilities of the day. Therefore, they are a good object of cultural exegesis in an effort to understand what makes our culture tick. Trying to articulate what makes our culture tick—or seeking a responsible understanding of our present cultural moment—is a larger project that I find endlessly fascinating and of great pastoral importance for our churches, which helps to explain what has led me to use this space to consider the selfie.

To speak of selfies as "normal" and ubiquitous is not to suggest that selfies are free of controversy and criticism. The selfie is a cultural phenomenon that is, in fact, easy to criticize, and Christians have spilled much electronic ink doing so. Those who spends hours producing and perfecting selfies are disparaged as self-aggrandizing and narcissistic, or starving for attention, or preoccupied with image. Critics have lamented the risks taken in—or the general inattentiveness to surroundings bound up with—the pursuit of the perfect profile picture, leading to some forty-nine fatalities while taking or attempting to take a selfie worldwide since 2014.[2] But another major criticism

---

[2]For a breakdown of the data, see Zachary Crockett, "The Tragic Data Behind Selfie Fatalities," *Priceonomics*, January 29, 2016, https://priceonomics.com/the-tragic-data-behind-selfie-fatalities. Statistics such as these led to the sensational (and, at several levels, nonsensical) 2015 headline, "Selfies More Deadly Than Sharks, Reports Show," FoxNews.com, September 22, 2015, www.foxnews.com/health/2015/09/22/selfies-more-deadly-than-sharks-reports-show.html.

of selfies, and one more obviously germane to the theme of this volume, has to do with the clear and at times tense relationship among selfies, sexuality, and body image. It is undeniable that the selfie is a prime instrument for sexual stimulation and attention, and this link is the main reason I want to consider the selfie.

SELFIES AND SEXUALITY

Sexually provocative and explicit self-portraits are common fare in today's unceasingly wired culture, with celebrity images in the vanguard. Thirty years ago, Richard Schickel commented wryly of on-the-scene television interviews that the language used by eyewitnesses to newsworthy events "imitates the shorthand clichés, the emblematic words and phrases, that they have learned at television's knee or read in the morning paper. They are like mirrors in that they can only reflect the images that pass briefly before them."[3] Schickel's words, only slightly reworked, serve as a fitting assessment of selfie culture. Most selfies that we mere mortals take and present to the world mimic the celebrity images that pass so briefly by us online. The poses and positions, the camera held above so as to produce a more slender appearance, the style of dress, the angle of head tilt, the duckface or "sparrow" compression of the lips—it's all learned at the Internet's knee. And it's typically—in varying degrees of explicitness and intentionality—sexually suggestive or in keeping with an expected sexual aesthetic.

This is not to say that the majority of selfies are lewd or risqué. Rather, they are like the images on one teenage girl's social media pages, which Nancy Jo Sales describes in *American Girls: Social Media and the Secret Lives of Teenagers*: "There were pictures of her playfully sticking out her tongue to the side, Miley Cyrus-style, and others where she was modestly exposing her cleavage or posing in short shorts. It was as if she were trying to present a sexualized self within the limits of what she knew would be seen as acceptable to parents, colleges."[4]

Of course, there are some self-images that are much more explicit, much more calculated for and successful at arousing lust—self-portraits in various

---

[3]Richard Schickel, *Intimate Strangers: The Culture of Celebrity* (Garden City, NJ: Doubleday, 1985), 290.
[4]Nancy Jo Sales, *American Girls: Social Media and the Secret Lives of Teenagers* (New York: Knopf, 2016), 111.

stages of undress. Developments in text messaging and apps providing images and videos with a temporary lifespan (Snapchat being one of the most outstanding examples) have led to more venturesome image sharing, perhaps fed by an illusion of privacy and ephemerality. In any case, "sexting" has become an important subset of selfie culture. Again, celebrities play a leading role, with celebrity mobile phone hacks not infrequently keeping celebrity news source TMZ's ratings up.

Here concerns are society-wide, as sexually explicit self-images interface with cyberbullying and "revenge porn." Of widespread concern is the production and circulation of sexually explicit self-portraits among minors. Two recent higher-profile scandals represent a larger problem. In early 2014, in rural Louisa County, Virginia, about a hundred nude or otherwise overtly sexual images of high school (and some middle school) girls were discovered on a secret Instagram page, leading to a massive investigation and the confiscation of hundreds of students' mobile phones with nude selfies of minors on them. According to chief deputy sheriff Donald Lowe, the people in and receiving the images came from "every race, religion, social, and financial status in the town. Rich, poor, everyone."[5] At the end of 2015, in Cañon City, Colorado, authorities discovered that a few hundred nude selfies and other explicit photos of over one hundred different high school and middle school students were circulating via mobile phones around the school district.[6]

As Hanna Rosin notes in a 2014 article in The Atlantic, "Surveys on sexting have found pretty consistently that among kids in their upper teens, about a third have sexted, making the practice neither 'universal' nor 'vanishingly rare' . . . but common enough in a teenager's life to be familiar."[7] Some studies suggest that as many as 40 to 50 percent of high schoolers have received a

---

[5]Hanna Rosin, "Why Kids Sext," The Atlantic 314.4 (November 2014): 66.
[6]Kassondra Cloos and Julie Turkewitz, "Hundreds of Nude Photos Jolt Colorado School," New York Times, November 6, 2015, corrected November 10, 2015, www.nytimes.com/2015/11/07/us /colorado-students-caught-trading-nude-photos-by-the-hundreds.html.
[7]Rosin, "Why Kids Sext," 68, quoting Elizabeth Englander. Lara Karaian observes that "sexting" is the adult or clinical term for the phenomenon; youth themselves typically do not refer to the messages in this way. See "What Is Self-Exploitation? Rethinking the Relationship Between Sexualization and 'Sexting' in Law and Order Times," in Children, Sexuality and Sexualization, ed. Emma Renold, Jessica Ringrose, and R. Danielle Egan (Hampshire/New York: Palgrave Macmillan, 2015), 337.

sexually explicit selfie.[8] In one survey of seven public high schools in East Texas, "boys and girls were equally likely to have sent a sext, but girls were much more likely to have been asked to—68 percent had been."[9]

Scandals and statistics like these rightly cause many people, and most Christians in particular, great alarm.[10] I have encountered different kinds of common responses among Christians to the undeniable, and oftentimes clearly problematic, link between selfies, sexuality, and sexual desire and arousal. One is preventative, seeking to set up strategic filters and systems of accountability on our Internet and cellular usage in an effort to protect ourselves and/or our children from viewing or producing explicit material. Such strategy is good and appropriate in most instances, but by itself it does little to offer a "Christian vision of sexuality," which is what we both hunger for and need. We are not merely seeking to avoid the bad but to delight in and pursue the true, good, and beautiful.

Another common response among Christians to the sexualization that is prevalent in selfie culture is to shun the producing and consuming of overtly sexualized self-images and to promote instead what we might call "positive" and "socially motivating" selfies. Selfies are, it is said, "just a tool" that we need not fill with filth but can, instead, fill with true and good "content" to use toward good ends (this is a prevalent, and perhaps typically evangelical, defense of media and technology). So we can laud #nomakeupselfies as a way of celebrating "natural beauty" and "being real," and we can enjoy #uglies as a way of playfully satirizing the sexualization of the self and obsession with body image.[11] With a more explicitly Christian agenda, we could make and share selfies at church events or on missions trips to stir up excitement and raise awareness for Christ's mission, or we could promote

---

[8]Donald S. Strassberg et al., "Sexting by High School Students: An Exploratory and Descriptive Study," *Archives of Sexual Behavior* 42 (2013): 15-21; Heidi Strohmaier et al., "Youth Sexting: Prevalence Rates, Driving Motivations, and the Deterrent Effect of Legal Consequences," *Sexuality Research and Social Policy* 11 (2014): 245-55.

[9]Rosin, "Why Kids Sext," 73. The study, not named by Rosin, is likely J. R. Temple et al., "Teen Sexting and Its Association with Sexual Behaviors," *Archives of Pediatrics and Adolescent Medicine* 166.9 (2012): 828-33.

[10]They also create no small amount of legal quandaries. See further Karaian, "What Is Self-Exploitation?," 337-51; and Rosin, "Why Kids Sext," passim, who notes the irony that "as it stands now, in most states it is perfectly legal for two 16-year-olds to have sex. But if they take pictures, it's a matter for the police" (69).

[11]Both strategies have, again, been spearheaded by celebrities such as Lorde and Cara Delevingne.

and engage in #ashtag Wednesday (which you can probably figure out on your own if you weren't already aware of it). To my mind, this is a much more problematic response than the merely preventative safeguarding against exposure to sexually explicit material. This is because the challenge posed by sexually explicit and sexually provocative selfies is, I suggest, not firstly or fundamentally *sexual* in nature. But to discern this, we need to review a few key historical and technological developments.

HISTORICAL AND TECHNOLOGICAL DEVELOPMENTS

Where did selfies come from? What are their historical antecedents? Self-portraits are most assuredly no new reality. Individuals as diverse as Rembrandt, Frida Kahlo, and Norman Rockwell have engaged in self-portraiture. But selfies are not simply self-portraiture. They are not even mere self-photography, despite the fact that Oxford Dictionaries, when selecting *selfie* as the 2013 "Word of the Year," defined the word as "a photograph that one has taken of oneself." Self-photographs have been around as long as daguerreotype; they were not uncommon in the days of the Polaroid; and many a 35 mm film roll has been retrieved from one-hour photo shops (now nearly extinct) with a surprise self-photograph among the developed pictures.[12] But self-photographs are not what caused such a spike in word usage in the last several years, nor are self-photographs responsible for what we can mean-ingfully and understandably call "selfie culture." A true understanding of the selfie necessitates the concluding clause in the Oxford Dictionaries' definition: "a photograph that one has taken of oneself, typically one taken with a smart-phone or webcam and uploaded to a social media website." The selfie that we are especially concerned with is the mass-producible self-portrait, made with the almost exclusive purpose of sharing and broadcasting to (mass) audiences. For that reality to take off, at least four developments were needed.

First was the technological development of small, user-friendly cameras, which made self-portraits easier to pull off for amateurs. Much more im-portant, second, was the rise of affordable digital cameras, particularly those

---

[12]See Marcy J. Dinius, "The Long History of the 'Selfie,'" *J19: The Journal of Nineteenth-Century Americanists* 3.2 (2015): 445-51; Kandice Rawlings, "Selfies and the History of Self-Portrait Pho-tography," *OUPblog*, November 21, 2013, http://blog.oup.com/2013/11/selfies-history-self-por trait-photography.

with LCD screens.[13] No longer did self-portraiture require waiting forever (i.e., a whole hour) to see how it turned out; instantly, we could see on the LCD screen how our images of ourselves looked. No longer did we have to waste film (and money) with repeat shots, but we could churn out ten, twenty, thirty photos of ourselves with no effort at all.

When, third, digital cameras joined forces with mobile phones, particularly mobiles with front-facing cameras, nearly all the pieces were in place for selfie culture to come into its own. Mobile phones with front-facing cameras have been around since the early 2000s, but the appearance of the iPhone 4 with a front-facing camera serves as an iconic turning point, being released in 2010, a mere three years before *selfie* would win the attention of Oxford Dictionaries. As one infographic puts it, now the "user has complete control over framing his/her selfie."[14] A fourth important historical and technological development was the rise of public forums for posting and viewing selfies (and, in general, the turn to the Internet for socializing), together with messaging apps for sharing selfies in a constant flow. The third and the fourth developments are roughly contemporaneous: the iPhone 4 appeared in 2010; Facebook overtook Myspace in number of users in 2009; Instagram launched in 2010; and Snapchat launched in 2011. The rise of social media sites and photo-sharing apps worked in synergy with camera phone development, for the camera phone was destined to be transfigured into the glory of the smartphone. With smartphones came the seamless integration of our selfies with our messaging and social networking forms of choice.

This brief (and lacunae-filled) survey of important historical and technological developments leading to the rise of the selfie and of selfie culture is necessary to understand the selfie. As Ken Myers has commented, "Cultural phenomena are not static and frozen bundles of meaning. They carry momentum. They came from somewhere, and they are going somewhere, and we can't be wise about where they are likely to be going if we are ignorant about the trajectories they are fulfilling."[15] To get the full picture of the selfie,

---

[13]As Rawlings notes, digital cameras were available to the consumer market in the 1990s, but it took about a decade for them to drop in price and to saturate the market. Ibid.

[14]See Irfan Ahmad, "The Rise of Selfies [INFOGRAPHIC]," *DigitalInformationWorld.com*, October 20, 2013, www.digitalinformationworld.com/2013/10/the-rise-of-selfies-infographic.html.

[15]Ken Myers, support letter to Mars Hill Audio subscribers, June 2008.

we must attend to much more than the material reality of self-taken self-portraits. We must discern historical trajectories. We must see how important precedents enabled the proliferation of these portraits in our photo collections especially for the purpose of sharing them (sharing our "lives") on conspicuously public platforms with our friends and family (and just maybe many others). We must, in fact, recognize that selfies are embedded in, the fruit of, and helping to perpetuate a larger cultural matrix. What newer technology and media enable is not simply the taking of more and better self-photographs. They sustain an orientation to reality in which selfies make sense. The proliferation of selfies in contemporary experience renders (more) plausible certain understandings of personal identity. Selfie culture encourages and sustains certain ways of interacting with others and receiving reality around us.

FUNDAMENTAL ANTHROPOLOGY AND ONTOLOGY

This is to say that selfies arise from and manifest a functional anthropology and ontology.[16] So we can and must ask after not simply the content of selfies, as it were, and the ends toward which they are used. We must also ask a more fundamental question: What assumptions about human being and identity make selfies seem normal, even attractive, prior to any question of content and ends? Without any pretense at comprehensiveness, I have four suggestions.

First, selfies, and selfie culture, operate on the assumption that who we are, the essence of our personal identity, is easily communicable. That is to say, what I refer to as "me" is something that I can communicate to you through the easy means of paragraphs and photos and timelines conveniently "post-able" to my website. To know "me" no longer requires the hard but glorious enterprise of spending five, fifteen, thirty years in the same place sharing resources, energies, experiences, and words. Getting to know and love me (or despise me, as the case may be) is a relatively easy endeavor, and so is (or should be) getting to know and love you. By listing the "most important" data about me (relationship status, religious affiliation, employment, favorite books and movies) and offering a plethora of photos of me and my close relationships and life experiences, I can give you a sufficient

---

[16]The language of "fundamental anthropology" and "ontology" comes from Michael Hanby, "The Civic Project of American Christianity," *First Things* 250 (2015): 34.

encapsulation of "me."[17] Selfies are considered self-expressions because the human self we imagine ourselves to be is a pretty simple (not complex) being that can be adequately expressed through various forms of media.

Second, the relationship between the "I" that is easily communicable and the body in which "I" find "myself" is instrumental. As Stanley Hauerwas puts it, the anthropological assumption of liberal societies is "that my 'body' is an instrument for the expression of my 'true self.'"[18] This is "the presumption that there is an 'I' that *has* a body," as opposed to the creaturely "I" who exists *as* a body. "Nowhere is such a view of the body better seen," observes Hauerwas, "than in the assumption, enshrined in modern medicine, that there is no limit to what we can and should do to overcome the limits of the body. Thus the difficulty of distinguishing torture from some forms of medical practice."[19] Selfies abound in liberal societies because selfies operate with and reinforce and amplify the same anthropological logic. "What matters," to steal Peter Leithart's expression, "is the 'me' lurking behind the roles I play and the things I do."[20] My body is but an instrument for the expression of that "me." Selfies are a matter of positioning and posturing my body, documenting my body's placement in exotic or culturally noteworthy locales, posing my body before celebrities, so that the "I" who is me may be noticed, so as to give expression to who "I" am and what "I" stand for.

Our selfie expressions are for an audience. So we can add a third anthropological assumption bound up with selfies: we are, at our core, performers. Our lives are performances for others. Again, selfies are not merely self-taken digital portraits but mass-reproduced self-portraits shared publicly through messaging and social media. Why post a selfie? Because it's "normal" to broadcast who I am to a watching world. It's

---

[17]As Nicholas Carr notes, these lists of personal data by which we present "who we are" to the public are, in fact, the scripts of who Facebook (or Amazon or Netflix) wants us to be or wants us to think of ourselves as. See Carr, *The Shallows: What the Internet Is Doing to Our Brains* (New York: Norton, 2010), 218-19; also Carr, *The Glass Cage: Automation and Us* (New York: Norton, 2014), 205-6.

[18]Stanley Hauerwas, "What Could It Mean for the Church to Be Christ's Body? A Question Without a Clear Answer," in *In Good Company: The Church as Polis* (Notre Dame: University of Notre Dame Press, 1995), 24. More defiantly, one might say, together with the indignant teenagers interviewed by Rosin, "This is my life and my body and I can do whatever I want with it." Rosin, "Why Kids Sext," 67.

[19]Hauerwas, "What Could It Mean," 24, emphasis original.

[20]Peter J. Leithart, *Against Christianity* (Moscow, ID: Canon, 2003), 84.

interesting and troubling to note that there is no clear line dividing what can be and what should be shareable publicly. So we post selfies of increasingly intimate experiences, whether it is the selfie when I first wake up sans makeup (#flawless), or the selfie postcoitus (#aftersex), or a cycle of selfies to document a belly's growth throughout a pregnancy. It's not limited to selfies. Much of our Internet activity is the sharing of our most intimate "selves" (under the names of "transparency," "authenticity," and "encouraging others"), sometimes through photos and videos, sometimes through words on blogs or Facebook. Christians are on the front lines. We post about our most intimate experiences: at funerals of loved ones, in morning devotions, in marital relations, in the teenage rebellion of our kids—selfies through words. It's what Ashley Samelson has described as "emotional immodesty."[21] But this is not simply ignoble narcissism, not merely an overstuffed sense of self-importance; it is prior to narcissistic tendencies in that performance is less something we do and more something we *are*. To broadcast one's self, to share a real-time flow of self-images, to perform before an ever-watching audience is what it means to be a normal human in the twenty-first century. In any case, it is economically responsible, since it's a waste of money to buy a phone with a front-facing camera and not use it!

Fourth, who we are is manufacturable. When we understand human personhood as easily communicable, with our bodies as tools for expression, and when we receive human existence as chiefly a matter of performance, the pieces are in place to imagine the human self to be fundamentally a production, an artifact of our own making. I can manipulate the "I" that I present to you and the world. The "I" proves to be a commodity to sell. I want you to buy "brand me." So what I do is "live life to the full," but not to experience a full life. I do so in order that, by way of documenting this "life to the full" in photos and (public) journaling, I can prove to the watching world that my life is worth paying attention to (i.e., purchasing). As Brett McCracken has commented, "Social media exacerbates our ever-growing tendency to approach cultural consumption as more of a public, performative act than an enjoyable, enriching experience. It becomes less about

---

[21] Ashley E. Samelson, "Emotional Immodesty on Facebook," *First Things Blog*, June 21, 2010, www .firstthings.com/blogs/firstthoughts/2010/06/emotional-immodesty-on-facebook.

the thing we consume and more about how our consuming of it fits our preferred image."[22]

Importantly, this doesn't have to be a vain effort to make our lives appear flashy and sexy so as to capture attention. Sometimes we can "manufacture" ourselves in more apparently commendable and modest ways. We can, with our selfies, seek to promote less "brand me" and more this or that Christian "lifestyle" or cause that we stand for. We can post the aforementioned "uglies," self-taken portraits highlighting our nonglamorized "selves." Indeed, "uglies" are lauded by Jessica Bennett as a "playful slice of authenticity in an age where everything seems airbrushed to perfection."[23] For Bennett, "uglies" are an expression of "authenticity." This is who we really are—our double-chins, our zits, ourselves with defenses down, facades removed, filters off. Yet for all that, they are still a presentation of our own choosing. I decide which selfies to post, which ones express the "real me." The "real me" is my self-presentation, a product of my making. Here artifice poses as authenticity.

CUTTING THE FRUIT WHILE WATERING THE ROOT

The anthropological and ontological sensibilities preserved and promoted in the proliferation of selfies involve viewing "me" as easily communicable, as instrumentally related to the body I "have," as fundamentally a performer, and as a product of my own making and knowing. Selfie culture is really a whole orientation to reality. The hundreds who turned their backs on Hillary Clinton to take selfies in late 2016 were not rejecting the reality before (or behind) them but seeking to experience and enhance it. The image gone viral from the Clinton rally encapsulates for us the meaning of the selfie. Selfies are the tips of the iceberg of a set of sensibilities about ourselves and how we communicate ourselves to others. They manifest an orientation toward reality and identity, an orientation that dominates contemporary society. And given this set of sensibilities and orientation, this functional and fundamental anthropology and ontology, is it any surprise

---

[22]Brett McCracken, "Selfie Deception," *MereOrthodoxy.com*, July 9, 2013, www.mereorthodoxy.com/selfie-deception.

[23]Jessica Bennett, "With Some Selfies, the Uglier the Better," *New York Times*, February 21, 2014, www.nytimes.com/2014/02/23/fashion/selfies-the-uglier-the-better-technology.html.

that increasingly we see people, old and young, wielding their sexuality (note the instrumental language) in public, performative, and ever-more provocative ways?

This is to say that the hypersexuality frequently appearing in selfie culture is not only or firstly a sexual problem but an anthropological and ontological one. In a tremendously helpful essay appearing in *First Things*, Michael Hanby asserts that "the sexual revolution is not merely—or perhaps even primarily—sexual . . . the sexual revolution is one aspect of a deeper revolution in the question of who or what we understand the human person to be (fundamental anthropology), and indeed of what we understand reality to be (ontology)."[24] I have chosen to spotlight selfies as a culturally prevalent and practical case study in order to demonstrate Hanby's point. If we live in a hypersexualized day and age, if selfies which typify our day and age are prone toward the titillating and explicit, it is not because we are salacious and libidinous. Or at least, those are not the only and most significant factors at work.

Consider, for example, a short piece that James Franco wrote for the *New York Times* in 2013. Franco, a celebrity well-known for the frequency with which he shares self-portraits, defended his obsession with selfies by frankly admitting that their importance to him lies in the power they lend him: "In this age of too much information at a click of a button, the power to attract viewers amid the sea of things to read and watch is power indeed. . . . Attention is power. And if you are someone people are interested in, then the selfie provides something very powerful, from the most privileged perspective possible."[25] Of particular interest in the essay is that Franco is well-aware that photos of himself topless are much more "liked," much more attention garnering, than those of him with his various "art projects."[26] This is no mere carnality; this is no mere self-preoccupation. This is a take on personhood and reality in which power goes all the way down.

Franco's candor is consistent with what I am proposing—namely, that sexually provocative selfies are more fruit than root. Selfies pose great

---

[24]Hanby, "The Civic Project of American Christianity," 34.
[25]James Franco, "The Meanings of the Selfie," *New York Times*, December 26, 2013, www.nytimes.com/2013/12/29/arts/the-meanings-of-the-selfie.html.
[26]Ibid.

challenges for Christians wanting to cultivate faithful, flourishing sexuality in the twenty-first century. But the challenges they pose lie deeper than many in the church may realize. Having simply a preventative strategy that seeks to filter out illicit content does not go deep enough to address the root anthropological and ontological issues. The fruit of disordered sexuality will keep coming back, perhaps in mutated forms. And such fruit will increase all the more if, not satisfied with simply taking preventative measures against sexually explicit content, we as a church attempt to harness the power of the selfie and social media for "good ends"—to promote "positive body image," to raise awareness and excitement for Christian endeavors, to motivate young people to participate in church life, and so on. In doing so we are not using neutral media to convey or consume true and good content. We are using media that sustain a vision of human nature in which embodied sexuality is not a gift to be received with gratitude and a moral calling to take up but an instrument to wield in our performances and self-making—all while trying to retain a traditional sexual ethic.

The church's cultural practice here—and likely also in several other areas—together with the sensibilities it sustains and gives form to, is incongruous with the sexual ethic we would seek to maintain.[27] Something must give. And clearly what we are seeing broadly in the church, and especially among younger generations, is the traditional sexual ethic giving, being reworked or discarded in favor of something new. This is unsurprising, given that the traditional ethic is incongruously and seemingly arbitrarily tied to the logic of our actual practice. Many are sniffing out the inconsistency. And in a laudable pursuit after consistency, many Christians are (not so laudably) abandoning the old paths that lead to life for self(ie)-made paths leading to this or that preferred "lifestyle." Saint Paul's words are true not only individually but also ecclesially: we reap what we sow. If we do not like the fruit we are reaping in the church, perhaps, instead of pointing the finger at hypersexual society "out there" or the immaturity of our younger

---

[27]I have focused on selfies and social media, in part because of their marked connection to sexuality. But I think we could find many practices and postures the contemporary American church takes up that reinforce the basic sensibilities we have discerned in selfie culture—the church's attitudes and practices with regards, for example, to food, to aesthetic taste in music, to the role (or the lack of any meaningful role) of the body in liturgical worship, to formality and standards of dress, or to Christian subcultural forms of spectacle and celebrity.

generations, we should consider what we as churches have been sowing and watering by way of our cultural practices and postures.

For Christians living in the post–sexual revolution era, the pursuit of "the Christian vision of sexuality" and of the "beauty, order, and mystery" to be found within those boundaries is no easy matter. It is all the more difficult if churches unwittingly reinforce and contribute to the very sensibilities in which sexual "freedom" seems normal. While the church has often done a fair job of seeking to cut off—or, at least, has frequently censured—the "fruit" that is sexual sin, it has often eagerly (if unwittingly) watered anthropological and ontological assumptions that form the roots of sexual "freedom." The church is too often trying to oppose with our left hand what we're creating space for with our right hand.

At very least, we should be aware of the oddness of our strategy. But more than that, I suggest that we make the effort to spell out the true Christian vision of sexuality and human nature upon which traditional Christian ethics are founded, as volumes like this one are seeking to do. And just as importantly, we should take stock of the anthropological assumptions and sensibilities that are given form in and sustained by our practices as churches. We may need, with wisdom, to limit or adapt or even strategically abstain from cultural and technological practices and postures that are in keeping with the anthropology and ontology of modernity. But I think we will also find that we can and should give more space to those practices most in keeping with, and that most promote the flourishing of, our humanity, whether male or female, young or old, Jew or Gentile—simple human practices such as sharing meals with brothers and sisters in Christ, standing and kneeling in liturgical worship and regularly partaking of the Eucharist, verbally confessing sins to one another and voicing forgiveness, praying and giving thanks to God together. It is in practices such as these that we begin to live true human life. It is in practices such as these that the Christian vision of sexuality is given space to grow into the fruit of mature, joyful, hope-filled men and women. It is in practices such as these that we press against the disordered sensibilities and structures of the world. And, of course, it is in practices such as these that we seek to be against the world for the life of the world.

7

The Transgender Test

DENNY BURK

OVER THE LAST SEVERAL YEARS I've written and spoken a great deal about transgenderism. That work has resulted in a good bit of feedback from folks who have either heard or read what I have had to say. A couple years ago, I received a heartbreaking letter from two parents of a transgender child. The letter tells the story of this family of four—a mother, a father, and two sons. One of the sons was killed in a tragic accident as a young adult. The other son grew up with gender-conflicted feelings. He had these feelings through most of his life, but as an adult he nevertheless got married to a woman and had children. After being married for a number of years, he decided to end his marriage and to "transition" his appearance to that of a female. Eventually, he even underwent gender-reassignment surgery.

In the letter the parents argue strenuously in favor of the idea that their son's transgender identity is the result of his brain sex being mismatched with his biological sex.[1] They believe that their "daughter" has always been

---

[1]Brain-sex theory holds that "there are areas of the brain that are different between males and females. . . . 'Brain sex' refers to ways in which the brain scripts toward male or female dispositions or behaviors." See Mark A. Yarhouse, *Understanding Gender Dysphoria: Navigating Transgender Issues in a Changing Culture* (Downers Grove, IL: IVP Academic, 2015), 67. On this theory, transgender identity emerges when someone's brain sex does not match their biological sex. This theory, therefore, attributes gender identity to nature and not to nurture. There is no agreement among scientists as to what causes transgender identity. Yarhouse concludes, "Our current understanding of etiology simply does not provide us with 'an empirically grounded detailed theory of the mechanisms and process of gender identity development'" (ibid., 80). See also Lawrence S. Mayer and Paul R. McHugh, "Sexuality and Gender: Findings from the Biological, Psychological, and Social Sciences," *New Atlantis* 50 (Fall 2016): 105: "Scientists have not established a solid framework for understanding the causes of cross-gender identification."

a female—at least in "her" mind. "Her" mind has always been female, even though "her" body has always been male. Because the brain is the "most important human sex organ," they believe that "she" had simply been born with the "wrong genitals." They claim that Scripture is silent about the biological factors that distinguish male from female and that there is no scriptural authority for prioritizing genital anatomy over brain structure and function. For this reason, they feel that their child's body needed to be transformed through surgery so that it would match the mind. Thus they have been fully supportive of their child's gender-reassignment surgery.

But they also lodge a strong critique against me personally. I have publicly gone on the record opposing the validity of transgenderism and of gender-reassignment surgery.[2] The reason the parents wrote me was to let me know that they thought my teaching on the subject was woefully in error. They argue that my failure to comprehend "the science" has left me with an unnecessarily low view of transgenderism. Moreover, they contend that to teach what the Bible has to say about the matter is insufficient. They even make the case that to teach what the Bible says is harmful to transgender people because it leads them away from "appropriate medical treatment" and condemns them to depression, self-loathing, and even suicide. They conclude with this challenge: "Could you live with knowing that your resolution opposing appropriate medical treatment of gender dysphoria led to the suicide of someone's precious child? . . . My husband and I don't think you want that on your conscience."

And so the letter ends. After sharing a narrative of what can only be described as devastating loss and heartbreaking turmoil for this family, this mother draws a lesson from her and her child's suffering: The Bible is insufficient to deal with the kind of turmoil and suicidal depression that my child has faced. If you insist that the Bible can meet our needs when science leads us in a different direction than the Bible, then you have blood on your hands. You are responsible for the death of suffering people like my child.

I'm not sharing this letter with you because this is just some one-off thing that lands in the inbox of guys who speak and write publicly about transgender issues. I'm sharing this because this is the kind of pushback

---

[2]E.g., Denny Burk, "Training Our Kids in a Transgender World," in *Designed for Joy: How the Gospel Impacts Men and Women, Identity and Practice* (Wheaton, IL: Crossway, 2015), 89-98.

that is coming every Christian's way very soon if it hasn't already. This is a conflict that all of us are going to face as Christians. And the question that we have to ask ourselves is, How are we going to respond in the face of this kind of conflict?

I would hope that our first response wouldn't be outrage but heartbreak. I don't know how anyone hears a story like this one above, and their heart does not break for this brokenhearted mother, who obviously loves her child and wants to relieve the suffering of her only surviving offspring. We need to feel the weight of pain that this mother has described. And as Christians, we need to feel the urgency to help this child and to relieve his suffering. On that much, we stand in solidarity with this mother.

Nevertheless our conflict is this: no matter how much we empathize and no matter how much our hearts may break and no matter how earnestly we desire to relieve the suffering of this child, our efforts will never measure up to the expectations of those who believe that the Word of God is harmful to people struggling with gender issues. In other words, it's not going to be enough *that* we want to relieve this child's suffering. We must also agree with them *how* that suffering is to be alleviated—even if that remedy disagrees with Scripture. And therein is our conflict.

And it is a real test for Christians. It is a test because popular opinion is moving against God's Word on gender issues. The dogmas of modernity and of the sexual revolution are coming home to roost. For Christians to oppose those dogmas with the Word of God doesn't just make us wrong. In the eyes of many, it renders us haters, bigots, people who should be banished to the margins of polite society. And so this is a real test for us because the stakes are so high. Who wants to be banished to the cultural margins? Are we going to love and care for hurting people in the way that Jesus tells us to do it? Or will we collapse under the pressure of those who hate the way Jesus has tells us to do it?

The conflict I'm describing is made even more acute by the fact that Christians aren't merely contending with secular culture over these questions. In some ways, we are contending with one another. Even among Christians who claim a connection to the evangelical mainstream, we are not all on the same page. Mark Yarhouse's 2015 book *Understanding Gender Dysphoria* is perhaps the most comprehensive response to the transgender question by someone in the evangelical movement. This book has made Yarhouse the go-to guy on this issue among evangelicals. *Christianity Today* had Yarhouse write a feature-length piece on transgenderism and gender dysphoria after Bruce Jenner made his transition in the summer of 2015—a piece based on the work he did in this book.[3] The review of this book on The Gospel Coalition website says that this book "marks a step forward in Christian engagement with gender issues."[4] And yet in this book, Yarhouse leaves the door open for transgender children to cross-dress and adopt cross-gender names for themselves. He also leaves the door open to gender reassignment surgery as one available treatment option for gender dysphoric adults. Is this a faithful response to the transgender challenge facing the Christian church? Apparently some people think that it is. I want to argue that it is not.

Before moving forward, it will probably be helpful for us to define a couple of terms. *Transgender* is a catchall term that refers to the many ways that people might perceive their gender identity to be out of sync with their biological sex. Until recently, the *Diagnostic and Statistical Manual of Mental Disorders* had classified this experience as a "Gender Identity Disorder." But in 2013, the DSM-5 removed this experience from its list of disorders and replaced it with the term *Gender Dysphoria*.[5] They did this in part to remove the stigma from the transgender experience—so that transgender people wouldn't have to say they had a psychological disorder. Instead, the DSM-5 just focuses on those who experience dysphoria (or mental distress) as a result of their perceived gender identity being out of sync with the gender they were assigned at birth.

So a relatively new issue (transgenderism) is making us confront some old questions. And it is a test of Christian conviction. There are three tests in particular that I want to highlight for the rest of this essay: (1) the test of biblical authority, (2) the test of biblical message, and (3) the test of biblical relevance.

---

[3]Mark Yarhouse, "Understanding the Transgender Phenomenon: The Leading Christian Scholar on Transgender Issues Defines the Terms—and Gives the Church a Way Forward," *Christianity Today* 59, no. 6 (July/August 2015): 44-50.

[4]Sam Ferguson, "Understanding Gender Dysphoria: Navigating Transgender Issues in a Changing Culture," The Gospel Coalition, July 15, 2015, www.thegospelcoalition.org/article/book-reviews -understanding-gender-dysphoria-transgender-mark-yarnhouse.

[5]American Psychiatric Association, *Diagnostic and Statistical Manual of Mental Disorders: DSM-5* (Washington, DC: American Psychiatric Association, 2013), 451-59.

TEST OF BIBLICAL AUTHORITY

"All Scripture is breathed out by God and profitable for teaching, for reproof, for correction, and for training in righteousness, that the man of God may be complete, equipped for every good work" (2 Tim 3:16-17).[6]

Our fundamental conviction as Christians is that we believe God has spoken to us in a book. Paul says that all "Scripture" is "breathed out by God." That word translated as "breathed out by God" is a term that appears nowhere else in Greek literature before Paul uses it here. In essence, Paul coins a term in order to describe the nature of Scripture. And he uses the term *theopneustos*—a compound word for "God-breathed." He is trying to say that the written word of Scripture *is* the very Word of God. When Scripture speaks, God speaks. The authority of Scripture, therefore, is nothing less than a shorthand for the authority of God.[7] It is his voice and his words, so it is his authority that we encounter in every word of Scripture that we read. If you have the Bible, you have the Word of God. And its teaching is sufficient for all your needs. What it says is always true. What it says is always right. What it says is always good for you. Why? Because God is the one who said it. And yet this authority is called into question by the transgender challenge.

In his book *Understanding Gender Dysphoria*, Mark Yarhouse distinguishes "three different frameworks for understanding gender identity concerns; these function as three lenses through which people view the topic."[8] They are *the integrity framework, the disability framework,* and *the diversity framework.*

The integrity framework or lens is the perspective of Scripture that emphasizes "God's creational intent and is the primary (or even exclusive) lens for most evangelical Christians."[9] This framework exposes that something is wrong when a person's perception of their gender identity doesn't match up with their biological identity.

The disability framework views gender dysphoria "as a result of living in a fallen world in which the condition—like so many mental health concerns—

---

[6]Scriptural quotations in this chapter are from the English Standard Version unless otherwise noted.
[7]N. T. Wright, *The Last Word: Beyond the Bible Wars to a New Understanding of the Authority of Scripture* (New York: HarperCollins, 2006), 25.
[8]Yarhouse, *Understanding Gender Dysphoria*, 46.
[9]Ibid., 47.

is a nonmoral reality."[10] Gender dysphoria is not a condition that people choose. It's just a result of living in a fallen world and in a fallen body. Because people don't choose to feel these conflicts, they are not moral. They just are.

The diversity framework views transgender issues as "something to be celebrated, honored or revered."[11] Diversity is good. Therefore diverse expressions of gender—even ones out of sync with biological sex—are also good. While evangelical Christians are rightly wary of this particular lens, we still have something to learn from it.[12] "The diversity framework helps the conservative Christian understand some of the limitations of more conservative (and sometimes rigid) scripts for gender identity and roles."[13]

So Yarhouse contends that Christians need to stop looking solely at the integrity framework (which is focused on biblical revelation). They need to balance Scripture against the other two "lenses," the *disability* and *diversity* frameworks. When we balance all three perspectives in what he calls "an integrated framework," it helps us to see that gender dysphoria is a "nonmoral reality" and enables us to focus on helping a person to "manage" his or her dysphoria.[14] And those management strategies might include crossdressing, cross-gender naming, and adopting a cross-gender identity.

Those aren't the only possible management strategies. But they are still listed among the options. But here's my question. Would those management strategies even be on the table if the authority of Scripture was held over and above the other two frameworks? Consider one Old Testament text that addresses the issue directly. Deuteronomy 22:5 (NASB) states, "A woman shall not wear man's clothing, nor shall a man put on a woman's clothing; for whoever does these things is an abomination to the LORD your God."

Notice that what they were to wear is not specified. What is specified is that no one should dress themselves in a way that obscures the sexual distinction between male and female. Where there are culturally encoded norms distinguishing the presentation of male and female, those norms are to be observed in order to affirm the Creator's distinction between male and

---

[10]Ibid., 48.
[11]Ibid., 50.
[12]Ibid., 51.
[13]Ibid., 52.
[14]Ibid., 53.

female. As P. J. Harland argues, "The prohibition of the wearing of clothes of members of the opposite sex . . . [was given] to safeguard the division between male and female."[15]

Consider also from Paul's writings 1 Corinthians 11:14-15 (NASB), "Does not even nature itself teach you that if a man has long hair, it is a dishonor to him, but if a woman has long hair, it is a glory to her? For her hair is given to her for a covering." For Paul, "nature" does not refer to human custom but to "the regular or established order of things"—the creational distinction that God made between male and female.[16] That creational distinction is not to be undermined by external presentations that would obscure it. As Tom Schreiner has argued,

> Nature teaches, then, in the sense that the natural instincts and psychological perceptions of masculinity and femininity are manifested in particular cultural situations. Thus, a male instinctively and naturally shrinks away from doing anything that his culture labels as feminine. So, too, females have a natural inclination to dress like women rather than men. Paul's point, then, is that how men and women wear their hair is a significant indication of whether they are abiding by the created order. Of course, what constitutes long hair is often debated—what is appropriately masculine or feminine in hairstyle may vary widely from culture to culture. . . . For a woman to dress like a man is inappropriate because it violates the distinction God has ordained between the sexes.[17]

Would cross-dressing be on the table if Scripture's authority was revered above the other two frameworks? I think the answer is no. And that is the problem with Yarhouse's approach. Balancing the three frameworks really amounts to relativizing the authority of Scripture. As Scripture is balanced against the need to find something good and praiseworthy about transgender experience, the authority of Scripture is diminished.[18]

---

[15]P. J. Harland, "Menswear and Womenswear: A Study of Deuteronomy 22:5," *Expository Times* 110, no. 3 (1998): 76.

[16]BADG, s.v. "φύσις."

[17]Thomas R. Schreiner, "Head Coverings, Prophecies, and the Trinity: 1 Corinthians 11:2-16," in *Recovering Biblical Manhood & Womanhood: A Response to Evangelical Feminism*, ed. John Piper and Wayne A. Grudem (Wheaton, IL: Crossway, 1991), 124-39.

[18]"The canonical Scriptures constitute the *norma normans* for the church's life, whereas every other source of moral guidance (whether church tradition, philosophical reasoning, scientific investigation, or claims about contemporary religious experience) must be understood as *norma*

Certainly we as Christians wish to help people who are navigating painful conflicts between their perceived gender identity and their biological sex. We love them. We feel compassion for them. And we want to see them whole and well and walking with God through Christ. But we aren't being loving, we aren't being compassionate, we aren't leading them to Christ when we in any way diminish the authority of Scripture.

So this is the test: Are we going to balance the authority of Scripture against these other concerns? Or are we going to insist that the Scripture stands over (and sometimes against) these other concerns? That is our test. And we have to stay true even if the whole world goes the other way.

TEST OF BIBLICAL MESSAGE

> But the Spirit explicitly says that in later times some will fall away from the faith, paying attention to deceitful spirits and doctrines of demons, by means of the hypocrisy of liars seared in their own conscience as with a branding iron, men who forbid marriage and advocate abstaining from foods which God has created to be gratefully shared in by those who believe and know the truth. For everything created by God is good, and nothing is to be rejected if it is received with gratitude; for it is sanctified by means of the word of God and prayer. (1 Tim 4:1-5 NASB)

Paul warns Timothy that false teachers are forbidding marriage and certain foods. Paul brushes aside their rules by appealing to the Bible. Paul says that God has created both marriage and food "to be gratefully shared in by those who believe and know the truth." Where do we read that God *created* everything, including food and marriage? We find that in the book of Genesis. Essentially, Paul is saying, "We know they're teaching error because it doesn't match up with the Bible."

Genesis 1 and 2 say that God created everything. Throughout the six days of creation, God looked at what he had made and said it was "good." After creating man, woman, and marriage on the sixth day, God says it is *very* good. The only time he said something wasn't good was when man was still

---

normata. Thus, normative Christian ethics is fundamentally a hermeneutical enterprise: it must begin and end in the interpretation and application of Scripture for the life of the community of faith." Richard B. Hays, *The Moral Vision of the New Testament: Community, Cross, New Creation: A Contemporary Introduction to New Testament Ethics* (New York: HarperOne, 1996), 10.

alone in Genesis 2:18. So God makes the woman and gives her to the man in marriage. Then everything is good. And that is why Paul says at the beginning of 1 Timothy 4:4 (NASB), "For everything created by God is good."

Paul tells Timothy that even though false teachers are saying marriage and food are bad, the Bible says marriage and food are good. For that reason, the church has to go with what God says, not with the false teachers who cannot tell the difference between good and evil. But notice how Paul generalizes. It's not just food and marriage that are good. He says "everything" created by God is good. And a part of what God creates at the very beginning is the sexual difference between male and female.

> Then God said, "Let Us make man in Our image, according to Our likeness."
> ... God created man in His own image, in the image of God He created him;
> male and female He created them. God blessed them; and God said to them,
> "Be fruitful and multiply, and fill the earth, and subdue it; and rule over the
> fish of the sea and over the birds of the sky and over every living thing that
> moves on the earth." (Gen 1:26-28 NASB)

There is a *sexual* complementarity embedded in God's good creation. But not only that, there is a *gender* complementarity that is also embedded into God's good creation. The "helper" corresponding to Adam designates a gender role for Eve—a role that is inextricably linked to her biological sex. Adam's role as leader, protector, and provider is inextricably linked to his biological sex. What does this mean? It means that God has so made the world that there is a normative, holy connection between biological sex and gender identity.

Let us state the principle again. This is the biblical message that is being tested right now. There is a normative connection between biological sex and gender identity. This is a connection that God established in the Garden of Eden before there was any sin in the world, and God calls that connection "very good." To deny that connection would be by definition "not good." Yes, that connection is defaced and injured by the fall and by sin. But that connection is God's original creation intent.

The letter that I shared at the beginning of this chapter was from a mother who believes that a person is transgender because their brain is hardwired to be a gender that doesn't match their biological sex. As I mentioned, her letter reflects what psychologists call a "brain-sex theory." It says that our brains "script" us toward male or female behaviors and dispositions.[19] But sometimes our brain's gender doesn't match up to that of our biological sex. When that is the case, many clinicians think that what a person *thinks* about him or herself should trump what God has *revealed* through biological sex.

In other words, what people perceive about their gender identity trumps what God's Word reveals about the normative connection that God establishes between biological sex and gender identity—a connection rooted in God's good creation. The severing of this connection is what makes transgender identities plausible to some people. It's also what makes people think they should resolve their gender identity conflict in a way that reshapes their body to conform to their thinking rather than reshaping their thinking to conform to their body. But we have to ask the obvious question: Is this the right way to think about things?

A couple years ago, I read about a thirty-year-old woman in Raleigh, North Carolina, who has always had a fascination with blindness.[20] She herself wasn't blind, but she always wanted to be blind. She says that since she was six years old, she always felt more comfortable at the thought of being blind. She had always felt like a blind person trapped in a sighted person's body. She had a condition that has come to be known as "Body Integrity Identity Disorder."

She had a perception about herself at odds with the biological reality that she could see just fine with her two eyes. Nevertheless, she wanted to be blind. But as an adult, she was unable to find a doctor willing to help her lose her sight. Finally, in 2006 she found a psychologist willing to help her. Over the course of many months, he gave her numbing drops for her eyes followed by drops of drain cleaner. After about six months of this excruciating treatment, she did finally lose her eyesight. She is now blind.

Most people hear that story and conclude that her mind was at odds with reality and that it is immoral and wrong to destroy healthy organs to accommodate that woman's misperception about herself. We don't deny that

---

[19]Yarhouse, *Understanding Gender Dysphoria*, 67.
[20]Ashton Edwards, "Woman Says She's Happier Than Ever After Fulfilling Lifelong Dream of Being Blind," *Fox 13 Salt Lake City*, October 1, 2015, http://fox13now.com/2015/10/01/woman-desperate-to-be-blind-had-drain-cleaner-poured-in-eyes-now-happier-than-ever.

she had a real desire to be blind and that she was experiencing real distress. We just believe that the best way to remedy that distress is not by destroying her eyes but by restoring her mind. We want to resolve her distress in a way that doesn't harm her body through destructive "medical" interventions.

Yet the prevailing view in "the mental health field is to address [gender dysphoria] through cross-gender identification and expression," which may lead to hormone treatments and gender-reassignment surgery.[21] In other words, the prevailing view in the mental health field is that psychological identity—one's own self-perception—should trump one's bodily identity. Yet that position is directly at odds with what Scripture teaches. It disputes with God about what is "good." It disputes with God about what he intends for us as male and female created in his image.

And that is why a Christian response must always seek to encourage people experiencing these conflicts to resolve those conflicts in keeping with their biological sex. But this is precisely the point that has come into dispute. In his book, Mark Yarhouse says that while he prefers the "least invasive" approaches to managing gender identity conflicts, he does not rule out other approaches. "Hormonal treatment and sex reassignment would be the most invasive. This is not to say a Christian would not consider the most invasive procedures; I know many who have. But they would not begin there, nor would they take such a decision lightly."[22]

> I see the value in encouraging individuals who experience gender dysphoria to resolve dysphoria in keeping with their birth sex. Where those strategies have been unsuccessful, *there is potential value in managing dysphoria through the least invasive expression* (recognizing surgery as the most invasive step toward expression of one's internal sense of identity).[23]

Notice that he doesn't rule out gender-reassignment surgery, but he leaves that possibility on the table. And he positively affirms "least invasive" measures, which include cross-dressing and assuming the gender role of the opposite sex. Likewise, Yarhouse recommends these least invasive methods for children with gender identity problems. But this is precisely where a Christian pastor or counselor cannot go. To allow these possibilities is to tell

---

[21]Yarhouse, *Understanding Gender Dysphoria*, 156.
[22]Ibid., 124.
[23]Ibid., 137 (emphasis mine).

people that God's creation is not "good" for them. And Christian pastors and counselors are not loving people well or serving people well if we lead them away from what God says is "good." As Vaughn Roberts has written, "Accepting our bodies as gifts from God certainly doesn't mean that it's wrong to try and correct what's wrong with them and seek to bring healing. But as we do so, we should follow the 'art restoration principle.' The aim is to restore the Creator's intention; but we are not to try to change it."[24]

TEST OF BIBLICAL RELEVANCE

"All Scripture is breathed out by God and profitable for teaching, for reproof, for correction, and for training in righteousness, that the man of God may be complete, equipped for every good work" (2 Tim 3:16-17).

This text says that this Word of God "equips" us "for every good work." That is a statement about the Bible's relevance to our lives. It's a statement about the sufficiency of Scripture. Everything that we need in order to know God, to believe in his Son Jesus, to be saved, and to walk in holiness and obedience is contained right here in this book. We are equipped for *every* good work. Not *some* of the good works. Not *most* good works except those good works that you need to rely on science to give you. No, it says it equips us for *every* good work. As Peter has said, "His divine power has granted to us all things that pertain to life and godliness, through the knowledge of him who called us to his own glory and excellence" (2 Pet 1:3).

He's given us "everything" we need? The apostles say, "Yes, everything." The question is, Do we believe that? Or are we going to cave in to the idea that the Scripture is sufficient for us except when it comes to navigating gender identity conflicts? Can we just forgo Scripture—as some people do—saying, "The Bible isn't a science book. It doesn't know anything about gender identity conflicts, and therefore it can't help us with that." Are we the first generation of Christians to deal with gender identity conflicts? Are we really going to believe that God left his people without resources to deal with these questions until the DSM-5 was published four years ago?

I don't think so. He has given us everything we need for life and godliness. We know about God's good creation of male and female in his image. We

---

[24]Vaughan Roberts, *Transgender*, Talking Points (Epsom, UK: The Good Book Company, 2016), 40.

know that even though that image has been marred by sin, he has made a way for us to get it all back through Christ. And we know that the grace of Jesus revealed to us in the Scripture is sufficient for every broken heart. That is what we have for ourselves. And that is what we have to offer to others.

that ever thought that image had been ... ed ... de ... much, we ... m ... ge ... all that thought ... thing. And we know that ... ge ... great ... ced to ... the sig ... ca ... so ... d it ... everywhere ... h ... that ... for ... i ... o ... un ... di ... g ... I ... hope ... have a plan ...

8

Put Pain like That Beyond My Power

A Christocentric Theodicy with Respect to the Inequality of Male and Female Power

GERALD HIESTAND

T HE LATIN POET OVID TELLS the poignant and tragic tale of Caenis, a young maiden who was once a "famous beauty, the loveliest of all the girls of Thessaly."¹ As is so often the case in classical myth, Caenis is pursued and ravished by a god—in this case the god Neptune. Neptune, while not quite contrite, nonetheless offers to grant Caenis a wish as a form of compensation for his deed. Caenis responds,

> This wrong you've done me needs an enormous wish—
> Put pain like that beyond my power. Grant me
> To cease to be a woman. Everything
> That gift will be to me.²

And so Neptune grants Caenis her wish. Caenis, now Caenus, "rejoicing in this gift," passed his days as a mighty warrior and a man.³

Ovid's *Caenis*, though a tale of divine and human interaction, captures well the tumultuous relationship that exists between men and women. This

---

¹The tale can be found in Ovid, *Metamorphoses*, trans. A. D. Melville (Oxford: Oxford University Press, 2008), XII.188, p. 279.
²Ibid., XII.100-104, p. 280.
³Ibid., XII.109, p. 280.

relationship, while often full of beauty, has nonetheless been fraught with suffering and abuse. Women throughout human history have too often been oppressed by an abusive use of male power. This abuse takes many forms—from subtle marginalization and exclusion to physical violence. We in the West live in a culture that, at least on the surface, champions the dignity and value of women, but we have not been able to wholly shake our Neptunian tendencies. Whatever our cultural ideals, women suffer at the hands of men far more than the reverse—as any police officer responding to a domestic call can attest. This disproportional suffering of women is the historically verifiable and motivating reality that has justifiably driven the variegated feminist movements throughout history (not least the feminist movements of our day). Even a casual survey—Aristotle's claim that women are mis-begotten males, to present-day Saudi Arabia's social and religious ban on women driving, to China's only recently abolished "one child" law that invariably preferenced boys over girls—shows that women have all too often occupied a second-class position with respect to men in ways that men have not typically had to occupy with respect to women.[4] The violence (whether physical or psychological or social) that has marked the war between the sexes has been asymmetrical.

The central premise of this chapter is that it is the man's greater power vis-à-vis the woman that accounts for much of this abuse. Here it is necessary to clarify what I mean by *power*. I do not have in mind *power* as an imma-terial construct, but more narrowly *power* as a capacity for "raw physical force." There are many forms of power beyond physical strength. Sexual power, intellectual power, social power, political power, relational power—all are forms of power that compete and often triumph over raw physical power. My claim here is not that women lack power, or that women are inherently less powerful than men. My claim is more simply that men have a greater capacity for physical force than women, and that this greater capacity for force is a primary occasion for male tyranny over women. Rape is the most vivid and tragic expression of this greater male capacity for force. But this same rapine impulse is manifested in a thousand lesser ways every time men use their greater physical power to marginalize and subject women.

---

[4] Aristotle, *De generatione animalium* 2.3.737a.

The greater levels of male physical power and its frequent misuse against women raises a serious question of theodicy: Why would God create humanity in such a way that there exists an inherent inequality of physical power between men and women, if this inequality has indeed resulted in such pervasive abuse and marginalization of women at the hands of men? The pagan god Neptune protected Caenis from further abuse by granting her desire to become a man and a great warrior. Neptune eliminated the potential for abuse by eliminating her femininity, by erasing the physical power gap between Caenis and the male world around her. Never again would a man force his will upon her, because she would have her own supply of god-given force to counteract the unwanted force of men. Neptune's initial assault not withstanding, is the God of the Bible less wise and compassionate than Neptune for failing to endow women with a capacity for force proportional to men? And most pressing, how should we navigate this power inequality? Are we to resist it as an evil, like Caenis—a thing to be feared and overcome? Or should we embrace it as a creational good? Or is there perhaps a via media between these two responses?

This paper seeks to provide (the beginnings of) a Christocentric theodicy that accounts for the divine wisdom in the physical power inequality between men and women and suggests a way forward for male/female relationships. Ultimately, I will argue that the physical power disparity between men and women has been purposefully ordained by God as a typological pointer to the gospel. Though often distorted by sin, power is not something to be shunned, but something to be deployed and shared in the service of sacrificial and empowering love. Toward this end, I will draw upon three main resources: the "third-wave" feminist Camille Paglia, the late Pope John Paul II, and St. Paul. We begin with Paglia.

CAMILLE PAGLIA: THE RELATIONSHIP BETWEEN BIOLOGY AND TYRANNY

In the preceding introduction I make the claim that the man's greater physical power vis-à-vis the woman has been a primary occasion for the oppression and abuse of women. It is intuitively obvious that such a claim is true with respect to physical violence. But my claim goes further. I am suggesting that it is the man's greater physical strength that has historically been a primary occasion for all types of abuse and marginalization of women—cultural, social, and political.

This is by no mean an uncontested claim. Many feminists (and others) argue instead that the main occasion for the historic male marginalization of women has little or nothing to do with biology and instead is sourced in the inequitable distribution of power within the political, social, and vocational structures of a given culture.[5] Just as certain races at certain points of history have been denied access to political, social, or cultural power, so too women have been denied the same. The solution then for gender equality from this perspective runs along the same lines as the solution for racial equality—a redistribution of political, social, and cultural power.

But third-wave feminist Camille Paglia disagrees. Paglia's breakthrough work is *Sexual Personae: Art and Decadence from Nerfertiti to Emily Dickinson*.[6] Paglia's writing is witty, aphoristic, and not without controversy among her fellow feminists. Paglia is one of the voices within third-wave feminism calling for feminists to recognize the innate biological differences between men and women and to reckon with how these differences relate to the feminist project: "Feminists grossly oversimplify the problem of sex when they reduce it to a matter of social convention: readjust society, eliminate sexual inequality, purify sex roles, and happiness and harmony will reign."[7]

For Paglia, the assertion of her fellow feminists that the problem is merely cultural, political, or social only begs the question of who it is that created such cultural constructs in the first place. Paglia's controversial answer is that human culture writ large is primarily the creation of men.[8] This claim

---

[5]Feminism is a variegated movement that cannot be easily defined, from the late nineteenth-century feminism in the West, with its focus on political equality for men and women, seen most clearly in the suffrage movement, to "second-wave" feminism with its emphasis on social and cultural equality, to what has now emerged since the 1990s as "third-wave feminism," which is in many respects a response to what has been seen by some feminists as the overreach of second-wave feminism. Though variegated, we can nonetheless speak of "feminism" if we limit our definition to something like the following: "Feminism is that movement, led by women, which has sought as its goal political, social, and cultural equality between men and women."

[6]Camille Paglia, *Sexual Personae: Art and Decadence from Nefertiti to Emily Dickinson* (New York: Vintage Books, 1991).

[7]Ibid., 1.

[8]For more from Paglia on this, see her *Time* essay, "It's a Man's World, and It Always Will Be," *Time*, December 16, 2013, www.ideas.time.com/2013/12/16/its-a-mans-world-and-it-always-will -be/. For a similar argument, see also Roy F. Baumeister, *Is There Anything Good About Men? How Cultures Flourish by Exploiting Men* (New York: Oxford University Press, 2010).

seems intuitively correct, just on a plain reading of human history, given that historically the distribution of cultural power has consistently favored men over women. Clearly we would expect a different distribution of political and social power between men and women if women had had an equal or greater share in creating the cultural power structures. Analogously, the cultural constructs in the United States have favored whites over blacks; such cultural, social, and political racial inequality is undoubtedly because the cultural constructs in the United States have largely been the product of whites. Following Paglia's logic, if a cultural construct favors one party over another, that's a sure sign it was created by the party the culture favors.

But we must press this further and ask the question of why it is that men have historically, with near universality, been able to act as the primary shapers of the cultural constructs that have advantaged men over women. Paglia's most basic answer is biology. "Feminists, seeking to drive power relations out of sex have set themselves against nature. . . . In nature, brute force is the law, a survival of the fittest."[9] Paglia, in a critique of her fellow feminists, argues that too much of the feminist movement has failed to grapple with this fixed fact of nature. Paglia is not endorsing the oppression of women, of course. Rather she is calling her fellow feminists to acknowledge that while women can and should seek political and social equality, they cannot get free from "contingency, that is, human limitation by nature or fate."[10] Paglia acknowledges that women have their own ways of oppressing and tyrannizing men. But she realistically acknowledges that men have a greater capacity for "brute force" vis-à-vis women, and that this greater capacity for force enables men to dominate and oppress women in ways that are not proportional or possible in the reverse. As Paglia poignantly states, when it comes to biology, "nature's burden falls more heavily on one sex."[11]

The appeals to racial oppression as analogous to gender oppression serve to confirm, rather than undermine, Paglia's claim. The oppression of the races throughout human history has been fluid—waxing and waning with the passing of time. No one race has unswervingly retained the upper hand

---

[9]Paglia, *Sexual Personae*, 2-3.
[10]Ibid., 3.
[11]Ibid., 9.

over another. The Philistines created cultural constructs that marginalized the Jews during the days of the judges, and then the Jews did the same to the Philistines under the Davidic dynasty. Latin Romans during the age of empire created power structures that marginalized indigenous Britons, Northern Europeans, and North Africans. When the Roman Empire crumbled, the barbarians on the Roman frontiers returned the favor. Examples of such cultural power shifts could be given ad infinitum.

But the cultural, political, and social oppression/marginalization of women at the hands of men has not been limited to particular times and places, such as we find with race. From the dawn of recorded human history the cultural constructs have—with almost no meaningful exceptions—advantaged men.[12] This is because culture is created by those who occupy the power position. Or again, culture is created by those who have the greatest capacity for force. This is certainly true with respect to race and cultural power. The Philistines oppressed Israel because they could, and Israel oppressed the Philistines because they could. And so on throughout human history. In a world that is (as Tennyson puts it) "red in tooth and claw," the physical capacity to force one's will on another—whether of entire nations, or individuals, or between gods and maidens—is nearly always the deciding factor in the success of tyranny. All other forms of power, when confronted in a do-or-die battle against raw physical power, must in the end, give way. The unarmed gladiator may have greater intellectual power than the lion, but on the sands of the coliseum, the lion is the winner every time.

Women are endowed with a great deal of power—intellectual, sexual, relational, emotional, etc.—in capacities that are equal to or supersede men. But physical power is the one type of power where men—as a gender—exceed women. And physical power is the one type of power that is indispensable for establishing the social, political, and vocational power structures of a culture.

Those who reject Paglia's claim about the priority of biology as a primary occasion for male tyranny over women must offer an alternate account of why men have historically tyrannized over women in ways that women have

---

[12]This assertion can be made notwithstanding the (highly) speculative feminists accounts of a human prehistory marked by a dominant matriarchal culture. Actual matriarchal societies have existed but constitute a tiny percentage of the overall anthropological data.

not tyrannized over men. Appeals to culture only push the problem down the street, since we must then ask why it is that men have been universally successful (with almost no meaningful exceptions) in creating cultures that have privileged men over women. Clearly there is something hardwired into the system that perpetuates the inequalities.[13] The history of our species teaches us that human beings seek their own advantage at the expense of others, and that apart from some outside influence, will continue to do so to the degree that they have capacity. This is, of course, a distinctly pessimistic way of conceiving of human nature. But it is also a deeply Christian way. In a fallen world cut off from divine grace, justice is, as Plato once cynically remarked, merely the advantage of the stronger.[14]

And it is here that we must confront the theodicy questions. Why would God create an asymmetrical power structure between men and women, given that this asymmetry is fertile soil for the marginalization of women? For the beginnings of an answer we now turn to John Paul II's account of the human body.

JOHN PAUL II: A THEOLOGY OF THE BODY

John Paul II's *Man and Woman He Created Them: A Theology of the Body* (hereafter *TOB*) is a wide-ranging series of addresses on the meaning of gender, sex, sexuality, sexual desire, and the body.[15] Basic to John Paul II's

---

[13]Were more space available, it would be worth pressing the point that it is not only the male's greater capacity for force, but his greater willingness to use it, that accounts for the male acquisition and keeping of cultural power. This psychological disposition too finds its roots in biology. See Dorian Furtuna, "Male Aggression: Why Are Males More Violent?," *Psychology Today Blog*, September 14, 2014, www.psychologytoday.com/blog/homo-aggressivus/201409/male -aggression; and Baumeister, *Is There Anything Good About Men?*, 47-59. Whether or not one grants my premise that men's greater capacity for physical force is a primary explanation for the larger cultural subjection of women writ large, the point still stands that men's greater physical capacity for force is very often the occasion for male physical violence against women in ways that are not symmetrical to female violence against men. The theodicy question remains.

[14]Said by Thrasymachus in Plato, *Republica* 338c.

[15]Most of my references to John Paul II are from John Paul II, *Man and Woman He Created Them: A Theology of the Body* (Boston, MA: Pauline Books and Media, 2006), hereafter cited as *TOB*. John Paul II has not been without his critics. See for example Patrick Snyder, *La femme selon Jean-Paul II. Lecture des fondements anthropologiques et théologiques et des applications pratiques de son enseignement* (Québec: Fides, 1999). The space limits of this essay allow for only a brief presentation of John Paul II's work, not a defense. For a defense of John Paul II against feminist critics, see Michele M. Schumacher, "John Paul II's Theology of the Body on Trial: Responding to the Accusation of the Biological Reduction of Women," *Nova et Vetera* (English ed.) 10, no. 2 (2012): 463-84.

work is his insistence that the human body contains a theology—that is, that our bodies tell us something about who we are as human beings and signify to us our purpose in the world.[16] In *Evangelium Vitae*, John Paul II captures the essence of his project when he states, "There is a truth of creation which must be acknowledged."[17] For John Paul II, biology is theology. Pushing back against modern and Cartesian notions of a depersonalized body, John Paul II rightly contends that our bodies are not merely arbitrary outer shells. The way we are shaped, the way the male and female bodies fit together, and the way in which conjugal love reproduces life—all inform our understanding of what it means to be human. Most fundamentally for John Paul II, the body "expresses the person."[18] Indeed, John Paul II's language blurs the lines between the person and the body when he writes, "Man does not *have* a body, he *is* a body."[19] Rather than merely finding the *imago Dei* in the intellect, as has been customary in much of Christian theology (e.g., Augustine and Aquinas), John Paul II insists that our bodies also reflect the *imago Dei*.[20] Man, as the visible *eikon* of the Creator, communicates through his body a true statement about God and his own humanity.

In *TOB*, John Paul II deploys this logic most specifically in service of expounding the beauty and meaning of marital love. But for the purposes of this essay, I wish to focus on John Paul II's fundamental insight that the human body communicates a theology (and anthropology) and use this insight to frame our understanding of gender and power. As has been observed, from the very beginning, creation invariably places the man in a position of physical power vis-à-vis the woman. While there are, of course, exceptions to the rule, social psychologist Dorian Furtuna notes that the average man has 75 percent more arm strength than the average woman, and that the upper male body is 90 percent stronger than the upper female body. He goes on to add, "Men are taller, they have denser and heavier bones, their

---

[16]This is an essentially Thomistic understanding of the body (see Thomas Aquinas, *Summa Theologiae* I, q. 91, a. 3), as Matthew Levering points out in his chapter on Thomas Aquinas's sexual ethics.

[17]John Paul II, *Evangelium Vitae*, English ed. (New York: Random House), 22.

[18]John Paul II, *TOB*, 14.5.

[19]Ibid., 12.15.

[20]The seeds for this type of theological anthropology can be found as early as Irenaeus, who insists that the body constitutes the image of God, prophetically and typologically reflecting the incarnate Son (*Adversus haereses* 5.16.2). Thus for Irenaeus, the image of God points to the embodied Son, rather than the nonembodied Father.

jaw is more massive, their reaction time is shorter, their visual acuity is better, their muscle/fat ratio is greater, their heart is bulkier, their percentage of hemoglobin is higher, their skin is thicker, their lungs bigger, and their resistance to dehydration is higher."[21] All of these physical differences give the man an advantage over the woman with respect to force. Adding to the physical disparity between men and women is the additional reality that the survival of our species depends on women carrying human life inside of them for the better part of a year. Physical mobility during pregnancy, recovery after pregnancy, and the unique dietary needs of an infant (handled exclusively via breastfeeding until only recently in human history) all increase the woman's vulnerability to male power.

From a Cartesian perspective the man's greater physical power can have no significance since the body has no essential meaning. Men are stronger than women, and women have babies. It all means nothing and says nothing about what it means to be a man or a woman. But following John Paul II's insight that biology is theology, one is compelled to ask what meaning the disparity of physical power between men and women has for our understanding of what it means to be a man and a woman. Unless one were to posit some sort of genetic diminishment of the woman as a consequence of the fall (a rather strange idea), we are left to grapple with the fact that God, for some reason, purposefully created men to be physically stronger than women. I do not recall anywhere in *TOB* where John Paul II notes the physical power disparity between men and women or draws any significance from it. But if we follow John Paul II's line of thought, surely it means *something*. What exactly it means is not revealed in the creation account.[22]

---

[21]Dorian Furtuna, "Male Aggression." Furtuna lists the following studies for his data: T. Abe, C. F. Kearns, and T. Fukunaga, "Sex Differences in Whole Body Skeletal Muscle Mass Measured by Magnetic Resonance Imaging and Its Distribution in Young Japanese Adults," *British Journal of Sports Medicine* 37 (2003): 436-40; and R. W. Bohannon, "Reference Values for Extremity Muscle Strength Obtained by Hand-Held Dynamometry from Adults Aged 20 to 79 years," *Archives of Physical Medicine and Rehabilitation* 78 (1997): 26-32. For more on the biological difference and how these differences affect social dynamics, see Anne and Bill Moir, *Why Men Don't Iron: The Fascinating and Unalterable Differences Between Men and Women* (New York: Citadel Press, 1999). For theological reflection on these differences (in keeping with the spirit of my essay), see Owen Strachan, "On Power and Fragility: Reflections on John Paul II's Theology of Bodily Womanhood," *Bulletin of Ecclesial Theology* 1.1 (June 2014): 61-72.

[22]Observe here that I am not making a natural law argument about how men and women should relate to each other. My deployment of John Paul II is not an effort to say *what* the physical disparity between men and women means, but rather more modestly to say that it means

But John Paul II points us in the right direction in *TOB*, cat. 86-102, where he exegetes Ephesians 5:21-23, drawing out the typological meaning of marriage. In this section, John Paul II argues, following Paul, that marriage is most fundamentally about Christ and the church. For John Paul II, Paul's treatment of marriage offers us an analogy wherein, "the reciprocal relationship between the spouses, husband and wife, should be understood by Christians according to the image of the relationship between Christ and the Church."[23] For this perspective, human marriage only makes sense in light of this fundamental context of meaning. For a full exposition of this meaning, we can now turn to St. Paul.

ST. PAUL AND MARRIAGE TYPOLOGY

Ephesians 5:21-32 is one of the New Testament's most developed treatments on marital relations. Paul's focus here is not primarily about power. Yet the manner in which he articulates the divine *telos* of the spousal relationship informs our larger theodicy question concerning the inequality of male/female power. Key to a proper reading of this passage is the observation that Paul pointedly describes the marriage relationship as an image of the spiritual relationship between Christ and the church. For Paul, marriage typologically points beyond itself to an ultimate fulfillment in Christ's marriage to the church. Which is to say, marriage is fundamentally about Christ and the gospel. Note carefully the significance of the last sentence of verse 32 within its context.

> For no one ever hated his own flesh, but nourishes and cherishes it, just as Christ does the church, because we are members of his body. "Therefore a man shall leave his father and mother and hold fast to his wife, and the two shall become one flesh." This mystery is profound, and I am saying that it refers to Christ and the church. (Eph 5:29-33)[24]

Throughout his treatment on marriage, Paul is discussing the relational dynamics of the husband and wife. And as he gives instruction to husbands

---

something. What that something is must be sought elsewhere—in this case St. Paul's Christ/church marriage typology.

[23]John Paul, *TOB*, 89.9; 90.

[24]All scriptural quotations in this chapter are from the English Standard Version unless otherwise noted.

and wives about how they are to treat one other, he draws a tight parallel between human marriage and Christ's relationship with the church. The way Christ treats the church, Paul tells us, serves as the pattern for the way in which a husband is to treat his wife. And the way the church relates to Christ is the way a wife is to relate to her husband. But by what logic does Paul ask husbands and wives to relate to one another as Christ and the church? The answer is found in verse 32. The oneness of human marriage, Paul tells us, "refers to Christ and the church."[25] Drawing upon the ancient marriage formula of Genesis 2:24, Paul reveals that sexual oneness within marriage was created by God, *from the beginning*, to serve as a typological foreshadowing of the spiritual oneness that has now begun to exist between Christ and his church—a oneness that has eternally existed in God's intent.[26]

And here we must press the *purposefulness* of the typological nature of human marriage. That marriage is a type of the gospel is not merely a happy coincidence of human history. But rather, by linking his comments to Genesis 2, the apostle assures us that *from the beginning*, God created the human marriage relationship to reflect the higher reality of the Christ/church relationship. Though human marriage came first historically, it is preceded logically by Christ's union with the church. Or again, human marriage is a type of Christ and the church, not the other way around. Or again, the Christ/church union precedes and supersedes all other marital unions. Human marriage is, from the beginning, full of divine intentionality.[27]

---

[25]For John Paul II, the marital commands would have no grounding if marriage were not fundamentally about Christ and the church. The analogy "illuminates the mystery, and is illuminated by the mystery," *TOB*, 90.2. The church has traditionally understood the marriage relationship through a typological framework. See 2 Clement 14:2; Augustine, *De peccatorum meritis et remissione* I.60; Thomas Aquinas, *Summa Theologiae* III.42.1; John Calvin, *Commentary on Galatians and Ephesians*, trans. William Pringle (Grand Rapids: Baker Books, 2003), 317-18; Luther, *The Babylonian Captivity of the Church*, trans. A. T. W. Steinhauser (Philadelphia, PA: Fortress, 1970), 223; Jonathan Edwards, "The Excellency of Christ, 1758," in *The Sermons of Jonathan Edwards: A Reader*, ed. Wilson H. Kimnach, Kenneth P. Minkema, and Douglas A. Sweeney (New Haven, CT: Yale University Press, 1999), 186; Karl Barth, *Church Dogmatics* III/2 (Edinburgh: T&T Clark, 1976), §45.3, 285-324. Many modern evangelical commentators embrace this typological interpretation as well.

[26]The two preceding paragraphs are drawn from Gerald Hiestand, "A Biblical Theological Approach to Premarital Sexual Ethics: Or, What Saint Paul Would Say About 'Making Out,'" *Bulletin of Ecclesial Theology* 1.1 (June 2014): 22-23.

[27]The New Testament's many references to the church as the "bride" of Christ, and to Christ as the "bridegroom" further highlights the typological nature of marriage—so too Christ's use of the wedding motif as an illustration of his return and consummate union with the church. And

All of this provides a theological rational for Paul as to the way Christians are to behave in marriage. Just as we give ourselves to Christ in the free surrender of ourselves to One who is sovereign over us, that we might joyfully receive him, so too the wife joyfully receives the husband.[28] And just as Christ in turn exercises his lordship over us in a way that does not seek his own ends but rather seeks our highest good, so too the husband gives himself to the wife.

And most significantly for our purposes, not only does the Christ/church analogy offer us a theological framework for understanding the New Testament's proscribed marital *behavior*, it also offers us a theological framework for understanding the divinely created marital *ontology*—why the man and woman exist as they do in relation to the other. Thus reflection on the power dynamics of the Christ/church relationship informs our understanding of the power dynamics between the husband and the wife, and then between men and women more generally.[29]

It is clear that Christ—as the heavenly bridegroom—occupies a position of strength in relation to the church. And it is likewise clear that the church occupies a position of vulnerability in relation to Christ. And this power disparity is not due to the debilitating effects of sin, but more deeply, to nature. Christ's divine nature gives him a native strength that the church does not inherently possess. And indeed, this inequality of power is central to the entire narrative of Christ and the church, for it is precisely because the church occupies a position of vulnerability that Christ comes as her suitor. If the church possessed by nature the same power and strength that Christ possessed, there would be no gospel story.

But it's important here to note how this power relation is worked out in the Christ/church relationship. Christ uses his greater power for the exaltation of

---

the book of Revelation explicitly refers to the wedding supper of the Lamb as inaugurating the dawn of the eternal age. See also 1 Cor 6:16-17, where Paul links the "one-flesh" union of a man and a woman with the "one spirit" union between Christ and the believer.

[28]John Paul II comments here that the wife's submission to the husband "consists in experiencing his love." See John Paul II, *TOB*, 92.6.

[29]Our larger discussion relates to power and gender dynamics beyond the spousal relationship. Yet the spousal relationship anchors all other male/female relationships, insofar as the spousal relationship stands uniquely and primordially at the headwaters of humanity's original creation. It is the divinely appointed means for the continuation of our species and cannot be relativized as merely one form of male/female relationship among many. As such, a close reading of the divine intent for marriage provides a framework for thinking more generally about the use and distribution of power in all forms of male/female relations.

his bride. This runs counter to the way the world typically uses power, where power is used to advance one's own agenda. Jesus shows us the proper use of power in the upper room. "Jesus, knowing that the Father had given all things into his hands," dressed himself as a servant and washed the feet of his disciples (Jn 13:3). The proper use of power is to put it in the service of sacrificial love. And even more fully, Jesus shows us the proper use of power at the cross. "Could I not call twelve legions of angels?" Jesus asks when the soldiers come for him. Yet rather than using the endless power at his disposal to seek his own safety, he used his power to secure the safety of his bride.

What's more, it is not simply that Jesus *uses* his power on behalf of his bride. He goes further and actually *shares* his power by sharing wholly of himself in such a way that all that he has becomes hers. Christ lifts up his bride to rule and reign with him in the age to come. He grants his "natural" strength—his deity via his Holy Spirit—to the church, and makes his bride a coruler with him of the kingdom of God. And for her part, the church (idealized in glory), entrusts herself to Christ and embraces/welcomes the benevolent use of his power on her behalf. She conveys her love for Christ through submission to his will. Yet she is not simply a passive presence in relation to Christ—a mere receiver of grace—but actively partners with him in his purposes now (2 Cor 6:1, "working together with him") and will reign with him in the coming kingdom (Rev 21–22). What's more, the church never confuses her exaltation *by* Christ with independence *from* Christ; she does not seize upon grace as an occasion for disregard. The fact that Christ has exalted her to a place of equality, to be a coruler with him, does not cause her to honor him less, but more.

Christ sacrifices himself for his bride that she might be glorified to a place of mutual dignity and respect. And it is precisely *because* of the power disparity between Christ and the church that Christ's love is so worthy of admiration. Sacrificial love can and does exist within egalitarian power relations, but it is magnified and amplified in nonegalitarian power relations.

LIVING FAITHFULLY INTO THE CHRIST/CHURCH TYPOLOGY

It is from this vantage point that we can begin to shape a theodicy with respect to the inequality of male/female power. Following John Paul II and the apostle Paul, we conclude that the woman was created to be physically vulnerable in relation to the man so that the selfless kind of other-exalting love that Christ expresses on behalf of the church, and the honor and deference the church shows to Christ, might be more readily manifest between the husband and the wife. The physical power disparity between husband and wife typologically matches the power disparity between Christ and the church. Like Christ, the husband is to use his greater physical strength not to advance his own agenda, but rather is to deploy his power for the betterment of his wife. And like the church, the wife is not to resent her husband's greater power but is to respect and honor it and gladly welcome its benevolent deployment on her behalf.

The power dynamics at play in Christ's relationship with the church and the husband's relationships with the wife provide for us a framework for thinking about the power relationship between men and women more generally. Following the ultimate pattern of Christ and the church, and the penultimate pattern of the husband and wife, those in positions of power (in this case, men, considered generally) are to use that power for the betterment and promotion of those in the less powerful position (in this case, women, considered generally).

The feminist movements have been good for women in many ways, most notably the way that they have drawn attention to the very real suffering and marginalization of women. But these movements have failed women insofar as they have tried to rectify this abuse by seeking, as their primary objective, the elimination of the power gap between men and women. We have too often sought the path of Caenis—to put pain beyond the power of women by attempting to eliminate feminine vulnerability. There is some wisdom in this approach. But Caenis's answer can never be the final answer. Paglia again: "Political equality for women, desirable and necessary as it is, is not going to remedy the radical disjunction between the sexes that begins and ends in the body."[30] Women will always occupy a position of vulnerability in relation to men. This cannot be changed insofar as it is inexorably connected to divinely ordered biology. It is God himself who has ordained the power gap, and he has done so precisely because the inequality of power allows for the unique demonstration of Christ-exalting, sacrificial love in

---

[30]Paglia, *Sexual Personae*, 21.

ways that would not be as possible in a completely egalitarian power structure. Thus the final answer to abuse is not a futile attempt to eliminate the power gap but trust in God's design and Christlike love.

In the intramural Christian gender debates, we can too often get caught up in arguing about who should be in the power position—as though we had the ability to rewrite this aspect of creation. The New Testament does not so much insist that husbands *should* be in the power position (as though this were determined according to arbitrary social constructs), but rather it simply and realistically acknowledges that husbands are, and then gives instruction about how men are to use their greater power.

Here it may be helpful to distinguish between "power as force" and "power as authority." While the two often run together, they are not the same. Authority can be possessed by those with a lesser capacity for force. A 5'6, 130-pound police officer has a level of authority equal to his 6'4, 270-pound partner, yet the latter has a greater capacity for force. In a physical altercation between the two officers and a violent noncompliant suspect, it is force, not authority, that is the decisive determiner. And of course, this is seen clearly in the fact that the noncompliant suspect has disregarded the authority of both officers and has moved straight into a raw power struggle. Many conversations around the topic of headship and submission in marriage focus too narrowly on the issue of authority without proper consideration of power. However much we might press toward an egalitarian *authority* structure in the spousal relationship, we cannot override biology and create a completely egalitarian *power* structure.

It is here that evangelical conversations on gender can lose their way. Too often our notions of gender equality conflate "equality of power" with "equality of worth" and thus assume that equality of power is the only kind of equality that counts. This is an essentially Nietzschian view of power and worth. If equality of power is the only way to affirm the equal value of the sexes, then male/female biology has doomed equality from the start. The Christ/church typological framework helps us see that an inequality of power is not inherently totalizing or demeaning, but rather has the potential to reveal the beauty of the gospel and sacrificial love.

But we must say more. The fact that God has hardwired a perpetual power gap into male/female relations does not logically lead to the conclusion that

God's design for men and women is a static power relationship. Here the Christ/church marriage typology needs to critique evangelical complementarian perspectives on gender. Too often complementarian notions of gender, while benevolent, fail to mirror the *empowering* reality of Christ and his relationship with the church. Christ doesn't just deploy his power on behalf of his bride; he *shares* his power with his bride. We are, according to Paul's Ephesians vision, raised up with Christ and seated with him "in the heavenly places, far above all rule and authority and power and dominion, and above every name that is named, not only in this age but also in the one to come" (Eph 1:20-23; see also Eph 2:6). If we lose sight of this aspect of Christ's relationship with the church, we inevitably end up with patronizing notions of male power. Women are pushed into overtly passive roles, while those in the power position (men)—even though exercising their power benevolently—feel no compulsion to share their greater power with women. What results is a static, nontransferable use of male power that all too often results in the subtle treatment of women as children rather than as coheirs of grace and corulers in the kingdom of God. Women are denied the opportunity to use their gifts in ways that lead God's people into a deeper relationship with Christ. This is a loss for both women and men. Any model of Christian gender relations that fails to meaningfully incorporate Christ's sharing of power with his bride misses the mark, and does not do justice to God's ideal.

Yet there is limit to how this power can be transferred. Christ does not transfer his power to the church in a way that makes the church independent of and no longer in need of Christ—as though Jesus were able to give away his power to the church like a rich person gives away money to a poor person, who now being in possession of wealth, is no longer in need of the rich person. Rather Christ's empowerment of the church comes in the form of his Spirit, which is his own presence. In this way, Christ shares his power only insofar as he shares himself; and the church rises on the high tide of Christ's power only insofar as the church dwells in relation to and lives in dependence upon Christ. The church's strength is always borrowed; we never become a divine person, eternal and uncreated.

The same pattern holds for how men share power with women. It is not possible for men to give away their greater capacity for physical force, as though it were a commodity; they can only share the benefit of this capacity, not the capacity itself. Thus while it is the duty and glory of the man to lift up and exalt the woman into a place of mutual equality, whatever the nature of this equality, it does not mean that the husband sends his wife into the basement at 2 a.m. to find out what that crashing noise was while he stays safely tucked beneath the blankets. The husband does not exalt the wife by cutting her off from his protective and sacrificial love; he cannot send his greater physical power with his wife into the basement while he remains in his bed. If we are not clear on this point, male attempts to "share power" become little more than male abdications of masculine responsibility.[31]

As such, male power-sharing can only occur when men dwell in benevolent and harmonious relation with women. Men must not quit the field, retreating into passivity, thinking that they can hand off their greater physical power like a commodity. Such misbegotten attempts ultimately leave women overburdened and underempowered. Like Paglia, I believe a primary mistake of the feminist movement has been its insistence (perpetuated by both men and women) that women can achieve equality with men independent of men.[32] It is precisely because the church embraces and consciously lives into Christ's greater power that she is exalted into a place of equality. In the same way, the greater power of the man is the very means by which the woman attains equality herself.

The Scriptures paint a clear picture of gender complementarity—the man is not independent of the woman, nor is the woman independent of the man. The story of Genesis is the story of life—the man shares his life with the woman and she in turn gives it back again. The life by which Eve lives is Adam's, for she is drawn forth from his side. But she is rightly called Eve—the living one, the Mother of Life, and the one through whom he finds his life again.

Conclusion

The year 2012 marked the hundred-year anniversary of the sinking of the Titanic; over fifteen hundred men, women, and children were lost. But the

---

[31]I am thinking here of women serving in military combat roles, as firemen, police officers, etc. The contemporary push to treat women as though they were men is a form of power-sharing that ultimately isolates women from the benevolent protection of male power. Complementarians will likewise see a logic here that extends to the debates regarding the ordination of women.
[32]See Paglia, *Sexual Personae*, 9.

casualties were not equally dispersed among the passengers. Only 20 percent of the men survived, compared with 70 percent of the women and children. But the contrasting survival rates weren't just rotten luck. The reason a higher percentage of women and children survived is because the majority of the men on the ship deployed their greater physical power in service of the women and children and because the women and children submitted themselves to this benevolent use of masculine power. And it is precisely the inequality of power that makes the sacrifice of the men of the Titanic so meaningful. They could have saved themselves; they could have used their greater physical power to preserve their own lives. But in sacrificial love they deployed their power for the sake of those in the vulnerable position. It was a distinctly Christian use of power.[33]

Ultimately, men are not called to go down with the ship because they are better at drowning but rather quite the opposite. In a strictly "tooth and claw" world, men are in fact much more capable of staying alive. And it is for precisely this reason that men are called first to die. The sacrifice of power on behalf of the vulnerable more closely reflects the beauty of the Christ/ church relationship. When men and women navigate the power structure of the male/female relationship in harmony with the Christ/church relationship—the man laying down his life in love in order that he might raise up the woman to a place of equality and glory, and the woman at peace with her vulnerability, honoring the man and embracing the deployment of benevolent power on her behalf, taking her place alongside him as a coregent of the coming kingdom—there is great beauty and happiness. The Caenis option, while seeming the safer and surer route to safety, in the end robs men, and most especially women, of their inherent beauty and dignity. Better to live into the way of Christ and his church, trusting that God, in his perfect time, will put all pain beyond our power—not by robing us of our vulnerability, but by perfecting and protecting us in Christ.

---

[33]In the same vein, millionaires John Jacob Astor and Benjamin Guggenheim refused to use their wealth and privilege to secure for themselves places on the lifeboats, choosing rather to give up their seats for the women and children and to go down with the ship.

9

Bent Sexuality and the Pastor

JOEL WILLITTS

If the door is open it isn't theft
You can't return to where you've never left

"Cedarwood Road," U2

Every shipwrecked soul knows what it is
To live without intimacy
I thought I heard the captain's voice
But it's hard to listen while you preach

"Every Breaking Wave," U2

M Y INTENTION IN THIS CHAPTER is to problematize sexuality by inviting us into our own stories of brokenness and harm. There are two realities that I want to uncover in this chapter. The first is the pervasiveness of sexual trauma. It's not the problem of a few; it's the condition of most of us. The second reality is the minimization or denial of our own trauma around sexuality. Because of our need to survive, to accomplish, to push beyond our own disquieted, restless hearts, we have worked hard, very hard to win the battle over sexual disorder. But among our tribe, the pastor, there have been many causalities—some dramatic and public, most quiet and hidden.

We've used the tools of discipleship to engage the struggle. And we have leaned on our own self-contempt to keep us in check in many cycles of acting out, confession, and spiritual flagellation after failure. But after decades of struggle, many of us in the middle of our lives are tiring out. We are fatigued and discouraged. We are fragmented and hiding. But the disquiet of our hearts, the isolation of our souls and bodies, is getting louder and stronger. Age is not bringing more holiness. Maturity is not what we thought it would be. Our past seems to be ever with us. As Bono so insightfully sings in U2's song "Cedarwood Road," "you can't return to where you've never left."

In an interview with Charlie Rose, Bono reflected on the retrospective nature of the songs on the album *Songs of Innocence* (2014) like "Cedarwood Road," which is about the violence he witnessed as a boy growing up in Ireland. At one point, prompted by Rose, Bono mused, "maybe you have to go back" to go forward.[1]

In general, our collective approach to sexual disorder has been to generalize it, to categorize it as sin, and then attempt to remove it with surgical precision from our lives. But there's the problem: sexual sin is not like gangrene or a tumor that can be cut out. It's not a demon that can be cast out. It's not like ritual impurity that can be removed through ritual purification. When we approach it categorically like this, we are unable to engage its meaning, and we cut ourselves off from attending to the deeper issues of the soul that concretize themselves in sexual bentness. The "sin" ceases to have the potential to be the invitation to go back and to heal.

The deep struggle—the bentness of our desire—has not led to curiosity, to the act of engagement with the story our bodies are speaking to us in their disorientation.

At the corporate level, in the attempt to keep our sexual disorder in check, we have created cultures of fear and contempt all around us. We have approached our human embodied condition not with fatherly attunement and curiosity but with detached judgments lacking a true empathy for the truly impossible burden of being human in the kind of world we inhabit.

It is my conviction that we, pastors that is, are far more sexually broken than we are even conscious of or willing to admit. I don't mean that this is a

---

[1] Bono, interview by Charlie Rose, *Charlie Rose*, PBS, September 20, 2016, https://charlierose.com /videos/29156.

willful suppression of some dark truth about ourselves—though it could be. As counterintuitive as this may sound, my experience tells me that we may be among some of the most self-unaware people on earth. And this is despite the fact that we think otherwise.

My contention in this chapter is that when properly understood, sexual trauma has affected all of us to some degree. Scripture and experience, I believe, bear witness to the assault by evil on our human sexuality. Surely, it is evil's most useful tool to fragment humans and hold them captive to shame, guilt, and self-contempt. It is evil's primary weapon to dehumanize further and to keep us from experiencing the depth of God's fatherly kindness. It seems there is nowhere in the world, there is no time in history, and there are no human peoples who are ever free from sexual trauma. Sexual trauma is a pervasive reality in the world we inhabit.

As I invite us into a place of vulnerability around these tender issues of the heart, I want to ask your permission "to share my life with you" as I also share the gospel, in the words of the apostle Paul (see 1 Thess 2:8). I ask that you, the reader, be kind to me as I vulnerably put to words elements of my own story that have deep shame attached. I need to name some things that are true that often remain unspoken. But I also ask that you show kindness to yourself. Something I write may bring flashes of memory you've not thought about. Deep emotion may surprise you. Be hospitable to those memories and be kind to that emotion by blessing it, by welcoming and honoring it. Let your body speak truth to you as you perhaps discover yourself in my story.

SEXUALLY BENT

The imagery of a godly sexuality is not a blessing. Instead it weighs on me like Cain's curse. The prospect of sexuality as a divine gift presents itself to me as a mere fanciful desert mirage. For me, sexuality feels dark and tainted—a space where God is not. First as an emerging adult and then as a fully formed middle-aged male, I have experienced my sexuality not as a holy and divine gift but as a constant source of ambivalence, shame, anguish, frustration, and hopelessness.

My sexuality is bent. It's warped, and I'm at home there. Strange and twisted as it may sound, this dark sexuality is for me a place of comfort, of kindness, of safety. Holy sexuality is foreign, awkward, terrifying.

My sexuality is a burden I have to bear, not a gift in which I take delight. In a moment of clarity not long ago, I told my wife, Karla, who has walked with me and has been willing to walk lovingly, patiently alongside me through my journey for twenty-three years, "I wish I didn't have a sexuality at all. I wish I didn't have to concern myself with sexual intimacy. Sex and intimacy are an impossible puzzle for me." Sex is little more than a bodily function that must be performed to regulate stress. Everything around it is chaotic and absurd.

My bent sexuality compelled Karla to ask me a question like, "Do you ever desire me sexually?" Vulnerable, honest, searching questions like that from her sink like millstones into my chest. I am filled with self-contempt, fear, confusion, and powerlessness. And all I can eek out in terms of a response is not much more than the whisper, "I don't know; yes, no." The only thing that is clear is the ambivalence. Even after many hours of therapy, my sexuality is an enigma I feel like I will never crack.

I am a survivor of childhood sexual abuse. My eighteen-year-old step-brother sexually abused me from age thirteen to sixteen. I'll spare the details here, but this man groomed me into a willing accomplice of his violent perversion. So brilliant a predator was he that I agreeably and enthusiastically became his disciple par excellence and partner in his sexually warping schemes.

And here's the terrible truth: I'm not alone. Conservative estimates say that one in four women and one in six men have experienced sexual abuse.[2] These figures woefully underestimate the real situation, however, and this is particularly true for men. Since nearly 90 percent of sexual predators are men, sexually abused men have increased levels of shame resulting from same-sex sexual contact, which results in far less self-reporting in the types of paper-and-pencil surveys that produce these figures.

In addition, most of us don't really know what constitutes sexual trauma in the first place. How would you define it, if asked to? You surely will think a story like mine fits any definition. But it took me several years before I ever thought to name what had happened to me "abuse." This is because I felt I had "enjoyed" and "participated" in the sexual relationship. How could it be abuse if I was joining in willfully? If I was the sidekick in this deceptive, dark

---

[2] "The 1 in 6 Statistic," 1in6.org, accessed March 2, 2017, https://1in6.org/get-information/the-1-in-6-statistic/.

scheme in the family? However, I had never considered the power dynamic that is always at work in abuse.

The first time I ever named my abuse to anyone was my sophomore year in college while serving as summer counseling staff at a Christian camp. One of my campers, late one night, shared that he had been molested by a youth worker. For the first time, I saw myself in his story.

DEFINING SEXUAL TRAUMA

When we understand what exactly sexual trauma is, we will find that more of us have been affected by abuse then we have ever realized. I've taken over this definition of sexual trauma from Christian therapist Dr. Dan Allender: "SA is a sexual experience initiated by a person of power (usually older) with a person who is not in a position to refuse (usually younger)."[3]

The anatomy of abuse then involves two components: (1) an invitation to a sexual experience of any kind and (2) an unequal power dynamic such that the victim cannot imagine refusing.

This proper understanding of SA reveals that many things we take for granted in our sex-crazed, post–sexual revolution culture are in fact sexual abuse. Take for instance the introduction of pornography by an older boy to a younger one. While this kind of thing is regularly viewed as "boys being boys," it is in fact an act of abuse—and, as attested by many men with whom I have spoken, has tremendous negative consequences on a person's sexuality. Often, this early introduction to sexuality creates a wound they forever carry around in their body.

Another recent example comes from the arena of NCAA Division I collegiate sports. In the fall of 2015, a sex scandal broke open involving the University of Louisville's basketball team when a former escort, Katina Powell, admitted in an exposé that she organized nearly two dozen stripping and sex parties from 2010 to 2014 inside Billy Minardi Hall, the on-campus

---

[3]Dan Allender, "Men and Sexual Abuse: Hope for Wounded Hearts," *Focus on the Family Daily Broadcast*, podcast audio, June 27, 2012, www.focusonthefamily.com/media/daily-broadcast /men-and-sexual-abuse-hope-for-wounded-hearts-pt1; see also Dan Allender, *The Wounded Heart: Hope for Adult Victims of Childhood Sexual Abuse* (Colorado Springs: NavPress, 2008), 47; Christine A. Courtois, *Healing the Incest Wound: Adult Survivors in Therapy* (New York: Norton, 2010), 22; Andrew J. Schmutzer, ed., *The Long Journey Home: Understanding and Ministering to the Sexually Abused* (Eugene, OR: Wipf & Stock, 2011), 5.

dorm for athletes. The parties were set up during recruitment visits. EPSN's *Outside the Lines* interviewed five former players, one of whom said they attended these parties. One of these players admitted to having sex after the graduate assistant paid for it; and another stated, "I knew they weren't college girls. It was crazy. It was like I was in a strip club."[4] The details of this scandal possess the two elements of sexual abuse: the invitation into a sexual encounter and an uneven power dynamic. It is hard to imagine a potential recruit having the maturity and courage to dismiss himself from this affair.

The subsequent sports talk—the main subject of so many in the week following—was disconcerting as many male sports radio hosts had little problem with the sexual exploitation of women and the sexual abuse of young men and seemed only to care about what the scandal meant for the already embattled hall of fame coach Rick Pitino. This episode reveals just how little our macho, sports-saturated North American culture understands its role in perpetuating sexual abuse, and reveals how little we still understand about its nature, in spite of the publicized cases like the Penn State Sandusky case or what is portrayed in the recent film *Spotlight*.

THE AFTERMATH OF SEXUAL ABUSE

What happens to a person who has been sexually traumatized? There are a variety of categories we could use to answer this question. I want to point out two very important categories of aftermath.

The first category is survival by any and every means. In his book *The Healing Path*, Dan Allender describes four basic paths survivors take in the aftermath of sexual trauma, all of which lead away from healing. Allender names the four routes: paranoid ("Life is difficult, then you die"), fatalistic ("Roll with it, Baby"), heroic ("What doesn't kill you makes you stronger"), and optimistic ("Just grin and bear it").[5]

The thing that all four of these paths have in common is the avoidance of pain. This intentionality to avoid pain has all kinds of negative effects. One of the most significant is the way these approaches "take the person out"

---

[4] John Barr and Jeff Goodman, "Former Louisville Recruit About His Visit: 'It Was Like I Was in a Strip Club,'" ESPN, October 20, 2015, www.espn.go.com/espn/otl/story/_/id/13927159/former -louisville-cardinals-basketball-players-recruits-acknowledge-stripper-parties-minardi-hall.

[5] Dan Allender, *The Healing Path: How the Hurts in Your Past Can Lead You to a More Abundant Life* (Colorado Springs: Waterbrook Press, 1999), 8-14.

emotionally in intimate interpersonal moments. Survivors share the struggle of staying present and often are perceived as aloof and difficult to know because of their hypervigilance in protecting themselves from further pain. Allender writes,

> The paranoiac avoids pain by seeing it everywhere and with everyone. He avoids disappointment by never being surprised by sorrow. The fatalist avoids pain by accepting it as normal and part of the impersonal "luck" of life. The hero avoids it by seizing it as an opportunity to grow without ever acknowledging need or weakness. The optimist avoids pain by seeing all the good surrounding it in other areas of life.[6]

The problem is, the only route to healing lies through the treacherous passes of the grief of our wounds. Our pain is an invitation to grieve what evil has done and is doing. Naming it with an empathetic and skilled loved one is the path to restoration.

But if we boil it down, victims of sexual abuse survive. And they survive by any and every means. Most often, though, survival strategies perpetuate the sexual dysfunction initiated by the predator, even if the abuser is well out of the picture, as in my case. I am told that 98 percent of men who struggle with sexual addiction have been sexually abused. These addictions, sins to be sure, are a kind of sinister kindness or false friend for the survivor; at one and the same time they act as friend and foe. As a friend, an addiction helps you survive an otherwise unsurvivable experience. An addiction like pornography can function as a place of kindness, rest, and safety for a survivor who is terrified of intimacy. But such disoriented practices are sinister because ultimately they enslave and dehumanize over time. I have often thought of addiction as something of an Egypt, a geography in the biblical story symbolizing both rescue and slavery at one and the same time.

The second category is bodily injury. Survivors have been injured bodily; some of the injury is at times visible, but much of it lies hidden in the brain. Brain science—known by a number of names, regularly called *neuroscience* or *neuropsychology*—today is teaching us that trauma leaves bodily injury deep in the structures of the brain. Trauma changes the physiology of the brain. In trauma, neuron pathways are created that affect the way we

---

[6]Ibid., 14.

respond to stimuli. Neurons are electrical messengers in our brain that control unconscious responses. Neuroplasticity is the term used to refer to the way neurons create neural networks in our brains. These networks facilitate easy travel between the domains of our brains that generate responses and patterns of thought.[7] Our brains have been literally shaped by traumatic experiences, and these patterns exercise influence on our bodies at a level below our consciousness. Christian therapist Joy Schroeder states,

> Memories of sexual abuse can be integrally bound up with the body. Some victims have visible scars, permanent injuries, chronic pains, sexually transmitted diseases, and pregnancy. For others, the scars are not visible, but memory of the abuse remains lodged in the psyche and as body memory.[8]

In his very important book *The Body Keeps the Score*, Bessel Van der Kolk explains something that could very well revolutionize how we approach spiritual formation when it comes to bent sexuality. He notes that the advances in neurological science

> help us understand why traumatized people so often keep repeating the same problems and have such trouble learning from experience. We now know that their behaviors are not the result of moral failings or signs of lack of willpower or bad character—they are caused by actual changes in the brain.[9]

Think about that! I know of few approaches to spiritual formation within the evangelical church subculture that adequately account for our body in the process of spiritual transformation.[10] I know of few that have yet understood the physiology of sexual brokenness and have taken it sufficiently into account in Christian formation.

---

[7]Curt Thompson, *The Soul of Shame: Retelling the Stories We Believe About Ourselves* (Downers Grove, IL: InterVarsity Press, 2015), 47.

[8]Jay Schroeder, "Sexual Abuse and a Theology of Embodiment," in *The Long Journey Home: Understanding and Ministering to the Sexually Abused*, ed. Andrew J. Schmutzer (Eugene, OR: Wipf & Stock, 2011), 193.

[9]Bessel Van der Kolk, *The Body Keeps the Score: Brain, Mind, and Body in the Healing of Trauma* (New York: Viking Pengiun, 2014), 3.

[10]Notable exceptions have been Dallas Willard, *The Spirit of the Disciplines: Understanding How God Changes Lives* (New York: HarperCollins, 1988), and the recent work of Curt Thompson in his two books: *Anatomy of the Soul: Surprising Connections Between Neuroscience and Spiritual Practices That Can Transform Your Life and Relationships* (Carol Stream: SaltRiver, 2010), and *The Soul of Shame* (Downers Grove, IL: InterVarsity Press, 2015); see also Victor Copan, *Changing Your Mind: The Bible, the Brain, and Spiritual Growth* (Eugene, OR: Cascade, 2016).

Now add to this ecclesial deficiency the fact that many people don't remember or recognize their own trauma around sexuality, either because of the tendency to minimize its impact ("it wasn't that bad") or because the memories have been repressed ("I've never been abused"). Minimization and dissociation are two of most common survival strategies a survivor uses.

In sum, left to themselves, survivors of sexual trauma are sexually dysfunctional, internally bodily wounded, and unable to be fully present emotionally. They fear and avoid intimacy and are hypervigilant in relationships. Often they either lack sexual desire completely or are hypersexual. And they have hidden wounds that are no less bodily than if they had lost a hand or a foot. What's more, tragically, many are walking around in quiet shame and despair because they are sexually bent and unaware of their own story.

ZERO TOLERANCE—CONTEMPT CULTURE

From this it is clear that sexual trauma significantly problematizes any attempt to simplify sexuality and Christian spiritual formation around sexuality. And this is true not only for a greater number of people in our church then we have realized, but also a greater number of us!

I was recently visiting with a dear friend of mine who is a pastor. We share a story of childhood sexual trauma, although our experience of it was very different. He shared with me that he finds he falls into pornography about once every four to six months. The cycle is nearly always the same. Pressures and tensions from around build up, there is a sense of isolation and frustration, a deep longing for relief that doesn't cost anything and the promise of rest. So after he "falls," he confesses to his accountability partner, he tells his wife, and he welcomes the voice of contempt as deserved. The accusations of death: "You call yourself a pastor?!" "You are a terrible husband and father!" "You are a hypocrite!" "You are a disappointment to Jesus!" He provides great hospitality to these accusations as he is keenly aware that as long as they stay he has resource to avoid acting out again. The words of accusation crush him into submission. Or sometimes they don't. Sometimes they drive him back to acting out. In both cases, however, my dear friend is imprisoned by evil, unable to know the joy of a heart open to the radical goodness of God.

Not that long ago I was working in a Starbucks deeply engaged in something that now I can't even recall. I was jolted out of my intense focus by the gregarious sound of my name: "Joel Willitts!" Looking up I saw an old acquaintance with whom I haven't talked in several years. We engaged in conversation. I don't know him well, but he had been in ministry and we had known each other in that context. He had left the ministry, several years ago, but I was not clear on why. He was now in finance, and I could sense some grief related to this career path. He seemed to me dislocated. I got curious, so he started to tell the story about his departure from ministry. During the final stages of ordination, which the denomination granted him, he was asked about pornography. He admitted he struggled with the temptation and had viewed porn within the last few months. The denomination granted his ordination and told him that they would be obliged to mention it to his senior pastor. This was a Friday. On Monday, his pastor called him into his office and fired him on the spot. The church had a "zero-tolerance" policy. Any staff member who looks at porn is dismissed, no questions asked. My friend admitted that he had known this policy upon being hired.

While it may be an extreme example, the culture of contempt, shame, and categorical handling of sexual sin is widespread in our churches. It's okay to have been struggling with sexual sin, but it's not okay to be struggling. Both of my friends in varying degrees are in church cultures that are threatening and dangerous for vulnerability. Given the cost of coming out, pastors stay hidden in the dark recesses of their compartmentalized lives.

Perhaps in part because of this compartmentalizing, we continue to hear pastors, predominately male pastors, preaching about sexuality in a jocular manner. Their "biblical" depiction of sexuality assumes things about male sexual desire that little reflect my own experience and many others who struggle with sexuality. My struggle is not with a wild, uncontrollable sexual desire that I'm tempted to exercise through the use of porn or sexual domination of another, but the opposite. I want nothing at all to do with sexual desire; and I want nothing more than to avoid it altogether.

Sexual dysfunction for many survivors of sexual trauma is not "getting away with something"—equivalent to an adolescent sneaking out of the second story window to exercise disoriented desire. It is not so much a desire gone wild as it is an attempt to minimize the desire. Sexual desire always feels to be a dark desire for the follower of Jesus who has deep woundedness.

While created good and holy by God, my sexual desire only seems to me a dark, unholy thing. So a pastor can announce to me "the truth" about sexuality, but my body tells me something very different; and because of where this knowledge resides, it is not something I can simply reprogram cognitively. Simply memorizing the logic of a spiritual equation like $2 + 2 = 4$ does not "fix" me. Because when I work out the equation in my logic, I always come out with 5; there is a short circuit in my neuron pathway. This is not a software problem; it's a hardware problem. My sexual bentness is in my bones, so to speak, not merely in my mind.

So the remedies for sexual sin and wholeness that my spiritual fathers, my youth pastors and pastors, offered me have only ever given me short-lived management strategies but never real lasting freedom. When I hear the boldly asserted promise of wholeness from sexual brokenness in Jesus—I'll be honest—I fight cynicism because I know how hard I have tried. After three decades of white-knuckle fighting, I continue to fail to curb my disoriented sexuality. And I feel the cold shadow of the evil one as he whispers words of accusation, contempt and shame into my ear: "You are just not disciplined enough; you are not surrendered enough; you don't love God enough; you are not enough; you have to work harder." I just want to scream, "To hell with it!"

I believe such preachers and writers are well-meaning. But they are doing more harm than good. The preacher who essentially offers something like "memorize two verses and call me in the morning" as the means of healing or overcoming sexual sin has not begun to grasp the complexity of sexuality and the irreducible connection between our body and our spiritual person.

Do I believe healing, wholeness, and restoration are both possible and available? Yes, I do. But most often the healing comes in fits and starts; it is the result of a long, painful process; and likely, it will not be completed until Jesus' return.

Why? Because our bodies continue to be made of the stuff of the earth, stuff that is still awaiting its restoration (Rom 8:22-23). Philippians 3:20-21 captures this long view; Paul puts the restoration of our bodies as the consequence of the second coming of Jesus. He says, Christ "will transform our lowly bodies so that they will be like his glorious body."[11]

---

[11]All scriptural quotations in this chapter are from the New International Version unless otherwise noted.

We have to come to grips with the fact that we are never on the "other side" of sin as long as we are in our bodies. The three-part evangelistic testimony we were taught and have likely taught to others is too simplistic and bordering on near erroneous. You know the one: (1) my life before I met Christ, (2) how I met Christ, and (3) my life since I met Christ. The obvious assumption of this narrative is a move from bad to good. "I was once a horrible person before I met Christ, wildly sexual and promiscuous. But then I had a traumatic experience and reached bottom. There in that moment of clarity I repented of my sins and trusted in Jesus for salvation. And now . . . Wow! Since then I've been growing spiritually these four decades. I am sexually pure. I easily overcome temptation and I have a great marriage with lots of sex because God loves sex!" Cynically I want to revise this three-part testimony to say instead: (1) my life before a broken home and sexual trauma, (2) the experience of a broken home and sexual trauma, and (3) my life after a broken home and sexual trauma.

This three-part structure is more honest about the deeply shaping experiences of my life. Jesus is awesome. I love and serve him. But what has most marked my life in deep, embodied ways is the trauma associated with a broken home and sexual abuse. We must develop an empathy for the utter difficulty it is simply to be human in the kind of world we inhabit. We need to recapture Jesus' invitation to openhearted living, living in the in-between of his first and second comings.

And the path to healing—if there really is one—is kindness, not contempt. For according to Paul, it's "God's kindness" that "is intended to lead you to repentance" (Rom 2:4).

"KINDNESS LEADS YOU TO REPENTANCE"—KINDNESS CULTURE

I received an email in response to a podcast I did with Preston Sprinkle on his show "Theology in the Raw." During the show I shared my own story of childhood sexual trauma.[12] The person (let's call her Brenda) shared with me an awful story of childhood abuse. The abuse began at six years of age and ended when she was twelve, after she became pregnant. She stated with aloof historical detail, "Three months after I turned thirteen I had the child

---

[12]You can find the podcast at "In Chicago with Dr. Joel Willitts," The Voice, May 11, 2016, www.941thevoice.com/in-chicago-with-dr-joel-willitts.

and gave him up for adoption." The even more tragic aspect of this story is in her following statement: "I went back to school with no counseling or professional help." She has struggled with addiction her whole life in the aftermath of these events and she is a Christ-follower. Her addiction, as for nearly all survivors, has been a sinister kindness, which has alternated between being both friend and foe. She labeled herself a recovering alcoholic and serial sex addict. Although these addictions have been in check for the last number of years, she wrote me for advice about her intense struggle with pornography.

She told me that she has been going to a therapist but was reluctant to bring it up. She named the overwhelming shame associated with it when the topic was brought up. Her candidness is familiar to all of us who have such tendencies. "I find it difficult to discuss it while trying to look someone in the eye." With that she added, "It is hard for me to see it as anything other than a shameful hypocrisy." Those are all too familiar words.

I want to close this chapter with my response to Brenda's email. It may represent a more radical position than you are comfortable with, but I offer it as an alternative path to the contempt culture of a majority of evangelical churches.

Please call me Joel. As I read the brief description of your experience, the word *pregnant* just crushed me. I'm imagining what a thirteen-year-old girl must have had to endure to give birth. Then to have to go back to school with no support is even more egregious. I'm so very, very sorry for the evil you've had to endure.

Words are impossible to find that could come close to reaching the extent of your wound. No words.

I am so encouraged to know that you've been going through therapy and finding levels of healing. Thanks for your questions. I'll seek to answer them as vulnerably as I can.

I heard Dan Allender say that one stops an addiction when one no longer needs an addiction. The reason you have a couple of addictions hanging on is because there is still more work to do in therapy. The addictions are signposts, I think, pockmarks left by an exploding shell. It's the crater left by a meteor. Its shape reveals something. What it can reveal is paradoxical. The addiction at the same time reveals both the power of the trauma and our beauty, dignity, and God-given longings and desires.

Let me ask you, have you conducted a dissection of your addictions? Let's take porn. Have you in the course of your therapy studied what about porn is so inviting to you? What does the experience of porn do? What is its story? What's porn's beginning, middle, and end for you? Each of us experiences porn differently. Each of us is attracted to it for different reasons. And we're attracted to different types of porn. What are you attracted by? What I'm suggesting is that you conduct a high-school-style science investigation of the details of your addiction in the context of therapy.

This kind of work blesses the addiction. It sees it for what it has been, a friend—what I call a sinister kindness. Given the hell you've been through, an addiction to porn has likely been something of a salvation for you—am I right? It's a way to show your troubled soul kindness in the safety of your own control. As you walk through the topography of your addiction, you'll see the contours of loss and neglect. You'll discover the sadness of your heart anew and have an invitation to grieve some more. It is the grieving that heals, I think. The grief brings with it grace and God's presence.

The fact is you're not yet ready to give it up. And you need to be kind to this fact about you. If you were to die tonight and go to heaven, Jesus is not going to condemn you because you watched porn. I believe he's going to wrap his arms around you and say, "I'm so sorry for what evil has done to you. You're home now. Rest, my dear, beautiful girl. I've been paying attention to you all these years and my heart is so broken over you. I'm so sorry." He's not going to show you contempt, that much I know for sure! Rest in God's extravagant kindness.

Let me tell you this, Brenda: if you ever do come to a point that you can give up porn, it will not be because of contempt or fear or guilt or shame or self-discipline. If you ever give up porn it will be because you have come to know God's kindness at the deepest level of your heart. Start being kind to yourself now because that is exactly how God will treat you through eternity. No sense waiting until then :)!

Now about me. No, I'm not yet on the other side of my porn addiction. The three decades of Bible memory, multiple accountability partners, and the intrinsic effect of ministry to limit immorality have not "fixed" me. My desires are too strong for those things to ultimately work. What's more, there is simply something more familiar and authentic in my bent sexuality than in godly sexuality. I despise that this is true. I'm offended by moralists who think people who watch porn are "getting away with something," who think that people who struggle with porn are having a good time doing it. As if struggling with a porn addiction is like dancing—if it weren't forbidden, everyone would do it (think *Footloose!*)! It's super fun! This may be true for a very few, but in my experience, it is far from the truth for most of us. This kind of thinking just increases shame and ensures deeper hiding. Yes, it's sin. Fine. We can agree on that. Yes, we need to stop it. No debate.

But we are sinners in need of grace and kindness. That's the gospel! I'm still trying to embrace the kindness of God toward me. This isn't something you just "learn." And until I do, I will struggle with this addiction.

Having heard this, you may not hire me to be your teaching pastor. That's fine. But I pray that it invites you to open your heart, to vulnerably enter your own story of trauma.

To tell the truth. To grieve. To come to vastly deeper awareness of the Father's kindness and care. To live under the banner of Jesus' eternal word to the exploited and willful sinner, "Neither do I condemn you. . . . Go now and leave your life of sin" (Jn 8:11).[13]

---

[13]For a detailed exposition of this story in light of sexual trauma, see my forthcoming chapter "Sexually Bent," in *Mere Sexuality: Rediscovering the Christian Vision of Sexuality*, ed. Todd Wilson (Grand Rapids: Zondervan, 2017).

10

The Wounded It Heals

Gender Dysphoria and the
Resurrection of the Body

MATTHEW MASON

THE HUMAN BODY IS centrally important to the Christian faith—from the goodness of creation, through Christ's incarnation, sufferings in our flesh, and bodily resurrection, to the resurrection of the dead. But what of those who experience a profound sense of alienation from their bodies, particularly those whose experience of their gender is one of being alienated from the biological sex of their bodies?

The experience of gender dysphoria and gender reassignment is deeply personal and often acutely distressing. Complex pastoral issues are involved, and we should beware responding in a detached and clinical way.[1] This paper is *not* my recommended pastoral response to a person who is experiencing gender dysphoria; for that, much patient listening and personal involvement is required. Rather, I am taking a step back from the pastoral frontline—although still wearing my pastoral spectacles—to consider the issue of gender identity and particularly what, if anything, the gospel has to say about it.

What follows aims to elucidate a Christian "moral ontology" as it relates to questions of transgender identity and gender dysphoria. Charles Taylor

---

[1]See Mark A. Yarhouse, *Understanding Gender Dysphoria: Navigating Transgender Issues in a Changing Culture* (Downers Grove, IL: IVP Academic, 2015).

describes a moral ontology as "the 'background picture' lying behind our moral and spiritual intuitions."[2] Building on Taylor, John Webster describes it as "an account of moral space . . . an account of what the good *is*, rather than what is *chosen* or *desired* to be."[3] As ethical agents, we live "'inside' moral space . . . circumscribed by a morally textured reality that is inexhaustibly independent of our private and public dispositions, that simply *is*."[4] More crudely, as I say to my congregation, there is such a thing as reality, and it's really real. This moral space is shaped by God in creation and redemption. So the question I am addressing is not how we would like to act, nor even primarily how we *should* act, but rather what is the moral space, given to us by God, within which we are called to act. This then has implications for how we ought to act. I shall argue that how we think about gender dysphoria is directly related to how we think about the resurrection.

RESURRECTION AND MORAL ORDER

In his seminal *Resurrection and Moral Order*, Oliver O'Donovan argues that "Christian ethics depends on the resurrection of Jesus Christ from the dead."[5] This is because "the foundations of Christian ethics must be evangelical foundations; or, to put it more simply, Christian ethics must arise from the gospel of Jesus Christ. Otherwise it could not be *Christian* ethics."[6]

In putting resurrection at the heart of his ethical project, O'Donovan offers a genuinely evangelical moral theology (e.g., Rom 1:1-5; 1 Cor 15:3-5; 2 Tim 2:8). He also avoids the trap of pitting gospel against creation and integrates both creation and the kingdom of God into his ethics. O'Donovan explains how the resurrection grounds a comprehensive Christian moral theology:

> In proclaiming the resurrection of Christ, the apostles proclaimed also the resurrection of mankind in Christ; and in proclaiming the resurrection of mankind, they proclaimed the renewal of all creation with him.

---

[2]Charles Taylor, *Sources of the Self: The Making of Modern Identity* (Cambridge: Cambridge University Press, 1989), 5-9.
[3]John Webster, *Barth's Ethics of Reconciliation* (Cambridge: Cambridge University Press, 1995), 216.
[4]Ibid.
[5]Oliver O'Donovan, *Resurrection and Moral Order: An Outline for Evangelical Ethics*, 2nd ed. (Leicester, UK: Inter-Varsity Press, 1994), 13.
[6]Ibid., 11.

The resurrection of Christ in isolation from mankind would not be a gospel message. The resurrection of mankind apart from creation would be a gospel of a sort, but of a purely gnostic and world-denying sort which is far from the gospel that the apostles actually preached. So the resurrection of Christ directs our attention back to the creation which it vindicates.[7]

Most evangelicals would agree on the gospel's centrality for ethics. But this raises the question of how one understands and articulates the gospel. As one pastor put it recently, "As evangelicals, we must be theologians of redemption, *not* theologians of creation." His claim was based on a right concern for the gospel's centrality but also on an understanding that the gospel is exclusively concerned with individual soteriology. However, the creation/redemption dichotomy is a false one. Redemption is the redemption not just of Christians (who are, in any case, creatures), but of Christians and with them the entire cosmos (Rom 8:18-25). This then pushes us to consider the creation that Christ died and rose to liberate and renew.

Penal substitutionary atonement and justification by faith alone are wonderful and vitally important truths. However, if we believe that individual soteriology exhausts the content of the gospel, we will find little that is genuinely evangelical to say to the ethical questions around transgender identity. What we do say will risk sounding arbitrary and moralistic, lacking any basis in how things really are. In contrast, O'Donovan's focus on the resurrection of Christ, humanity's consequent resurrection, and creation's renewal enables him (without denying the atonement and personal soteriology) to articulate a more biblical, robust, and comprehensive gospel. It also provides a properly evangelical foundation for a rich and coherent account of the body and why what we do with it matters.

The resurrection points us *back*, to the created order, and *forward*,

> to the end of history when that particular and representative fate [i.e., the resurrection of Jesus] is universalized in the resurrection of mankind from the dead. "Each in his own order: Christ the first fruits, then at his coming those who belong to Christ" ([1 Cor] 15:23).[8]

---

[7]Ibid., 31.
[8]Ibid., 14.

In so framing ethics, O'Donovan sits within a venerable theological tradition of relating creation, redemption, and consummation—or, nature and
grace. So, for example, Aquinas's famous dictum states, "Grace does not
destroy nature but perfects it."[9] More fully, for Herman Bavinck, "The essence of the Christian religion consists in the reality that the creation of the
Father, ruined by sin, is restored in the death of the Son of God and re-
created by the grace of the Holy Spirit into a kingdom of God."[10]

John Bolt argues that "the fundamental theme that shapes Bavinck's
entire theology is the trinitarian idea that grace restores nature."[11] Matthew
Roberts alters Bolt's summary of Bavinck and brings it more closely in line
with O'Donovan, noting that grace *restoring* nature might imply that grace
simply restores nature to its prelapsarian state. He argues that it is better to
speak of grace redeeming, restoring, and renewing creation, bringing it to
the eschatological glory God always intended.[12]

In a passage of great beauty, from which the title of this paper is taken,
Bavinck summarizes the scope of God's work in the gospel: "Christianity
does not introduce a single substantial foreign element into the creation. It
creates no new cosmos but rather makes the cosmos new. It restores what
was corrupted by sin. It atones the guilty and cures what is sick; the wounded
it heals."[13] As O'Donovan maintains, "New creation is creation renewed, a
restoration and enhancement, not an abolition."[14] This insight is fundamentally important in considering the nature of our bodies and its relationship
to transgender experiences.

In directing our attention to creation in both its protological and eschatological aspects, the resurrection directs us to a moral order because "we
must understand 'creation' not merely as the raw material out of which the
world as we know it is composed, but as the order and coherence *in* which

---

[9]Thomas Aquinas, *Summa Theologiae*, Latin-English ed., trans. Dominican Fathers of the English
Province (Scotts Valley, CA: NovAntiqua, 2008), I q. 1, a. 8, ad. 2.

[10]Herman Bavinck, *Reformed Dogmatics I: Prolegomena*, ed. John Bolt, trans. John Vriend (Grand
Rapids: Baker Academic, 2003), 112.

[11]John Bolt, "Editor's Introduction," in Bavinck, *Reformed Dogmatics I*, 18.

[12]Matthew P. W. Roberts, "Thinking Like a Christian: The Prolegomena of Herman Bavinck,"
Ecclesia Reformanda 1/1 (2009): 81.

[13]Herman Bavinck, "Common Grace," trans. Raymond C. van Leeuwen, *Calvin Theological Journal*
24 (1989): 61.

[14]Oliver O'Donovan, *A Conversation Waiting to Begin: The Churches and the Gay Controversy* (London: SCM, 2009), 99.

it is composed."[15] Creation is meaningful, not random; it has a coherent structure, which reveals what is good.

In relation to questions about gender, the good, God-given structure of creation is as follows: God has created us in his image as male *and* female.[16] This reality is clearly inscribed on our bodies, which (with rare exceptions) are unambiguously either male *or* female.[17] This bodily reality is not simply biological; it is personal, because our bodies are personal. We are not androgynous persons who happen to have, as a matter of indifference, either a male or female body. We are either male or female persons. Our gender (masculine or feminine), although shaped by culture and tradition, is inscribed in our bodies and blossoms forth from the root of our biological sex. Our bodies, therefore, give us our gender identity, which is inextricably linked to our bodily form as male or female. Transgender questions highlight this, because the desire to reassign one's gender by means of surgery assumes that one's body clearly marks one personally as male or female.

This assumption—that creation is ordered and meaningful, providing an objective moral ontology—differs markedly from modern assumptions about morality. These pay little or no attention to the created order and focus instead on the individual willing subject, who is free to order her own life and moral world as she prefers.[18] In modernity, freedom is "radicalized . . . turned into the very root of human authenticity and dignity." Free moral action becomes self-construction. Law, "the norms by which we govern action," is disconnected from nature and "radically internalized."[19] The only external limit is "Thou shalt do no harm."[20] Someone experiencing gender

---

[15]O'Donovan, *Resurrection and Moral Order*, 31.

[16]I unpack this at length in "The Authority of the Body: Discovering Natural Manhood and Womanhood," *Bulletin of Ecclesial Theology* 4.1 (forthcoming, 2017).

[17]I cannot pursue questions of intersex conditions here. I think they are best understood as Disorders of Sexual Development (DSDs), consequences of the fall, a natural evil, akin to something like congenital blindness. The natural, creational form of humanity is male and female.

[18]"Western moral thought since the Enlightenment has been predominantly 'voluntarist' in its assumptions. . . . It has understood morality as the creation of man's will, by which he imposes order on his life, both individually and socially." O'Donovan, *Resurrection and Moral Order*, 16; cf. John Webster, "Evangelical Freedom," in *Confessing God: Essays in Christian Dogmatics II* (2005; repr., London: Bloomsbury, 2016), 215-18.

[19]Webster, "Evangelical Freedom," 215-16.

[20]For a rich analysis from a liberal-progressive perspective of why the "do no harm" principle is insufficient, see Jonathan Haidt, *The Righteous Mind: Why Good People Are Divided by Politics and Religion* (London: Penguin, 2012).

dysphoria should therefore be free to realize his or her "true" gender identity through gender reassignment.

What does the gospel say to this? We now turn to 1 Corinthians 15 to consider creation's renewal and perfection through Christ, whose bodily resurrection is the firstfruits of our resurrection.

RESURRECTION: CONTINUITY AND TRANSFORMATION

In 1 Corinthians 15, Paul argues from the resurrection of Christ to the future resurrection of all believers in Christ against some in Corinth who were denying the resurrection of the dead (v. 12). Christ has been raised as the firstfruits of those who have died (vv. 20, 23), thus guaranteeing the resurrection of believers. Paul sets up a contrasting parallel between Christ and Adam (vv. 21-22, 44-49), which establishes two things. First, there is an organic connection between the resurrection of Christ and the resurrection of all in Christ. He was not raised in isolation. He is the eschatological Adam, the representative head of a new humanity, raised as the firstfruits of a great harvest. Second, there is an organic connection between protology and eschatology, between Adam's body in creation (and the bodies of those who bear his image), and Christ's body in the resurrection (and the bodies of those who bear his image).

From 1 Corinthians 15:35 onwards, Paul answers the objection, "How are the dead raised? With what kind of body do they come?"[21] His answer is rooted in the Genesis creation account. He argues for both continuity and transformation, on analogy with sowing a seed (v. 37). This enables him "to walk a fine line, asserting both the radical *transformation* of the body in its resurrected state and yet its organic *continuity* with the mortal body that preceded it."[22] Paul observes the many types of flesh and bodily glory within creation (vv. 39-41). It is important to note, although it is little noted, that he is working with the categories of Genesis 1. First Corinthians 15:39 lists the main categories of creatures from days five and six of creation (Gen 1:20-28): humans, animals, birds, and fish, which are also the main categories of creatures over which humans have dominion (Gen 1:26, 28). Then he contrasts

---

[21] All scriptural quotations in this chapter are from the English Standard Version unless otherwise noted.

[22] Richard B. Hays, *First Corinthians*, Interpretation (Louisville, KY: Knox, 1997), 270.

heavenly bodies and earthly bodies (1 Cor 15:40-41), and the heavenly bodies—sun, moon, and stars—are those listed on the fourth day (Gen 1:14-19). Thus, Paul's argument for the resurrection is rooted firmly within God's ordered creation, implying that we best understand the resurrection by reflecting on the original creation, for in the resurrection creation comes to fruition and completion.

Importantly for our argument, as Paul uses the analogy of the body as a seed to be sown he states, "But *God* gives it a body *as he has chosen,* and to each kind of seed its own body" (1 Cor 15:38 emphasis mine). Note first God's authority over the kind of body with which the dead are raised. It is he, not we, who gives the form of the body, and he does it in accordance with his choice, not ours. (The application to transgender questions should be obvious.) Note also the contrasting tenses of *didōsin* (present tense, "he gives"), and the aorist tense of *ēthelēsen* ("as he purposed"). Anthony Thiselton, quoting G. G. Findlay, explains, "The aorist in this context denotes 'not "as he wills" (according to his choice or liking) but *in accordance with his past decree in creation,* by which the propagation of life on earth was determined from the beginning.'"[23] Thus, Paul's initial answer to the question, "With what kind of body will the dead be raised?" is "With the God-given bodily form that corresponds to his initial purpose in creation."

This matches what we know of Jesus' resurrection appearances. He was raised bodily, able to be seen and touched, to eat fish with his disciples (Jn 20:27; Lk 24:31, 37-43). The tomb was empty; he rose with the same body in which he was crucified. Therefore, he was raised in his male body, which the Father had prepared for him in the incarnation (cf. Heb 10:5). Although the disciples were at first kept from seeing who he really was (e.g., Lk 24:16; Jn 20:14-15), when their eyes were opened, they saw him as immediately recognizable from his bodily form, which included the wounds he received in his death (Jn 20:20, 27). Thus Jesus, the firstfruits of our resurrection, was raised with the same body and therefore the same sex and gender as was given to him in God's creational purposes. To be sure, John later sees the risen Christ radically transformed and glorified (Rev 1:12-16). But even here he sees him

---

[23]G. G. Findlay, *Expositor's Greek Testament* 2:934 (London: Hodder and Stoughton, 1901), quoted in Anthony C. Thiselton, *1 Corinthians* (Grand Rapids: Eerdmans, 2006), 1264. Italics mine.

as "one like a son of man" (Rev 1:13), recognizably continuous with the Son of Man in his earthly ministry.[24]

Nevertheless, as we observed with the seed analogy, not only is there bodily continuity in view in 1 Corinthians 15, there is also transformation, the transformation from a "natural body" (*sōma psychikos*) to a "spiritual body" (*sōma pneumatikos*). First Corinthians 15:42-44 is notoriously easy to misunderstand, and the NRSV does not help matters by translating *sōma psychikos* as "physical body," which might be taken to imply a difference in substance between something material and something immaterial.[25] However, Paul has already contrasted *psychikos* and *pneumatikos* in 1 Corinthians 2:14-15. There the contrast is clearly not between material and immaterial. Rather, as the NRSV recognizes, Paul there contrasts the "unspiritual" or "natural" (*psychikos*) person, who does not accept the things taught by the Holy Spirit, and the "spiritual" (*pneumatikos*) person to whom the Holy Spirit has revealed God's wisdom. So in 1 Corinthians, the *psychikos/pneumatikos* contrast is between two modes of existence: one without the Spirit and one under the Spirit's guidance.

In speaking of a *sōma psychikos* (1 Cor 15:44), Paul seems to be alluding to Genesis 2:7, which he quotes in 1 Corinthians 15:45. When God breathed into Adam's nostrils the breath of life, Adam became "a living being" (LXX *psychēn zōsan*). But the last Adam, in his resurrection, has become "a life-giving Spirit"[26] (v. 45). This does not imply "ontological fusion" between Christ and the Spirit, but rather that Christ is so identified with the Spirit that the Spirit becomes *his* Spirit (see Rom 8:9-11): "to have the Spirit is to have Christ; to have Christ is to have the Spirit."[27] Hence the risen Christ breathed the Spirit into his disciples just as God breathed the breath of life into Adam (Jn 20:22). The distinction between the "natural body" and the "spiritual body" is therefore one not of substance, but of "mode of existence."[28] This fits well with

---

[24]Note also that in the preview of his resurrected glory granted to Peter, James, and John in the transfiguration, it was recognizably the man, Rabbi Jesus, who was transfigured (Mk 9:2-9, par.).

[25]Thiselton, *1 Corinthians*, 1275.

[26]"Spirit" should be capitalized here as a reference to the Holy Spirit; cf. Sinclair B. Ferguson, *The Holy Spirit* (Leicester, UK: Inter-Varsity Press, 1996), 54; Herman Ridderbos, *Paul: An Outline of His Theology*, trans. John Richard De Witt (Grand Rapids: Eerdmans, 1975), 88.

[27]Ferguson, *Holy Spirit*, 54; see also Ridderbos, *Paul*, 87-88.

[28]Thiselton, *1 Corinthians*, 1276; cf. Gordon D. Fee, *The First Epistle to the Corinthians*, New International Commentary on the New Testament (Grand Rapids: Eerdmans, 1987), 786.

the contrasts of 1 Corinthians 15:42-43, where *en* is modal and implies not a different body, but a different mode of existence for the same body.[29] Thus the Jerusalem Bible captures well the meaning of verse 44: "When it is sown it embodies the soul, when it is raised it embodies the [S]pirit."[30]

The resurrection, therefore, heralds a glorious transformation as our weak, dishonorable, dying bodies are so infused and governed by the Holy Spirit that they will be transformed into living, glorious, powerful bodies. But they will nevertheless be the bodies our Creator gave us in creation. 1 Corinthians 15:53-54 confirms this. Thiselton notes "the fourfold use of *touto*, this" in these two verses. It is *this* body that will be transformed. How? *This body* will put on (*endysasthai*) immortality "like a new set of clothes."[31] In general, Thiselton makes a little too much of the discontinuity between the two embodied states, and Calvin is better. Against "those fanatics who invent the notion that men are to be given new bodies . . . this verse plainly confirms that we shall rise in the very same flesh that we have now, for the apostle has assigned it a new quality, as if it were a garment."[32] *This* body, given to me by my Creator according to his original purpose, including its biological sex and the personal gender identity that entails, is the body that will rise on the last day—transformed, powerful, immortal, and glorious beyond my imagining.

Where Thiselton is very helpful is in suggesting a musical analogy. He describes "the postresurrection mode of life as *a purposive and dynamic crescendo of life.*"[33] In the light of creation and resurrection, how should we think of our ourselves and our bodies with their sex and gender? Imagine a symphony, with the theme announced at the beginning in frail pianissimo on the woodwind. As the symphony develops, the theme grows, is challenged, and disappears. But then, at the climax of the final movement, with a magnificent crescendo, the same theme triumphantly returns fortissimo, scored for full orchestra, with brass and percussion to the fore. The same theme, but gloriously transformed.

---

[29]Thiselton, *1 Corinthians*, 1276.

[30]JB, corrected to refer to the (Holy) Spirit rather than the (human) spirit. Hays claims that this is "by far the most graceful translation." Hays, *First Corinthians*, 272.

[31]Thiselton, *1 Corinthians*, 1297. Emphasis original.

[32]John Calvin, *1 Corinthians*, trans. John W. Fraser (Grand Rapids: Eerdmans, 1960), 344.

[33]Thiselton, *1 Corinthians*, 1279. Emphasis original.

Augustine confirms this line of argument with an observation from Jesus' discussion with the Sadducees about marriage and the resurrection (Lk 20:27-40). Augustine counters earlier patristic claims that women would be raised as men, noting that Jesus could have answered the Sadducees by saying, "Do you not realize that she will be raised as a man?" Instead, he said, "'They shall not be given in marriage,' which applies to females, and 'Neither shall they marry,' which applies to males." In the resurrection, vice is removed, but nature is preserved. "And the sex of a woman is not a vice, but nature." Thus, "He . . . who instituted two sexes will restore them both."[34] Notice Augustine's logic: God will restore and perfect his original creation pattern.

RESURRECTION CAUTION AND COMFORT

We have seen that, in relation to our bodies and their sex and gender, creation has a God-given moral order, which is reaffirmed, renewed, and perfected through the resurrection. This speaks to questions of gender dysphoria and especially to ethical questions surrounding gender reassignment. And it speaks a hard word. This must be spoken with sensitivity, gentleness, and patience, but also with clarity. We are not autonomous moral agents possessing absolute authority over our bodies and their sexual form; we live in moral space that is shaped by God's purposes in creation and its renewal in the resurrection. Through the resurrection, the gospel speaks clearly about the appropriate form of our bodies. We do not decide for ourselves whether we are male or female; God has already decided for us. The resurrection shows that he is committed, eternally committed, to that decision. My body's biological sex at birth is also the biological sex of the body in which I shall be raised. It therefore defines my gender now. Put starkly, the resurrection of the body shows that gender reassignment is a rebellion against the moral order God has written on our bodies in creation in their sexual form as male or female. It also indicates that whatever hormone therapy someone has undergone, and whatever reconstructive surgery has taken place, his or her true sex and gender has not changed; there is an underlying, consistent, God-given, God-affirmed ontological reality. Again, to put it starkly, if someone was born male, he remains male,

---

[34]Augustine, *The City of God*, trans. R. Dyson (Cambridge: Cambridge University Press, 1998), 22.17.

whatever the outward form of his hormonally and surgically altered body may indicate.

However, if this speaks a hard word for some, there will be occasions when it speaks comfort and hope to others. Some who undergo gender reassignment later regret their decision and desire to transition back again.[35] This can be prohibitively expensive, and given the extent of the hormone therapy and surgery they underwent, a full return to the appearance and function of their birth sex may be impossible. But only in this life. Augustine comments on 1 Corinthians 15, "People are amazed that God, who made all things from nothing, makes a heavenly body from human flesh. . . . Is he who was able to make you when you did not exist not able to make over what you once were?"[36] Human physicians cannot make over perfectly what they have unmade imperfectly, and whatever they attempt, even if somewhat successful, will come at the cost of great physical and emotional pain. But the Great Physician will one day remake us perfectly, without pain, in a moment, in the twinkling of an eye (1 Cor 15:51-52). This may also provide incalculable comfort and hope to the parents of a child who has undergone, or is planning to undergo, gender reassignment.

RESURRECTION HEALING

We have one more step to take. For most of us, news of the renewal and transformation of this weak and dying body in the resurrection is obviously good news. But what of those who might recoil in horror when confronted with the reality that the body they were born with is God's eternal design for them? Can *this* gospel be good news for someone who is so alienated from his body and its sex that he identifies as a person of the opposite gender? Yes, it can, because the gospel does not leave us simply confronted by an objective reality.

Having established the integrity of the created order, O'Donovan goes on to consider us as moral agents. Here too the resurrection is good news,

---

[35]See Walt Heyer, "I Was a Transgender Woman," *The Public Discourse*, April 1, 2015, www.thepub licdiscourse.com/2015/04/14688/; Walt Heyer, "'Sex Change' Surgery: What Bruce Jenner, Dianne Sawyer, and You Should Know," *The Public Discourse*, April 27, 2015, www.thepublicdis course.com/2015/04/14905/.

[36]Augustine, "Sermons for the Feast of Assumption" 264:6, quoted in Gerald Bray, ed., *1-2 Corinthians*, Ancient Christian Commentary on Scripture (Downers Grove, IL: InterVarsity Press, 2006), 178. Obviously he did not have gender reassignment in mind, but surely his words apply here also.

because it means our renewal and reintegration as moral agents.[37] Christ is risen as life-giving Spirit. And he shares his Spirit with his people not just to renew and transform our mortal bodies but to transform and renew us entirely, to the very depths of our beings and even in the darkest and most troubled corners of our lives. The Lord who is the Spirit is even now renewing us day by day, transforming us from glory to glory into his image (2 Cor 3:17-18). We have this treasure in jars of clay, but in our weakness, afflictions, and perplexity, God's power is working so that we are not crushed or forsaken or driven to despair; even in death-like experiences of distress, the life of Jesus is made known in our mortal bodies (2 Cor 4:7-11). Our renewal will not be completed in this life, which will continue to confront us with unsearchable depths of brokenness and pain. But viewed from the perspective of the resurrection, these seventy, eighty, or ninety-year burdens are light, momentary afflictions that are preparing an eternal weight of glory beyond compare (2 Cor 4:16-18).

In the resurrection, our renewal and reintegration will be complete; brokenness and alienation will be healed, entirely, forever. Given what we have seen about the resurrection and our bodies, perhaps we can speculate that when the Lord Jesus calls us from our graves for judgment (Jn 5:25-29), for those who experience gender dysphoria but reject him in this life, one of the horrors of hell will be an eternity trapped in a body and a sexual identity they reject, because they reject the loving intentions of the Creator who gave it to them. But for those who experience gender dysphoria but cling to Christ for mercy and hope, surely one of the glories of the new creation will be to receive back the body they were originally given, transformed and glorified, to inhabit that body as their Creator and Redeemer's loving gift, and finally to be at rest.

All of us are wounded by Adam's fall. All of us experience ourselves, our gender, and our sexuality, in ways that are fractured by sin, guilt, and shame. This plays out in many ways. The experience of gender dysphoria is but one, albeit peculiarly agonizing, way that this primal tear in the fabric of our humanity plays out in human experience. Amid this bewildering confusion, the resurrection of Jesus Christ provides solid ground on which to stand. It

---

[37]O'Donovan, *Resurrection and Moral Order*, 101-2.

reaffirms God's purposes in creating us as personal embodied creatures, male and female, and so it shows that God's purposes in giving me the body that I have—including its particular sex—were and remain good purposes. It promises that God will bring these good purposes to their glorious completion, when this fragile, tired, and dying body will clothe itself in glory and immortality, and I shall be perfectly renewed in the likeness of the Man of Heaven. It therefore teaches us that our bodies, including their form as male and female, provide a moral and sexual true north to orient the compass of our gender identity now, as we await the Savior from heaven who will one day come and transform our lowly bodies to be like his glorious body (Phil 3:21). For some, that orientation and that waiting will be far more painful than for others. But still, in the light of the gospel, all of us can wait in hope. For Christ is risen, and he will make all things new. "[He] restores what was corrupted by sin. [He] atones the guilty and cures what is sick; the wounded [he] heals."[38]

---

[38]Bavinck, "Common Grace," 61.

Part Three

BIBLICAL and HISTORICAL REFLECTIONS on GENDER and SEXUALITY

11

Imaging Glory

1 Corinthians 11, Gender, and Bodies
at Worship

AMY PEELER

F EW NEW TESTAMENT TEXTS offer a more sustained reflection on the
beauty, order, and mystery of God's gift of sexuality than the eleventh
chapter of Paul's first letter to the Corinthians. It is also the case that few New
Testament texts are more contested. As a pristine example of that great
paradox of the New Testament, Paul's thoroughgoing culturally defined instructions—telling men and women the appropriate way to fix their hair
nonetheless—become the vehicle for God's word through the ages, offering
instructions for conduct in worship and insights into a Christian perspective
on gender. As a testimony to the fact that Christians serve the God of creation who became incarnate, Paul affirms that bodies matter even and especially in a context in which the Spirit is active through prayer and prophecy.
In fact, bodies matter so much because they become the vehicles for dis-
playing the glory of God.

The voluminous literature on this section of 1 Corinthians provides fertile
ground for debate. One can take a position on the contested meaning of
almost every phrase, from the historical (Does Paul want the women to put
their hair up or keep it covered?) to the supernatural (In what way are angels
involved here?) to the theological (What is the meaning of *kephalē* and what
does it say about Christology, anthropology, theology, and gender?). I,

however, will not be approaching this text as an arena for debate. Instead, admonished by Paul's closing word against contentiousness and encouraged by the CPT to highlight what unites faithful pastor theologians rather than what divides them, I will explicate those points of widespread agreement. Maybe unsurprisingly for such a passage as this, it seems to me that there are only two, and two rather simple ones at that. First, Paul assumes that both men and women pray and prophesy in worship, and second, as they do so, Paul wants women to have long hair and men to have short. As distant as these particular instructions for a congregation in first-century Corinth might seem, these beacons of clarity amid a great haze of confusion—both in historical exegesis and in contemporary culture—offer some profoundly meaningful and practical principles for liturgy and theology. When we gather for worship in which everyone participates, our bodies should image the glory of the God we are worshipping, the creative God of life.

POINT ONE OF CLARITY: MEN AND WOMEN
PRAYING AND PROPHESYING

The first clear point upon which a spectrum of interpreters agree is this: Paul assumes that both men and women are praying and prophesying in the gatherings of the Corinthians.[1] Interpreters recognize that 1 Corinthians 11 signals a shift to issues of Christian worship; here Paul discusses behavior and dress amid these gatherings, then the Lord's Supper, and finally the communal exercise of spiritual gifts when instruction, conviction, and conversion can happen.[2] In other words, "instructions for the actions performed when

---

[1] Unsurprisingly, interpreters who favor the full ministerial participation of women call attention to this reality. See Richard B. Hays, *First Corinthians*, Interpretation (Louisville, KY: John Knox, 1997), 182-83; Anthony C. Thiselton, *The First Epistle to the Corinthians*, New International Greek Testament Commentary (Grand Rapids: Eerdmans, 2000), 828. Gordon D. Fee explicitly denies any possibility for the subordination of women from this passage. Fee, *The First Epistle to the Corinthians*, rev. ed., New International Commentary on the New Testament (Grand Rapids: Eerdmans, 2014), 565, 579-80. Yet this recognition appears also in the theologians who do not believe women can participate equally in worship leadership. Adam Hensley, who argues that women cannot offer all kinds of prophecy, acknowledges that women do participate in some kinds of public prophecy. Hensley, "Σιγαω, λαλεω, and ὑποτασσω in 1 Corinthians 14:34 in Their Literary and Rhetorical Context," *JETS* 55 (2012): 355. Even Wayne A. Grudem, who argues for the inappropriateness of women teaching, does state, "That is why women can prophesy." Grudem, *Evangelical Feminism and Biblical Truth* (Sisters, OR: Multnomah, 2004), 231.

[2] Richard Hays titles this section, which includes 11:2–14:40, "Community Worship" and states, "Paul has grouped these issues together because all of them pertain to the actions of the community gath-

they are gathered together as a believing community"—that is what Paul offers in these chapters. In so doing he affirms, instructs, and critiques their ecclesial behavior.

In this particular section the focus is on prayer and prophecy. In 1 Corinthians 11:4 he begins, "every man . . . while praying or prophesying," followed by verse 5, which demonstrates the parallel for women, "every woman . . . while praying or prophesying."[3] Later, in 1 Corinthians 11:13, he mentions again that women are engaged in the act of prayer. Based on this unambiguous statement, no one who seeks to align themselves with the revealed Word of the Scriptures could prohibit either men or women from praying or prophesying in public worship.

This is quite a bold statement. Immediately following such a statement must be the recognition that a difficulty and hence disagreement arises with the meanings and the entailments of first-century Christian prophecy. What does Paul mean and what do the Corinthians understand by "prophesying" (*prophēteuō*)? Again it seems wise to begin with that which is clear from the text. First, when Paul speaks about prophesying, it is a speech act heard by others. "The one who prophesies speaks to people" (*anthrōpois*, 1 Cor 14:3 ESV). Just a few verses later, Paul contrasts speaking in tongues with speaking in a prophecy (1 Cor 14:6).

Second, it is also clear that this is a gift Paul desires everyone to pursue and practice. At the beginning of 1 Corinthians 14, he admonishes all of them to pursue love (clearly his great desire as made manifest in 1 Cor 13) and all of them to seek the spiritual gifts, "especially that you may prophesy" (1 Cor 14:1). Again in 1 Corinthians 14:5, "I want you all to speak in tongues, but even more to prophesy" (ESV).[4]

The difficulty lies in discerning the nature of prophesying. To limit myself to the Corinthian context, Paul states here that it involves upbuilding, encouragement, and exhortation (1 Cor 14:3). This is an ecclesial activity that

---

ered for prayer and worship." Hays, *First Corinthians*, 181-82. The more critical reading of Hans Conzelmann, who argues for certain tensions within the chapters, recognizes that all deal with "conduct at divine worship." Conzelmann, *1 Corinthians*, Hermeneia (Philadelphia: Fortress, 1975), 182.

[3]All scriptural quotations in this chapter are NASB unless otherwise noted.

[4]It seems that Paul makes some kind of differentiation between this practice of prophecy, which all should do, and the gifting of being a prophet, which according to 1 Corinthians 12, might not be given to all (1 Cor 12:10, 28-29). This could be a distinct office or a gift that comes at different times to different people. Thiselton, *Corinthians*, 1095.

builds up the church (1 Cor 14:4-5). For unbelievers who might join the service and experience prophesying (done one by one, 1 Cor 14:31), they experience reproof and judgment, which results in worship and a recognition of the presence of God (1 Cor 14:24). Thiselton summarizes prophecy this way:

> Prophesying in Paul's theology and in his argument in this chapter is the performing of intelligible, articulate, communicative speech-acts, the operative currency of which depends on the active agency of the Holy Spirit mediated through human minds and lives to build up, to encourage, to judge, to exhort, and to comfort others in the context of interpersonal relations.[5]

Because Paul assumes that women pray and prophesy, it seems that he assumes they participate in this kind of activity.

What then of 1 Corinthians 14:34-35, where Paul says that women should be silent in the churches, that they are not allowed to speak, that it is in fact shameful for a woman to speak in church? Some way forward must be found because if Paul has said that women prophesy—speak publicly—he cannot mean here, just a few chapters later, that women must be utterly silent. Therefore, some have concluded these verses could be an interpolation or a quote from the Corinthians with which Paul disagrees or that he is prohibiting chatter, disruptive speech.[6] I find most convincing the arguments of Witherington, Thiselton, and Hensley that Paul is prohibiting evaluative speech, interrogating speech that calls into question, in a shameful way, the prophecies of others.[7] This kind of speech draws the focus away from God into human disagreements, and especially if this is wives charging husbands publicly with hypocrisy when they try to prophesy—that is "too much information," which should be handled at home.

For point one, my conclusion is this: we do not all have to agree about leadership, teaching, or sacramental authority. But we can all agree along

---

[5]Ibid., 1094.

[6]For the interpolation view, see Fee, *Corinthians*, 782: "The two text critical criteria of transcriptional and intrinsic probability combine to cast considerable doubt on their authenticity." The view that this is a quote with which Paul disagrees is found in Marshall Janzen, "Orderly Participation or Silenced Women? Clashing Views on Decent Worship in 1 Corinthians 14," *Direction* 42/1 (2013): 55-70. On the prohibition of chatter, see Fee, *Corinthians*, 786-87.

[7]Ben Witherington III, *Women in the Earliest Churches* (Cambridge: Cambridge University Press, 1988), 99; Thiselton, *Corinthians*, 1156, 1158-61; Hensley, "Σιγαω, λαλεω, and ὑποτασσω," 343-64.

with Paul that the Holy Spirit gives to both men and women the gift of encouraging speech to be practiced vocally and publicly in the gathered Christian assembly. This much boldness, then, is warranted: any church that does not allow women a place to speak publicly has misread 1 Corinthians 14 and is simply ignoring 1 Corinthians 11.

POINT TWO OF CLARITY: HAIR

This point of consensus, however, almost immediately leads to one of the most contested issues in this passage. When men and women do pray and prophesy, what should they look like, especially with regard to their head? Paul begins with the men: when they pray and prophesy, if they have something "against the head" (*kata kephalēs*), then they shame their head (1 Cor 11:4). Later he states in verse 7 that a man ought not to cover the head, and finally in verse 14: "Does not nature itself teach you that if a man wears long hair it is a disgrace for him?" (ESV). The first two phrases give rise to intense debate: in 1 Corinthians 11:4 and 7, does Paul warn against men having long hair or against men wearing a covering over their head? Solid arguments exist for both.[8] Depending on the geography, the setting, the occasion, and their rank, at times men were expected to wear head coverings; at other times, they were not. It varied depending on the situation.

The last instruction to men about their heads, thankfully, is not so ambiguous. The verb *komaō* means to wear long hair, and across various ethnicities and settings in the ancient world it was widely assumed that men were to keep their hair short.[9] So while scholars are undecided on the issue of head coverings for men, they are agreed that Paul instructed the men of Corinth not to let their hair grow long.[10]

The converse for women is also true. The debate over whether Paul prohibits head coverings or unloosed hair intensifies with Paul's increased word count to the women's situation, but his words leave no room for confusion on the point that he believes women should not have short hair. The rhetoric

---

[8]See the thorough discussion of the two options in Thiselton, *Corinthians*, 822-26.

[9]Fee, *Corinthians*, 583.

[10]Men should "take no pleasure in curling their hair with the iron." Ovid, *The Art of Love and Other Poems*, trans. J. H. Mozley, rev. G. P. Goold, LCL 232 (Cambridge, MA: Harvard University Press, 1979), 47. "Uncared for beauty is becoming to men," but they should not let "stubborn locks be spoilt by bad cutting; let hair and beard be dressed by a practiced hand." Ibid., 49.

of his argument only works based upon the assumption that to be sheared (*exyrēmenē*) or to be shorn (*keirasthō*) is a major source of shame.[11] Whether head coverings were involved or not, Paul again aligns himself with a widespread cultural agreement that women's hair should be kept long.[12]

Paul offers both a negative and a positive reason for his admonitions concerning the length of hair. First, inappropriate lengths could visually insinuate sexual aberration.[13] Men who allowed their hair to grow long might do so to signify their role as sexual partners for other men or to display themselves as set apart for the service of a god, the worship of which might include sexual expressions.[14] For women, short hair could also convey sexual deviancy. Either this suggested that she was a lesbian or it denoted that she had been exposed in adultery and punished by the cutting of her hair.[15] If men adopted long hair or women adopted short, they very well might bring shame upon themselves, each other, the angels with whom they joined in worship, and God himself.[16] As they worshiped God, they could look like those whose lives were not commensurate with God's standards.

If my reading here is correct, then Paul would urge the same principle, if not the same specific instruction, upon contemporary congregations. It becomes immediately clear that my context, at least, does not assign the same meanings to hair length. Are we going to tell the godly, sweet elderly ladies in our churches, who wear their hair curled, teased, and short (in the style of the 1940s and '50s) to grow their hair long? On the other side, are we going to demand frequent cuts from our younger men whose hair touches

---

[11]Caroline Vander Stichele and Todd C. Penner, "Paul and the Rhetoric of Gender," in *Her Master's Tools? Feminist and Postcolonial Engagements of Historical-Critical Discourse*, ed. Caroline Vander Stichele and Todd C. Penner (Leiden: Brill, 2005), 294.

[12]"It is usual for men to have their hair cut and women to let it grow." Plutarch, *Moralia*, vol. 4, trans. Frank Cole Babbit, LCL 305 (Cambridge, MA: Harvard University Press, 1979), 27.

[13]Unusual hairstyles could also be an indication of mourning. See Plutarch, *Moralia* 4.267A-B.

[14]Martial describes a male slave used sexually as a "wanton long-haired one." Martial, *Epigrams* 3.58.30-1 (Bailey, LCL). See the discussion in John Pollini, "Slave-Boys for Sexual and Religious Services: Images of Pleasure and Devotion," in *Flavian Rome: Culture, Image, and Text*, ed. A. J. Boyle and W. J. Dominik (Leiden: Brill, 2003), 149-66. See also Juvenal, *Satirae* 2.14-16; Apuleius, *Metamorphoses* 8.24-27.

[15]Vander Stichele and Penner, "Paul and the Rhetoric of Gender," 292. Lucian, *Fugitivi* 27 *Dialogi meretrici* 5.3. The possibility of adultery appears in Dio Chrysostom, *De fortuna ii (Or. 64)* 3.

[16]Many commentators adopt the view of Paul's comment about the angels that they participate together with angels in the worship of God. Thiselton lists Augustine, Peter Lombard, Aquinas, Grotius, Estius. Thiselton, *Corinthians*, 839-40.

their shoulder—not unlike the common image of Jesus—which actually was popular since the 9th century?[17] Speaking from my own cultural context, long hair on men and short hair on women no longer carry any kind of connotation of sexual misconduct. Contemporary public advertisements about our sexuality include much more focus on the body. Are there certain cultural markers that denote prostitution or sexual flagrancy? Definitely. We would not want a believer, especially one who was going to take on the public role of praying or speaking the word of God publicly, to dress in such a way that many congregants would wonder if he or she is involved in such practices. It is more difficult to imagine sartorial examples for a member of either gender to indicate by dress that he or she participates in same-sex behaviors. Certain stereotypes exist, but they have not been—and are becoming even less—uniform. The principle issues forth then not in a specific dress code, but in a more general reminder: when you come to worship, adorn your body in such a way that you do not look shameful, that you do not project a dissonant message that you are both a worshiper of God and *pornos*, to use the New Testament catchall term for any sexual deviancy.

Paul offers a positive motivation for his instructions as well. The head of men and women, in addition to conveying sin, could also be a location for projecting glory. The second reason why men should not be covered (*katakalyptesthai*) is that they are the image and glory of God (1 Cor 11:7). Paul's use of image language, *eikōn*, evokes the creation text of Genesis 1, where man is created in the image of God (Gen 1:26, although the LXX of this passage uses the broader term *anthrōpos*, rather than Paul's more narrowly defined *anēr*). Paul's reader, familiar with the text of Genesis, or one whose ears are on alert for statements of inequality, might immediately counter that women too are made in the image of God, as Genesis 1:27 states unequivocally.

The following verses of 1 Corinthians 11, I contend, reveal that Paul too is aware of this because he structures his words precisely in the direction of this mutual male and female image bearing. Verse 8 immediately speaks of the creation of woman: for man is not from woman but woman from man. Then verse 9 repeats it: man wasn't created through the woman but woman

---

[17]Michele Bacci, *The Many Faces of Christ: Portraying the Holy in the East and West, 300 to 1300* (London: Reaktion Books, 2014), 116-40.

through the man. Possibly Paul repeats this reality twice to "put women in their place" and remind them of their order in creation.[18] It is not outside the realm of possibility that some women in Corinth needed to be reminded that the world did not begin and end with them. But it seems we can also read this double affirmation of the order of creation as a reminder that man, *anēr*, does not bear the image of God alone. My point is that Paul's statement follows the same pattern of Genesis 1:26-27: the creation of one man as the image and likeness of God, then the creation of male and female. We might wish Paul to have been more explicit, to affirm the *imago Dei* of women with a phrase that kept the balance, but it seems a responsible reading to see this affirmation in the order of his statements. In the narrative of creation, man imaged God, but only for the brief period of time before woman at his side imaged God as well. This is the case in Genesis, and by mentioning the story of the creation of woman, Paul's words recount the same events. The order leads to this truth: when humanity reflects the image of God, it does so in interdependence between men and women.

A difference arises, however, with the concept of glory, a term not found in the creation narratives. Paul states that man is the glory of God and woman is the glory of man. That which constitutes God's glory is a multifaceted concept for Paul, including God's immortality (Rom 1:23; 1 Tim 1:17), truthfulness (Rom 3:7), faithfulness (Rom 4:20; 2 Cor 1:20), holiness (Rom 3:23; 1 Cor 6:20), reconciliation (Rom 5:11), light (2 Cor 4:6), grace (Rom 5:2; 2 Cor 4:15), salvation (2 Tim 2:10), power (Eph 3:16), honor (1 Tim 1:17), riches (Phil 4:19), and kingdom (1 Thess 2:12). Here, specifically, uncovered, short-haired men are God's glory.

What then does Paul mean by glory *here*? How do men show the glory of God, while women, whose long hair gives to them glory (1 Cor 11:15), show the glory of men (1 Cor 11:7)? My contention is that Paul defines glory here as the glory of creating life. Paul expresses a resonance between God's glory and life in several other instances, so these can be for him related ideas.[19]

---

[18] Jorunn Økland, *Women in Their Place: Paul and the Corinthian Discourse of Gender and Sanctuary Space*, JSNTSup 269 (London: T&T Clark, 2004), 188, 194; Antoinette Clark Wire, *The Corinthian Women Prophets: A Reconstruction Through Paul's Rhetoric* (Minneapolis: Fortress, 1991), 130.

[19] Rom 2:7: "To those who by perseverance in doing good seek for glory and honor and immortality, [God will render] eternal life"; Rom 6:4: "Therefore we have been buried with Him through baptism into death, so that as Christ was raised from the dead through the glory of the Father,

Moreover, it is a repeated idea that God's glory is displayed in his creation (Ps 19:1; 97:6; Rev 4:11) to which Paul himself refers in Romans 1:18-23. The first support in this specific passage for this "creating life" connotation of glory is that it is, as every interpreter cannot miss, replete with creational imagery.[20] Genesis 1 and 2 reverberate throughout, leaving unmistakable echoes. Second, Paul refers to the subsequent creation of life throughout the millennia. Since creation, life has repeated when the man has come through the woman. With this dual focus on the creation of life—first and subsequent—it seems possible that this is the particular aspect of glory in view here. The head of men should be visible because when one looks upon a man one is reminded of God's creation of the first man, Adam.[21] One is reminded of the glory of God in the creation of life. Conversely, when one looks upon a woman with long hair, which indicates that she is not sexually deviant in any way, one is reminded of her ability to partner with man to complete his glory, namely his ability to create life.[22]

Again, we might wish that Paul had said both men and women equally provide a vision of the image and glory of God. Theologically Paul cannot be charged with gender inequality in value, in sinfulness, in the possibility of redemption, and in giftedness for both men and women. But here, if the issue is sexuality in the context of creation, it makes sense for him to draw a distinction. Men, properly unadorned, give a picture of the first creation of a human, and women, properly adorned, give a picture of the subsequent creation of all other humans. Looking at a man with short hair and visage uncovered, one could think, He reminds me of Adam! God has the ability to create life! God is glorious! Looking at a woman with long hair arranged with propriety, one would think, Through her, man has the ability to create life! Man is glorious.

---

so we too might walk in newness of life"; Col 3:4: "When Christ, who is our life, is revealed, then you also will be revealed with Him in glory."

[20]Conzelmann, *1 Corinthians*, 186-88; Thiselton, *Corinthians*, 811, 833-37; Fee, *Corinthians*, 567-73; Richard A. Horsley, *1 Corinthians*, Abingdon New Testament Commentaries (Nashville: Abingdon, 1998), 153-55; Hays, *First Corinthians*, 186-87.

[21]Thiselton traces the meaning of *kephalē* whereby head functions as a representative of the whole. Thiselton, *Corinthians*, 816-20.

[22]A common view among both Greeks and Jews was that men supplied the seed and woman nurtured the seed. See Andrew Lincoln, *Born of a Virgin? Reconceiving Jesus in the Bible, Tradition, and Theology* (Grand Rapids: Eerdmans, 2013), 256-58. It is certainly possible that this kind of view underlies Paul's statements here.

This comparison exposes a vital difference. God can create a full human on his own. Man cannot do so. To put it another way, man was the finished product of God's creation. Woman is not the product of man, but his indispensable partner. Just as was true with the concept of image, there is also a mutuality of glory here. Man shows God's glory of creativity, the glory of life; but if God had stopped there, that glory of life would have been limited to just one human creation. The plenipotentiary glory of God's creative life is surely not singular, but exponential. As Paul says in 1 Corinthians 11:12, all things come from God. Hence, after revealing his glory in creating a life, the fashioning of woman from man was the way in which God designed to show his glory of replicating life. God's glory is revealed in both the man (first creation) and the woman, who as the partner of the man, shows his glory of continuing to create life, through the mystery, beauty, and complexity of sexuality.

I am only now ready to make comment on the contested verse at the beginning of the section, 1 Corinthians 11:3, in which Paul states that he wants the Corinthians to know that Christ is the head of every man, man is the head of woman, and God is the head of Christ. It should be clear from my foregoing exegesis that I find "source" to be a much better meaning than "leader." This is not because I've counted more references to *kephalē* in *Thesaurus Linguae Graecae* as "source" than "headship," but because it seems clear to me that this entire section has as its major focus the creation of life.[23] Paul says that God is the source of all things, which would include Christ. I do think this leaves open the possibility of "eternal begottenness," even if Paul himself might not have been thinking of those terms. In addition, Paul has stated (three times actually: 1 Cor 11:8, 9, and 12) that woman comes from man, so man is the source of woman. Finally, the two other times when Paul uses the phrase "image of God," he does so as a reference to Christ (2 Cor 4:4; Col 1:15). Christ, then, as the ultimate image of God is the source for the first human to be the image of God. Again, room is left for the theological development of Christ as the template for humanity, but Paul has left

---

[23] I maintain, however, that word studies do have their place. See Lynn H. Cohick, "Tyranny, Authority, Service: Leadership and Headship in the New Testament," *Ex Auditu* 28 (2012): 74-89; and (for the opposite view) Wayne Grudem, *Evangelical Feminism & Biblical Truth* (Sisters, OR: Multnomah, 2004), 552-99.

the dots that can be connected later.[24] *Kephalē* as source seems the best fit because of context, but that does not mean that in and of itself it can bear the full weight of an egalitarian reading. Room for debate about the implications of source certainly remain.

Having discussed the challenging issues of image, glory, and head, I can now return to Paul's positive motivation for instruction in this passage: dress in a way that shows the glory of God's creativity. When you come to church don't just avoid dressing like a prostitute; the mere embrace of this negative could devolve into dour presentations. Instead, adorn yourself to show that you are worshiping the God who created life in the beginning and, through men and women, continues to create life today. Demonstrate through self-control the protection of sexuality, but also through freedom the beauty of God's creativity.

A focus on the creation of life might suggest that Paul is concerned about biological fecundity alone, thus honoring and privileging the married couples of Corinth over and against the unmarried. But while acknowledging this unmistakable biological creational lens, a proper exegesis of this passage also has to take into account Paul's privileging of singleness just a few chapters earlier, where he invokes his own story and that of his Lord. He would never advocate practices in a congregation that elevate the procreative function in such a way so as to alienate those who are unable to reproduce or who are gifted with singleness. Therefore, I want to be careful to acknowledge, as other commentators have argued, that Paul's instructions here do not apply only to married men and women but to the community as a whole.[25]

It is easy to see how male and female ontology, considered independently of each other, exhibits God's creative power. Men, by their existence, reveal God's creation of the first human whether or not they can have biological children, even as they testify to God's ongoing creation as a being who came from a father and a mother. Likewise, nonchildbearing women, simply by their existence as daughters, demonstrate God's continual creation of life.

Yet demonstrating this creative glory through bodily appearance is most difficult for that woman who cannot partner with a man to bring about the

---

[24]Edward Schillebeeckx, *Jesus: An Experiment in Christology* (New York: Crossroad, 1979), 626-36.
[25]Conzelmann, *1 Corinthians*, 184; Hays, *First Corinthians*, 185.

creation of new biological life, because of either singleness or barrenness, or age. If this message is for every man and woman, as Paul states in 1 Corinthians 11:4 and 5, then how can the nonchildbearing woman demonstrate glory through her bodily presentation, even the glory of the man, hence the glorious partnership of creating life? The key lies, it seems, in Paul's "Christological reinterpretation" of 1 Corinthians 11:11. While some interpreters take this as a sharp adversative to what has come before, it is also possible to read this statement as building upon the creational theology of the previous verses.[26] Just as the image and glory of God were almost immediately reflected in the first male and female pair, so too in the Lord it is explicitly the case that women and men cannot be apart from one another. This is the new community, the new family, where all have a relationship with God through Christ. Paul's powerful phrase "in the Lord" testifies to the possibility of the creation of life that is not just biological.

"In the Lord" is Paul's way of speaking of the Christian community (1 Cor 16:19). And even more interestingly, in the nine uses of this phrase in 1 Corinthians, it resonates with themes of glory and creative life. In three of the instances, *en kyriō* redefines family. Paul calls Timothy his child "in the Lord" (1 Cor 4:17). He tells the slave, a member of the household, that he is truly free "in the Lord" (1 Cor 7:22). The woman who has been widowed can establish a new family, but only "in the Lord" (1 Cor 7:39). In addition, Paul contrasts a boast in the flesh with a boast that is "in the Lord" (1 Cor 1:31). He talks about the Corinthians as his creative work "in the Lord" that proves his apostleship (1 Cor 9:1-2), and he encourages them to do work "in the Lord" that will be fruitful (1 Cor 15:58). In the Lord is where one's flesh provides neither privilege nor hindrance because in the Lord one can produce fruit, the fruit of a vocation of evangelism and discipleship, the fruit of new relationships, the fruit of freedom, the fruit of a spiritual child. In the Lord, in the Christian community, men and women are vitally necessary for one another because they can create life through the power of God, even if that life is not biological. The man and woman unable to bear physical children can

---

[26]For the adversative view, see Alan G. Padgett, *As Christ Submits to the Church: A Biblical Understanding of Leadership and Mutual Submission* (Grand Rapids: Baker Academic, 2011), 118; Thiselton, *Corinthians*, 842. Fee reads *plēn* as an adversative and translates it "nonetheless" (*Corinthians*, 578n128). For the creational theology view, see Conzelmann, *1 Corinthians*, 190; Hays, *First Corinthians*, 155.

still give a visual picture of the glory of God's ability to create life. And truth be told, Paul would argue that these members can actually create more life than those who can produce biological children. Numerous issues have changed, so we might not share the opinion Paul holds forth in 1 Corinthians 7 that singleness is to be preferred. Nevertheless, his vigorous argument there, and here in 1 Corinthians 11 with his fulsome phrase "in the Lord," bars any contemporary diminishment of the nonfertile Christian. In nature and the church, men and women are dependent upon one another because all things naturally and spiritually find their source in God, who is Creator of all and the Father of the household of the Lord's followers. If all things come from God, then women and men, married and single, childbearing or no, can visually demonstrate in their bodies the full creative power of God.

It exceeds the bounds of this essay to postulate what this passage might say to those Christians who do not easily fit into the male/female binary.[27] To mention such contested ground, which in the present climate would be irresponsible to ignore, compels us even more desperately to hear the closing verse of this section: "If anyone is inclined to be contentious, we have no such practice, nor do the churches of God" (1 Cor 11:16 ESV). If anyone proposes to be a lover of victory, to use one-upmanship, to be contentious, Paul says that he doesn't have such an ethos, and neither do the churches of God. The issues of 1 Corinthians should not be grounds upon which we demand our rights. Instead, we should all hear the words Paul has said to the Corinthians and by the inspiration of God's Spirit, hear those words proclaimed to the church today: You are all invited to worship, you are all invited to pray and prophesy, and when you do so, you cannot dress any way you please. Bodies matter in worship. Do not in some kind of gnostic fashion (be it anarchist or ascetic) think that they do not. When you gather for worship, you have the chance to display the glory of life, both biological and spiritual, both of which are demonstrations of life in the Lord. You have the chance to image in your body creative life—in word and deed, content and form, proclamation and aesthetic—and in so doing give glory to God.

---

[27]In his recent book on the issue, Mark Yarhouse defines the situation in this way: "Experiences of gender identity in which a person's psychological and emotional sense of themselves does not match or align with their birth sex." Mark A. Yarhouse, *Understanding Gender Dysphoria: Navigating Transgender Issues in a Changing Culture* (Downers Grove, IL: IVP Academic, 2015), 19.

12

Thomas Aquinas on
Sexual Ethics

MATTHEW LEVERING

I N ACCORD WITH MOST MODERN biblical scholarship, N. T. Wright
holds that "Genesis 1 is in fact a 'temple'-vision, God making a heaven-
and-earth house for himself in which he would place, at its heart and as the
climax of creation itself, the humans who would be his image-bearers, his
royal priesthood, summing up the worship of creation and reflecting his
wise order into his world."[1] In this essay, I wish to consider what it means
for human image-bearers to reflect God's "wise order into his world" specifically with regard to sexual desire. My argument is that God's *temperate*
eschatological people are true priests and "image-bearers" who give him
praise and reflect "his wise order into his world." Temperance with respect
to sex belongs to the eschatological restoration of God's people and their
reigning in the world as his royal images, as a "new family" that lives together in a "way that declare[s] to the world that Jesus, the crucified and
risen one, [is] the world's true sovereign."[2]

My account of the eschatological restoration of God's people presumes
Genesis 1, where "God created man in his own image, in the image of God
he created him; male and female he created them" (Gen 1:27).[3] I take this

---

[1] N. T. Wright, *Paul and the Faithfulness of God* (Minneapolis: Fortress, 2013), 1509.
[2] N. T. Wright, *After You Believe: Why Christian Character Matters* (New York: HarperCollins, 2010), 228.
[3] All scriptural quotations in this chapter are from the Revised Standard Version, Catholic Edition unless otherwise noted.

unity and differentiation of humanity—"man" is created "male and female," and "a man leaves his father and his mother and cleaves to his wife, and they become one flesh" (Gen 2:24)—to be foundational for sexual ethics.[4] However, in our fallen condition this one-flesh union, which serves as the foundation for family life and for the raising of children, is plagued and undermined by lust. Paul notes that men and women can be "aflame with passion" (1 Cor 7:9) to such an extent that they choose to engage in sexual acts that are not in accord with spiritual union with Christ. When we are "aflame with passion" in lust, we no longer perceive the locatedness of our sexuality within the broader context of self-giving love in the service of the family (and of the restored family of God). Thomas Gilby describes this broader context as, among other things, "a child's right to a family background," namely the right to be raised by one's mother and father.[5] This "right" identifies one of "the inherent goods of creaturely existence."[6] As Janet Smith puts it, our "natural urge for sexual pleasure" is good in itself, but in our fallen condition we require chastity to learn "how this urge must be put in service of the goods of the persons whom that urge affects."[7]

N. T. Wright comments that God's restored family already experiences "the transformation not only of the heart but of the entire life" and reflects God's wise order for human sexuality into a deeply confused and disordered world.[8] Since over the course of time God taught Israel much about this wise order, Paul can retain important elements of "classic Jewish sexual ethics" in his teaching of the Gentiles about sexual ethics in Christ.[9] Since believers are still fallen, Paul finds himself having to inform the Gentile Corinthians that "there is immorality among you, and of a kind that is not

---

[4]See Alexander Pruss, *One Body: An Essay in Christian Sexual Ethics* (Notre Dame: University of Notre Dame Press, 2013); John S. Grabowski, *Sex and Virtue: An Introduction to Sexual Ethics* (Washington, DC: Catholic University of America Press, 2003), 96-103.

[5]Thomas Gilby, "Appendix 3: Natural and Unnatural in Morals," in Thomas Aquinas, *Summa Theologiae 43: Temperance (2a2ae. 141-54)*, trans. Thomas Gilby (London: Eyre & Spottiswoode, 1968), 254.

[6]Oliver O'Donovan, *Church in Crisis: The Gay Controversy and the Anglican Communion* (Eugene, OR: Cascade Books, 2008), 98.

[7]Janet E. Smith, "The Universality of Natural Law and the Irreducibility of Personalism," *Nova et Vetera* 11 (2013): 1129-47. See also Karol Wojtyła (the future Pope John Paul II), *Love and Responsibility*, trans. H. T. Willetts (San Francisco: Ignatius Press, 1981).

[8]Wright, *Paul and the Faithfulness of God*, 1037.

[9]Ibid., 1508.

found even among pagans; for a man is living with his father's wife" (1 Cor 5:1). Similarly, in the same letter, Paul is compelled to warn against sexual intercourse with prostitutes: "Shall I . . . take the members of Christ and make them members of a prostitute? Never! Do you not know that he who joins himself to a prostitute becomes one body with her?" (1 Cor 6:15-16). In condemning such behavior, which Gentiles had previously assumed to be acceptable for men, Paul points out that whereas "every other sin which a man commits is outside the body," "the immoral man sins against his own body" (1 Cor 6:18). This is particularly disastrous for Christians, whose bodies should "glorify God" (1 Cor 6:20). Commenting on 1 Corinthians 6:19-20, Wright remarks, "Those who already stand on resurrection ground, and must learn to live in this new world, need to be reminded that what they do with their bodies in the present matters, because the spirit who dwells within them will cause them to be raised as the Messiah was raised."[10]

In exploring the virtue of chastity, I will underscore that, as Wright remarks, "the common life of the church . . . seems to have functioned from the first in terms of an alternative family. . . . If one belonged to it, one did not belong any more, certainly not in the same way, to one's previous unit, whether familial or racial."[11] Among Christians, families remained important, even while in certain ways being transcended through a friendship with Christ that encompasses all who love the Lord. Wright states that Paul's ethic "reflects Paul's vision of the coming divine rule over the whole creation, and of humans being called to share in this rule," so that Christian moral life is about becoming "the sort of people through whom the one God will establish his sovereign rule, bringing his wise order into the world."[12] In sexual ethics, we royally reign with Christ when we bring "his wise order into the world." God's eschatological family must image God with respect to sexuality in a manner that fosters the flourishing of human families. Freed "from the dominion of darkness and transferred . . . to the kingdom of his beloved Son" (Col 1:13), we are able to overcome the vices of fallen sexual desire that have long undermined family life: "immorality, impurity, passion" (Col 3:5).

---

[10]Wright, *Paul and the Faithfulness of God*, 1112.
[11]N. T. Wright, *The New Testament and the People of God* (Minneapolis: Fortress, 1992), 448.
[12]Wright, *Paul and the Faithfulness of God*, 1113.

John Grabowski has observed that Thomas Aquinas's treatment of chastity "successfully integrates an account of human nature and its inclinations into a larger framework of virtue. Chastity enables the person's sexual powers to be exercised intelligently and freely in accord with the goods of human nature—particularly the inclination to procreate, educate, and care for offspring."[13] Given our fallen human condition, we often find ourselves desiring to live out our sexual desire in ways that, directly or indirectly, undermine the likelihood that children will be raised by their own mother and father. Today, we often imagine that our sexual acts have no consequences outside ourselves and consenting participants. In fact, when for example humans fornicate, commit adultery, or engage in homosexual acts, these actions undermine the stable bond of mother and father as the context for raising children. We need the grace of the Holy Spirit to be able, as Adrian Thatcher puts it, "to embody the divine love that sent the Son into the world" through well-ordered sexual desire and family life.[14] For Aquinas, therefore, chastity is not only about human nature and virtue, but also belongs to the graced self-giving life of the Christian toward the weak and the vulnerable so that (as Grabowski says), "understood spiritually, the essence of chastity is found in charity and the other theological virtues."[15]

In this essay I will emphasize that, for Aquinas, chastity belongs to the "inbreaking of God's Kingdom and the invitation to discipleship in the area of sexuality and marriage," an invitation that above all requires Christlike love and that also requires obedient attention to the New Testament's identification of sexual "sins that break down the Christian community."[16] Scripture contains numerous teachings about sexual ethics, as for example when Jesus warns against lust and adultery in his Sermon on the Mount. Aquinas understands Scripture as authoritatively teaching us about holiness of life, including the acts by which we love other persons "through the body," as temples of the Holy Spirit.[17] I will address Aquinas's discussion of chastity

---

[13]Grabowski, Sex and Virtue, 82.
[14]Adrian Thatcher, Theology and Families (Oxford: Blackwell, 2007), 45. However, Thatcher argues for "extending the rite and the right of marriage to couples of the same sex." Ibid., 137.
[15]Grabowski, Sex and Virtue, 83. Grabowski cites Thomas Aquinas, Summa Theologiae II-II, trans. Fathers of the English Dominican Province (Westminster, MD: Christian Classics, 1981) q. 151, a. 2.
[16]Grabowski, Sex and Virtue, 52, 61.
[17]Ibid., 63. Grabowski adds, "Life in the Spirit is enfleshed in the body and indeed in sexuality." Ibid., 64.

and the sins against chastity. I argue that Aquinas's theology of chastity makes manifest the eschatological restoration of God's family accomplished by Jesus Christ, who enables his followers to reflect God's wise order in their sexual actions.

AQUINAS ON THE CREATOR GOD'S "WISE ORDER" AND OUR PARTICIPATION IN IT

Wright holds that in God's kingdom-project, God aims to build up a people (Israel as reconfigured around the Davidic Messiah-king) "through whom . . . God will establish his sovereign rule, bringing his wise order into the world."[18] Aquinas envisions a quite similar reality in his own ethics. To understand God's "sovereign rule" and "wise order" according to Aquinas, we need first to appreciate his theology of law and then to unite it to his theology of Christ's cross and its fruits.

Like Wright, Aquinas makes clear that God knows the wise order of human flourishing, the flourishing of God's royal images who possess (as rational animals) "a natural aptitude for understanding and loving God."[19] Aquinas explains God's wise order using philosophical language, but his point is fundamentally the same as Wright's and originates in his theology of God's creative work. In terms drawn from Augustine (who adapts them for Christian purposes from Stoic philosophy), Aquinas states that "the whole community of the universe is governed by Divine Reason. Wherefore the very Idea [*Ratio*] of the government of things in God the Ruler of the universe, has the nature of a law."[20] For Aquinas, *law* does not mean merely positive law—that is to say, human laws. God's understanding of the wise order of all things to their proper flourishing is itself a law, promulgated in the Word (from the outset of creation) by the divine Ruler of the cosmos. God knows the wise order of good human actions that lead to human beatitude.[21] When actions deviate from this order, they are bad and lead away from true human flourishing. Aquinas terms this divine knowledge by which all things are ordered rightly "eternal law."[22]

---

[18]Wright, *Paul and the Faithfulness of God*, 1113.

[19]Aquinas, *Summa Theologiae* I, q. 93, a. 4.

[20]Aquinas, *Summa Theologiae* I-II, q. 91, a. 1.

[21]See Aquinas, *Summa Theologiae* I-II, qq. 1-5.

[22]See especially Aquinas, *Summa Theologiae* I-II, q. 93, aa. 1-6. For Aquinas, as J. Budziszewski

How can mere humans know God's eternal wise order for good human actions? Aquinas identifies three ways: divine revelation, human reason, and the structure of the human body. With regard to the last named source of knowledge, Aquinas observes that "all natural things were produced by the Divine art, and so may be called God's works of art."[23] We can see that the human body is a divine work of art because the human body is clearly made for the kind of rational creatures that we are. For instance, the human body possesses a large brain, possesses hands and fingers that enable writing and making things, stands erect with eyes pointing outward rather than toward the ground, and has a mouth and tongue suited for speech. All of these aspects show the way in which the human body is "most suited to such a form" (namely the rational soul) and "to such operations" (namely rational activity and communion).[24] The human body, therefore, can help us to discern God's wise order for the flourishing of his royal images.

Birds or stars participate in God's wise order, but they do not know that they do. By contrast, humans participate rationally in God's wise order by discerning rationally what pertains to our flourishing. Cain knows, despite his envy, that he should not murder Abel. Cain kills Abel anyway, but Cain himself greatly fears to be killed (see Gen 4:14). Aquinas describes this rational participation in God's eternal law as our participation in "the Eternal Reason, whereby it [the rational creature] has a natural inclination to its proper act and end: and this participation of the eternal law in the rational creature is called the natural law."[25] By "natural inclination," Aquinas means our rational inclination toward that which pertains to our individual and communal flourishing, such as to do good and avoid evil, to preserve our lives, to know the truth (including truth about God), to procreate and raise children, to live in society, and so forth.[26] Aquinas emphasizes that "natural

---

points out, "Eternal law is the foundation and origin of all law, its *sine qua non*. . . . If eternal law does not exist, then neither does natural law. In fact, properly speaking, we have no nature at all." Budziszewski, *Commentary on Thomas Aquinas's "Treatise on Law"* (Cambridge: Cambridge University Press, 2014), 159.

[23] Aquinas, *Summa Theologiae* I, q. 91, a. 3.

[24] Aquinas, *Summa Theologiae* I, q. 91, a. 3.

[25] Aquinas, *Summa Theologiae* I-II, q. 91, a. 2. For discussion and bibliographical material, see Matthew Levering, *Biblical Natural Law: A Theocentric and Teleological Approach* (Oxford: Oxford University Press, 2008), chapter 4.

[26] Aquinas, *Summa Theologiae* I-II, q. 94, a. 2.

law" is not first and foremost a set of external precepts, but rather is the mind's constitutive participation in God's providential ordering of us to what is good for us. As Aquinas states, "the light of natural reason, whereby we discern what is good and what is evil, which is the function of the natural law, is nothing else than an imprint on us of the Divine light. It is therefore evident that the natural law is nothing else than the rational creature's participation of the eternal law."[27]

The "wise order" of God, which befits his "sovereign rule" and which should be reflected by his royal images in the world, is therefore known through the divine art that is our body and through human reason's participation in God's eternal law. With regard to the latter, however, Aquinas notes that "though there is necessity in the general principles, the more we descend to matters of detail, the more frequently we encounter defects."[28] For example, we may agree that we should not murder innocent humans, but with respect to defining who is innocent and who is human, we often err. Therefore, in order to renew his human images, God needed to reveal even precepts of the natural law, and God also needed to heal our wills so that we could obey these precepts. Like Wright, in accord with Scripture, Aquinas holds that God has done this through Christ. In Aquinas's view, the Mosaic law "showed forth the precepts of the natural law, and added certain precepts of its own" in preparation for Christ.[29] For its part, the divinely revealed "law of Christ" (Gal 6:2) is more, but not less, than the natural law as expressed in the Ten Commandments and the Golden Rule ("whatever you wish that men would do to you, do so to them" [Mt 7:12]). The "law of Christ," taught in the Sermon on the Mount and elsewhere (including by Paul), defines the ethics of what Aquinas calls "the Gospel of the kingdom."[30]

AQUINAS ON CHASTITY, VIRGINITY, AND LUST

Aquinas notes that in our fallen condition, our sexual desire easily slides into lust. For this reason, "*chastity* takes its name from the fact that reason

---

[27]Aquinas, *Summa Theologiae* I-II, q. 91, a. 2.
[28]Aquinas, *Summa Theologiae* I-II, q. 94, a. 4.
[29]Aquinas, *Summa Theologiae* I-II, q. 98, a. 6.
[30]Aquinas, *Summa Theologiae* I-II, q. 106, a. 4, ad 4. See Servais Pinckaers, *The Sources of Christian Ethics*, trans. Mary Thomas Noble (Washington, DC: Catholic University of America, 1995).

chastises concupiscence, which, like a child, needs curbing."[31] This chastising should not be imagined as arbitrary. It is rather a matter of living according to what is truly reasonable, and not allowing concupiscence to lead us away from God's wise order. In chastity, a person makes "moderate use of bodily members, in accordance with the judgment of his reason and the choice of his will."[32]

In Scripture, the people of Israel are often presented as God's bride, and in this capacity they are often described as unchaste due to their worshiping other gods. In a verse quoted by Aquinas, the prophet Jeremiah expresses the Lord's condemnation of Israel as follows: "You have played the harlot with many lovers" (Jer 3:1).[33] As Aquinas recognizes, this prophetic usage is a metaphor for a lack of spiritual "chastity." Spiritual chastity consists in the human mind delighting "in the spiritual union with that to which it behooves it to be united, namely God," and at the same time refraining from "delighting in union with other things against the requirements of the order established by God."[34] Describing the restoration to spiritual chastity, Aquinas quotes 2 Corinthians 11:2, where Paul rejoices in having "betrothed you [the Corinthian community] to Christ to present you as a pure bride to her one husband."[35] In faith, we can be sure that God, through his restored people or family, is accomplishing what Paul describes in marital imagery in Ephesians 5:25-27 (which Aquinas does not quote here, but which he quotes often in the *tertia pars*): "Christ loved the church and gave himself up for her, that he might sanctify her, having cleansed her by the washing of water with the word, that he might present the church to himself in splendor, without spot or wrinkle or any such thing, that she might be holy and without blemish."

In accomplishing this restoration, God gives his people not only spiritual chastity for the upbuilding of the family of God, but also bodily chastity for the upbuilding of human family life. Aquinas fully recognizes the strength of the concupiscible pleasures, which are rooted in our natural desire to preserve human nature by eating, drinking, and sexual intercourse. If

---

[31] Aquinas, *Summa Theologiae* II-II, q. 151, a. 1.
[32] Aquinas, *Summa Theologiae* II-II, q. 151, a. 1, ad 1.
[33] Cited in Aquinas, *Summa Theologiae* II-II, q. 151, a. 2.
[34] Aquinas, *Summa Theologiae* II-II, q. 151, a. 2.
[35] Cited in ibid.

concupiscence were not strong, then it would not need the curbing or chastising influence of the virtue of chastity. Chastity involves the way in which we think about, look at, and touch others, and so chastity also involves purity. In this regard, Jesus intensifies the Torah: "You have heard that it was said, 'You shall not commit adultery.' But I tell you that anyone who looks at a woman lustfully has already committed adultery with her in his heart" (Mt 5:27-28 NIV).

Jesus' warning would be unnecessary, of course, if chastity were easy for members of the inaugurated kingdom. Aquinas, therefore, must give serious attention to the vice of lust (*luxuria*), in which we follow our sexual desire in ways that betray God's wise order, undo his reign, and fail to image his self-giving love. The term *lust* can be used to express disordered pleasures other than sexual ones, but Aquinas notes that it applies preeminently to disordered sexual pleasures. Just as enjoying the pleasures of eating and drinking must have a proper relation to sustaining bodily life in order to be good, so also enjoying the pleasures of the sexual organs must have a proper relation to procreation in order to be good. This does not mean that sexual acts must actually lead to the procreation of a child, but it does mean that sexual acts that are deliberately or intrinsically closed to procreation (as distinct from simply being infertile) fall outside God's wise order, which Aquinas calls "the order of reason."[36]

In response to the objection that "everyone can lawfully make use of what is his" and so "there can be no sin in venereal acts," Aquinas quotes 1 Corinthians 6:20, "you were bought with a price. So glorify God in your body."[37] There is no autonomous possession of one's own body, certainly not within the kingdom of God (where the Spirit indwells the body), and not even "outside" this kingdom, since the Creator God "is the Supreme Lord of our body."[38] Aquinas notes that God is not an arbitrary Supreme Lord, arbitrarily refusing to let us use our sexual organs in any way we like. Rather, God seeks our flourishing. We flourish as individuals, families, and communities—and as the family of God in Christ—when we use our sexual organs according to the order of reason, whereas "lust

---

[36] Aquinas, *Summa Theologiae* II-II, q. 153, aa. 2 and 3.
[37] Aquinas, *Summa Theologiae* II-II, q. 153, a. 3, obj. 2 and ad 2.
[38] Aquinas, *Summa Theologiae* II-II, q. 153, a. 3, ad 2.

consists essentially in exceeding the order and mode of reason in the matter of venereal acts."[39]

What happens when lust overcomes a person? The person enjoys satisfying the concupiscible appetite's desire for sexual pleasure, a desire generally motivated by the strength or "vehemence of the pleasure."[40] But there are obviously consequences for casting aside the wise order of God and instead being guided by one's sexual desire. Aquinas refers to Daniel's condemnation of the unjust judges of Israel who, impelled by their sexual desire for Susanna and for other young women, fell into crimes of lust and thereby into other crimes as well. Daniel says, "Beauty has deceived you and lust has perverted your heart" (Dan 13:56).[41] When we simply follow our sexual desire, we become blind both to the good end of an act and to what should (and should not) be done in attaining the end of the act. Whatever satisfies the sexual desire becomes what the lustful person rashly does. The lustful person can also fall into a "*hatred of God*, by reason of His forbidding the desired pleasure," along with a disordered "*love of this world*, whose pleasures a man desires to enjoy," and a "*despair of a future world*, because through being held back by carnal pleasures he cares not to obtain spiritual pleasures, since they are distasteful to him."[42]

Realistically, Aquinas is aware that sexual desire is not easily ordered to human flourishing. Strengthened by the Holy Spirit, some persons "refrain from lustful pleasures chiefly through hope of the glory to come," but in the face of concrete temptation, this hope can lose its hold.[43] Human flourishing requires that male and female sexual desire be ordered and acted upon rationally so as to foster stable, self-giving bonds of familial communion that allow for true caring for children, the aged, and needy neighbors. To be able to order our sexual desire in this way, we need "right reason." Cajetan Chereso explains that "virtue moderates and proportions man's life according to the spiritual clarity of reason."[44] As a perfection or "rectitude"

---

[39] Aquinas, *Summa Theologiae* II-II, q. 153, a. 3.
[40] Aquinas, *Summa Theologiae* II-II, q. 153, a. 5.
[41] Cited in ibid.
[42] Aquinas, *Summa Theologiae* II-II, q. 153, a. 5 (italics in original).
[43] Aquinas, *Summa Theologiae* II-II, q. 153, a. 4, ad 3.
[44] Cajetan Chereso, *The Virtue of Honor and Beauty According to St. Thomas Aquinas* (River Forest, IL: The Aquinas Library, 1960), 44. Chereso adds that "right reason shines forth in a life of virtue, because such a life is full of the light and clarity of the eternal law—a light and clarity participated by first principles, and by truths which they, in their turn, illumine."

of the appetite, moral virtue requires "the virtue of prudence in reason," so that we reason rightly about matters of action.[45] As fallen humans, moreover, we need the grace of the Holy Spirit to sustain us in right reason. Otherwise we remain enslaved to "the works of the flesh," which Paul describes as "immorality, impurity, licentiousness, idolatry," and so forth (Gal 5:19-20).[46] Living in accord with right reason as members of the Christian community— and thus, in Paul's words, as people committed to repenting "of the impurity, immorality, and licentiousness which [we] have practiced" (2 Cor 12:21)— we reflect God's love and "spiritual beauty" as his royal images and share in his reign as his restored people, his family called to "inherit the kingdom of God" (Gal 5:21).[47]

The task then is to discern what sexual acts are not in accord with God's wise order. Aquinas's answers flow from biblical revelation and rational discernment. Logically, he points out that a sexual act can fail to be in accord with right reason either because of the wrong circumstances or because of something bodily that does not accord with the ordering of sexual desire toward the rational end of procreation and the raising of children. Aquinas's critique of fornication, then and now a popular pastime (perhaps even more so now that effective contraception is available), is especially instructive here. On biblical grounds, Aquinas rejects fornication because it "debars a man from God's kingdom."[48] Since fallen humans have long practiced fornication, many great patriarchs and rulers of Israel were fornicators. Aquinas notes the case of Judah, who had sexual intercourse with his daughter-in-law Tamar when she was posing as a prostitute, and many more cases could be noted, since as Jesus says, "out of the heart come evil thoughts, murder, adultery, fornication, theft, false witness, slander" (Mt 15:19).[49] Paul observes that "the immoral man sins against his own body" (1 Cor 6:18) and takes "the members of Christ" and makes them "members of a prostitute" (1 Cor 6:15).[50]

---

[45]Ibid., 45.

[46]Aquinas quotes Gal 5:19 in *Summa Theologiae* II-II, q. 154, a. 1, obj. 6.

[47]Aquinas quotes 2 Cor 12:21 in *Summa Theologiae* II-II, q. 154, a. 1, obj. 5.

[48]Aquinas, *Summa Theologiae* II-II, q. 154, a. 2, *sed contra*.

[49]For the instance of Judah, see Aquinas, *Summa Theologiae* II-II, q. 154, a. 2, obj. 3. Aquinas does not here quote Mt 15:19.

[50]These two verses of 1 Corinthians are cited by Aquinas in *Summa Theologiae* II-II, q. 154, a. 3, obj. 2 and 3.

On the basis of rational discernment, Aquinas explains the sinfulness of fornication as being due to the fact that it undercuts the wise order of God's plan for human flourishing. It might seem that the fornicator (male or female) is simply using his or her body to obtain and give sexual pleasure. But as Aquinas explains, fornication—and of course adultery as well— undermines the stability that children need their mother and father to have. The fornicating man and woman have made no binding promises to each other; their act is simply one of satisfying desire for sexual pleasure. The result is that the formation of the stable unions that enable the flourishing of individuals, families, and societies is greatly undermined by fornication. For its part, adultery, which is condemned in the Decalogue (see Ex 20:14), violates the marital vow, jeopardizes the stability of the marriage(s), and results in children not knowing who their father is. With reference to Sirach 23:22-23, Aquinas explains that adultery involves "a twofold offense against chastity and the good of human procreation. First, by accession of a man to a woman who is not joined to him in marriage, which is contrary to the good of the upbringing of his own children. Second, by accession to a woman who is united to another in marriage, and thus he hinders the good of another's children."[51] The emphasis on the damage that our disordered sexual acts do to the most vulnerable among us is illuminating.

Aquinas compares humans in this regard to other emotionally sensitive animals. He argues that God's creative order aims to ensure that where two parents are needed for raising the offspring, indeterminate fornication is avoided. In the case of dogs, where puppies grow up very quickly and "the female suffices for the offspring's upbringing," sexual union is naturally "indeterminate."[52] But a human child does not grow to maturity for many years, and the raising and educating of a human child to function well in the world is difficult. Aquinas remarks that "the upbringing of a human child requires not only the mother's care for his nourishment, but much more the care of his father as guide and guardian, and under whom he progresses in goods both internal and external."[53] Since human children need both their mother and their father, the practice of fornication harms children by

---

[51]Aquinas, *Summa Theologiae* II-II, q. 154, a. 8.
[52]Aquinas, *Summa Theologiae* II-II, q. 154, a. 2.
[53]Ibid.

promoting familial instability and the absence of fathers. It is reasonable, then, that humans direct themselves to individual and social flourishing by avoiding acting upon sexual desire to fornicate, and by instead directing sexual desire to conditions of stable marriage in which the end of procreation (which includes raising the children) can be more suitably attained.

On the basis of the historical fact of the existence of the institution of marriage across cultures and times, Aquinas considers that generally speaking, "human nature rebels against an indeterminate union of the sexes and demands that a man should be united to a determinate woman and should abide with her a long time or even for a whole lifetime."[54] Yet he has no trouble admitting that "among the Gentiles, fornication was not considered unlawful."[55] He grants that his own rejection of fornication is rooted primarily in biblical revelation, which teaches us how to discern and instantiate God's wise order. Uninstructed by revelation, reason does not generally suffice for discerning right and wrong, given the "corruption of natural reason" caused by the fall.[56] He still thinks that fornication can be shown by right reason to be opposed to God's wise order for human flourishing, but he does not pretend that right reason will be able to draw this conclusion easily or generally outside of divine revelation and the grace of the Holy Spirit. After all, for Aquinas "man's reason is right, insofar as it is ruled by the Divine Will, the first and supreme rule"—a rule in which human reason participates in by natural law.[57] Fallen humans have turned away from God, and it is no wonder that they cease to act reasonably in the way that best pertains to true human flourishing.

In contrast to fornication, which modern culture widely embraces, Aquinas and contemporary culture find agreement in opposition to rape.[58] It is evident that such an act does not serve human flourishing, since one of the participants is unwilling and suffers terrible assault. Rape also stands against the ordering of sexual desire to the procreation and raising of children, since such violence attacks the very basis of human community. Likewise, although a sexual relationship between close relatives (incest) is

---

[54] Aquinas, *Summa Theologiae* II-II, q. 154, a. 2.
[55] Aquinas, *Summa Theologiae* II-II, q. 154, a. 2, ad 1.
[56] Ibid.
[57] Aquinas, *Summa Theologiae* II-II, q. 154, a. 2, ad 2.
[58] See Aquinas, *Summa Theologiae* II-II, q. 154, a. 7.

now legally accepted in some European societies, even post-Christian coun-
tries tend to agree with Aquinas that it is morally wrong. Aquinas notes that
Leviticus 18 contains commandments against incest, and he reflects that
"there is something essentially unbecoming and contrary to natural reason
in sexual intercourse between persons related by blood, for instance between parents and children who are directly and immediately related to one
another."[59] It is not reasonable to turn the family into a place of sexual relations, outside of those between husband and wife. Parents and children owe
each other debts of love, but the kinds of love appropriate to close familial
relations do not include forming a new family through sexual intercourse.

Like the Old Testament and Paul, Aquinas does not think that homosexual acts belong to God's wise order for human flourishing. Homosexual
acts employ the sexual organs in ways that violate human sexuality's intrinsic ordering to procreation and the raising of children, by forming male-
male or female-female pairings. Such sexual acts affect not only the individual participants but also inevitably families and communities, as can be
seen today in the redefinition of marriage as not needing a man and a
woman, thereby turning the nature of marriage "into a sterile, unisex affair,"
and also in the now-commonplace production of children through invitro
fertilization or through a surrogate mother.[60] In such situations, the children
born are unjustly deprived from the outset of either their mother (because
the parent and the adoptive parent are two men) or their father (because the
parent and the adoptive parent are two women). With respect to homosexual acts in themselves, it cannot be said that the acts possess an ordering
to a procreative end. Only male-female sexual acts can possess such an ordering. In this sense, Aquinas classifies homosexual acts under lust, because
the ordering of these acts separates sexual pleasure from the end of the
procreation and raising of children, and because "use of the right sex [namely
male or female] is not observed."[61]

Aquinas holds that prior to the fall, sexual intercourse between Adam
and Eve would "have been without lust," but certainly not without strong

---

[59] Aquinas, *Summa Theologiae* II-II, q. 154, a. 9, ad 3.
[60] Douglas Farrow, "Marriage and Freedom: The Splendor of Truth in a Time of Denial," *Nova et Vetera* 11 (2013): 1138.
[61] Aquinas, *Summa Theologiae* II-II, q. 154, a. 12, ad 4.

sexual desire and sexual pleasure, which belong properly to chaste sexual intercourse.[62] Indeed, Aquinas considers that the "sensible delight" that characterizes sexual intercourse would "have been the greater in proportion to the greater purity of nature and the greater sensibility of the body."[63] Commenting on Aquinas's theology of chastity, the Catholic moral theologian Albert Plé observes that what is morally important "is not the intensity of pleasure, but the way (oblatory or narcissistic) in which the power to love is affected."[64] Chastity, therefore, does not aim to "suppress desires and pleasures of the senses."[65] Instead it moderates sexual desire for the sake of fostering a stable family in which children are raised by their mother and father and in which the "one-flesh" communion of the man and woman (Gen 2:24) can image the love of "Christ and the church" (Eph 5:32). I should underscore that for Aquinas, when the married couple is infertile, their sexual intercourse still possesses the appropriate intrinsic ordering to the procreative end of marriage as well as to the strengthening of their marital bond.

These two ends of sexual intercourse are well summed up by the Catholic philosopher J. Budziszewski:

> One is procreation—the bringing about and nurture of new life, the formation of families in which children have moms and dads. The other is union—the mutual and total self-giving and accepting of two polar, complementary selves in their entirety, soul and body. These two meanings are so tightly stitched that we can start with either one and follow the threads to the other.[66]

Separating them is the mark of unchastity, because sexual intercourse is not the work of a soul using a body, but rather of the integrated soul-body person in which the spiritual and bodily ends of sexual intercourse are united. When human sexuality is cut off from its intrinsic connection to the upbuilding of families in which children are raised by their mother and

---

[62] Aquinas, *Summa Theologiae* I, q. 98, a. 2, ad 3.
[63] Aquinas, *Summa Theologiae* I, q. 98, a. 2, ad 3; see also Aquinas's discussion of the nature and function of pleasure in I-II, qq. 31-34, including his position that all good operations will be pleasurable in some way.
[64] Albert Plé, *Chastity and the Affective Life*, trans. Marie Claude Thompson (New York: Herder and Herder, 1966), 124.
[65] Ibid., 125.
[66] J. Budziszewski, *On the Meaning of Sex* (Wilmington, DE: ISI Books, 2012), 24.

father, this harms the person or persons involved in the sexual acts. It also profoundly undermines the stability and flourishing of families, including the family of the inaugurated kingdom of God, the eschatological marriage of Christ and his church that husband and wife are called to image.

CONCLUSION

Jesus does not condone judgmentalism or moralism. He commands his followers not to judge the interior moral condition of others and to "first take the log out of your own eye" before trying to deal with the speck in a neighbor's eye (Mt 7:5). But his eschatological teaching is fully consistent with Paul's warning to the Corinthians: "Do not be deceived; neither the immoral, nor idolaters, nor adulterers, nor homosexuals, nor thieves, nor the greedy, nor drunkards, nor revilers, nor robbers will inherit the kingdom of God" (1 Cor 6:9-10). Specific actions matter. Fortunately, we can repent and, in faith, live in Christ. Thus Paul immediately goes on to say, "And such were some of you. But you were washed, you were sanctified, you were justified in the name of the Lord Jesus Christ and in the Spirit of our God" (1 Cor 6:11).

With Wright, I emphasized that we are called to be royal and priestly images of God in Christ, and to reflect God's wise order in the world. This wise order can be known in various ways, including through human reason's participation in God's "eternal law" or wise plan for human flourishing, whose pattern is not separable from the divine artwork of human bodies. But fallen humans need God's teaching through Scripture if we are to follow the "script" of the inaugurated kingdom. As underscored by God's teachings in Scripture, God intends for sexual desire to be operative in modes that build up stable human families in which the father and mother love each other self-sacrificially and raise and educate their children in Christ. Notwith-standing our frequent failures and the vehemence of our sexual desire, these modes cannot wisely be separated from the channeling of sexual activity within the intrinsic ordering of human sexuality toward procreation and the raising of children.

13

One Soul in Two Bodies

Icons of Sergius and Bacchus
Then and Now

MATTHEW J. MILLINER

IN 1982, A YOUNG YALE PROFESSOR named John Boswell, both gay and Catholic, was in London to give an address to the Gay Christian Movement. His book *Christianity, Social Tolerance, and Homosexuality* (henceforth *CSTH*) had been published two years before, and he was quickly rising to prominence.[1] *CSTH* had proven—for many gay people at least—that Christianity was not the enemy.[2] The book had much in its favor, bearing what might be called an imprimatur and nihil obstat from Michel Foucault himself, and winning the 1981 American Book Award in history.[3] But in 1982, the attacks were mounting. Boswell claimed Christianity emerged in an atmosphere of tolerance to homosexuality (thesis 1) and that to read the Scriptures or early Christians as hostile to homosexuality is simply wrong (thesis 2).[4] Such assertions were countered by many Christian voices as bad exegesis and bad history and were likewise attacked

---

[1]John Boswell, *Christianity, Social Tolerance, and Homosexuality: Gay People in Western Europe from the Beginning of the Christian Era to the Fourteenth Century* (Chicago: University of Chicago Press, 1980).

[2]Mathew Kuefler, *The Boswell Thesis: Essays on Christianity, Social Tolerance, and Homosexuality* (Chicago: University of Chicago Press, 2006), 12.

[3]Foucault's endorsement is emblazoned on the back of the first edition hardcover: "A truly groundbreaking work. Boswell reveals unexplored phenomena with an unfailing erudition."

[4]Kuefler, *Boswell Thesis*, 2.

by gay voices for whom Christianity was still to blame.[5] Indeed, the first two insights of what has come to be called the Boswell Thesis don't sit comfortably together, nor have such insights aged well. The dilemma is straightforward enough: the more one succeeds in proving the first thesis—that homosexuality was well known in the Greco-Roman world—the more difficult it is to make the case that Paul didn't know precisely what it was he was condemning.[6] Moreover, David Halperin complained early on that a one-hundred-year-old category is not a strong enough net to gather the variegated historical instances of same-sex erotics.[7] One of the frustrations—but also delights—of reading Boswell is that he understands this but proceeds with abandon nonetheless, recruiting what he will call "gay saints" like Sergius and Bacchus to his cause. But more was required to buttress his theses. And so at that talk in London, as the critiques were mounting, he unveiled for the first time a crowning insight upon his previous book that could fend off the critics. He claimed to have discovered ample documentation for same-sex unions—properly qualified, he would even say gay marriage—in premodern Europe. It is that claim that I wish to focus on in this chapter. Boswell delivered on his promise twelve years after that 1982 address in *Same Sex Unions in Premodern Europe* (henceforth *SSU*). Tragically, it was published the same year as the brilliant John Boswell died, at only forty-seven years old, of AIDS.

My aim here is to contextualize Boswell's achievement. Indeed, it is even possible to say that only now, well over thirty years after his initial claim about premodern same-sex unions, are we in a place to understand the phenomenon he uncovered. In so doing, I also want to investigate something else about this book—namely, its iconographical repercussions. Boswell, or

---

[5]Responses to the book are catalogued at the Fordham University webpage, "People with a History: An Online Guide to Lesbian, Gay, Bisexual, and Trans History: John Boswell Page," Fordham University, last updated April 11, 2007, http://sourcebooks.fordham.edu/pwh/index-bos.asp, accessed March 3, 2017.

[6]In his well-regarded study of sexuality in late antiquity, Kyle Harper inveighs that "any hermeneutic roundabout that tries to sanitize or soften Paul's words is liable to obscure the inflection point around which attitudes toward same-sex erotics would be forever altered." Kyle Harper, *From Shame to Sin: The Christian Transformation of Sexual Morality in Late Antiquity* (Cambridge, MA: Harvard University Press, 2013), 95. Boswell has certainly been the most famous of such hermeneutical roundabouts.

[7]David M. Halperin, *One Hundred Years of Homosexuality: And Other Essays on Greek Love* (New York: Routledge, 1990).

perhaps his publisher, chose to place a sixth-century Sergius and Bacchus on the cover of *SSU*. The icon shows both saints, executed for their Christian faith under the emperor Maximian (r. 286–305), holding the martyr's cross. They are dressed for the imperial court in jeweled torques, and their individual halos are elegantly unified by their Lord who hovers between them.[8] The ancient Christian trope used to describe such brotherhood was "one soul in two bodies."[9] Jesus—not their parents—bound them together. Notwithstanding its original context, the placement of this icon on the cover of *SSU* is what catapulted Sergius and Bacchus into their present status as gay icons. In this chapter I will trace the claims of *SSU*, how such claims have been most recently contested, and how that might help us grapple with the book's iconographical progeny today.

SERGIUS AND BACCHUS AND SAME-SEX UNIONS

SSU begins by admitting that because premodern societies did not have the heterosexual/homosexual distinction we have today, the question "Were they homosexual?" is anachronistic and "to some extent unanswerable."[10] But Boswell aims to answer it anyway, even if exercising the normal skills of a historian amid antigay prejudice of our time is like "attempting to perfect the breast stroke against a riptide."[11] Building upon the thesis of *CSTH*, he feels justified in assuming that sex was going on. He even goes so far as to refer to Jesus and John as a "same-sex couple," adding that the description of them in the Bible is "intimate if not erotic."[12] But his star case is Sergius and Bacchus.[13] "Peter and Paul may have been

---

[8]For a catalog entry of the original icon, see Robert S. Nelson and Kristen M. Collines, eds., *Holy Image, Hallowed Ground: Icons from Sinai* (Los Angeles: J. Paul Getty Museum, 2006), 127. Whether the icon is fifth or sixth century is debated.

[9]Claudia Rapp, *Brother-Making in Late Antiquity and Byzantium: Monks, Laymen, and Christian Ritual* (New York: Oxford University Press, 2016), 32. Hereafter *BMLB*.

[10]John Boswell, *Same-Sex Unions in Premodern Europe* (New York: Villard Books, 1994), xxv. Hereafter *SSU*.

[11]Ibid., xxvii.

[12]Boswell adds that Jerome's attempt to emphasize John's youthful virginal status did not succeed because "unmarried men were expected to provoke desire among older men." Ibid., 139.

[13]It is well worth hearing Boswell describe these "gay saints" in a recording of a University of Wisconsin in 1986. John Boswell, "Jews, Gay People, and Bicycle Riders," YouTube video, 47:07–50:12, from a lecture presented by Nothing to Hide, Madison, WI, 1986, posted by "georgelmosseprogram," October 20, 2012, www.youtube.com/watch?v=DwEAZNdJ-J4.

overinterpreted as romantic pairs," he admits, "but Serge and Bacchus were probably correctly so understood."[14]

Boswell translates the life of Sergius and Bacchus in the appendix, where readers will encounter several things that seem to resist his interpretation that these two men were gay lovers. First, the central passage that Sergius and Bacchus prayed together, as if with one mouth, was from Romans chapter one. "Because they walk in the darkness of their unknowing; they have exchanged your glory, uncorruptible, God, for the likeness of corruptible men and birds and beasts."[15] No doubt some readers might have known what comes in the following two verses. And what stitches these saints together, moreover, is the recitation of the great Psalm of the Law, 119. "We will delight ourselves in thy statutes: we will not forget thy word. . . . I will run the way of thy commandments, when thou hast enlargened my heart."[16] Boswell translates his key line of evidence in this way: "For the crown of justice for me is with you."[17] However, he changes the translation in the main text to read, "For the crown of justice for me is *to be* with you."[18] This is quite the flourish of interpretation. But even if we grant it to him, Boswell doesn't seem to realize that this may actually reflect a motif from the New Testament, rather than a confession of desire of two men to be romantically entwined for eternity. First Thessalonians 2:19-20 reads, "For what is our hope or joy or crown of boasting before our Lord Jesus at his coming? Is it not you? Yes, you are our glory and joy!" (NRSV). Boswell, furthermore, claims that this kind of emotional intimacy—the desire to be with one another in the afterlife—is unique. But it is actually a common trope in the Byzantine world. We have numerous stories of saints bonded together, buried together, and hoping to be united in the life to come.[19] "For we will shortly depart from this world," says Paul to John in an early fifth-century saint's life, "and in the company of our Lord we will forever rejoice with one another."[20]

---

[14]Boswell, *SSU*, 219.
[15]Ibid., 378.
[16]Ibid., 382, 385.
[17]Ibid., 385.
[18]Ibid., 150.
[19]Rapp, *BMLB*, 145, 152-53.
[20]Ibid., 145.

But why then do Sergius and Bacchus appear in the same-sex union ceremonies, which they do? Moreover, Boswell calls them marriages. "According to the modern conception—i.e., a permanent emotional union acknowledged in some way by the community—it was unequivocally a
marriage."[21] But when we read them—for Boswell encourages us to judge
for ourselves—we encounter the same kind of mitigating factors that seem
to ward off the kinds of interpretation Boswell encourages.[22] In one of the
ceremonies, there is even a mention of how "love saved Lot from the
Sodomites."[23] Far more significantly, in these brother-making ceremonies
we repeatedly read that these unions should take place "without offence or
scandal." Even Boswell admits this "might be read as warnings against a
sexual component."[24] In fact, we have a case where just such a scandal *did*
involve homosexual associations.[25] That is, we have a monastic situation
where the possibility of homosexual activity uses the word *skandalon*, which
shows up in the ceremonies.

But it will not do to just comb through Boswell's translations and dispute
them. That has been done in countless reviews and is rather tedious. What
is needed is a full-scale understanding of what these rituals are and why
Sergius and Bacchus played a role in them. In the endless responses to
Boswell's book, Claudia Rapp is acknowledged—by a project very friendly
to Boswell—as the "best place to start" to assess his project.[26] She is deemed
fair-minded, and she does not resort to ad hominem attacks as so many
people have. Rapp's balanced 1997 review has now become a full-length
study on *Brother-Making in Late Antiquity and Byzantium* (henceforth
BMLB). Rapp takes pains to point out at the beginning she is in "no way
attempting to undermine the legitimacy of seeking recognition for same-sex

---

[21]Boswell, *SSU*, 190.
[22]Ibid., 191.
[23]Ibid., 293. While Boswell attempted to distance Sodom from homosexuality in *CSTH*, in a *SSU*
footnote he confesses that he missed "an occurrence of the noun *arsenokoitai* in Eusebius that
connects it to Sodom." Ibid., 219.
[24]Boswell holds out hope that "without offense or scandal" in the brother-making ceremonies
might just be that they would only have sex with each other and not partners external to the
union. He bases this on the fact that "'chastity' is never mentioned or appealed to in same sex
unions." Ibid., 205-6. It is quite the stretch to call this the "only reasonable interpretation" of the
warnings against scandal.
[25]Rapp, *BMLB*, 146. In other cases it is difficult to determine. Ibid., 163, 168.
[26]"People with a History," Fordham University.

partnerships in current societies." Her concern is instead the historical record. Rapp is appreciative of Boswell, but she claims the "ecclesiastical ritual of brother-making was not formulated with a view to the sexual dimension." Adding, of course, that "it is difficult to see any further than that when the bedroom lights are out."[27]

SPIRITUAL FRIENDSHIP

Rapp's method in *BMLB* begins with disputing the marriage analogy to brother-making ceremonies. It is not, as Boswell insisted, "inescapably clear" that the term *adelphopoiēsis* meant "lover" or "form an erotic union" to "contemporaries."[28] This is why Rapp chooses the much more direct translation "brother-making," whereas Boswell chose "same-sex unions" (which he termed the "only honest methodology").[29] When, furthermore, Orthodox marriage customs are understood, it is quite clear that "the ritual of *adelphopoiēsis* does not show any significant resemblance to that of marriage during the Byzantine period."[30] There are no rings, and there is no crowning—key ingredients to any Orthodox wedding. A better analogy for the brother-making ceremonies is the baptismal rites of Christian initiation or godparenthood.[31]

Moreover, the deep roots of the practice are not marriage but the intimacies of monasticism. Gregory of Nazinanzus and Basil of Caesarea, for example, experienced *erōs* for one another, which Rapp translates as "'fervent attraction' without the slightest hint of a physical component."[32] Lest one think it is concealed prudery demanding such interpretations, such an approach is also a cutting edge of queer theory. James Davidson has tried to transcend "sodomania" to realize there were multiple kinds of homosociality in ancient Greece, many of them not including a genital component.[33] Chaste same-sex friendships in antiquity afforded a precedent for the

---

[27]Rapp, *BMLB*, 47.
[28]Boswell, *SSU*, 19.
[29]Ibid., 25.
[30]Rapp, *BMLB*, 76.
[31]Boswell never quite tells us whether he had seen any of the manuscripts in person. Rapp has personally handled 43 out of the 66 that survive. Ibid., 59.
[32]Ibid., 38.
[33]James Davidson, *The Greeks and Greek Love: A Radical Reappraisal of Homosexuality in Ancient Greece* (London: Weidenfeld & Nicolson, 2007).

relationships enjoyed by Christian monks. Christians transposed the pagan notion of friendship—already quite high in Aristotle—to an even higher key, "adding God as the *tertium quid*."[34] The ritual of *adelphopoiēsis* grew from this fertile soil.

When viewed within the entire history of Byzantine monasticism, brother-making appears quite normal. Intimate bonds of union formed. And while we just can't know if sex occurred, we can know heterosexual or homosexual activity was continually, explicitly condemned for monks, who had taken the path of celibacy. In the urtext of monasticism, for example, the spirit of lust vanquished by Antony appears to him as a boy.[35] Monks frequently lived in close contact between two men or very small groups. We have archaeological evidence of their close quarters (and texts that match) to show they could be roomed in singles or pairs—but pairs of brothers in these contexts were standard.[36] Rapp explains that these men "substitute[d] biological ties and perhaps those of marriage with a new society of men who share the same purpose of spiritual advancement."[37] The abbot was your father, the monks your siblings, a relationship perfectly expressed in the "not bound by nature, but by faith" lines in the brother-making ceremonies.[38] In fact "the language of kinship became so normative and pervasive in the monastic context that it was biological brotherhood that called for additional qualifiers."[39] Obviously, these relationships could be emotionally intense, and "the possibility of sexual relations can never be excluded,"[40] but precautions were taken to avoid sexual improprieties.[41] Some incidents surviving in the written record can be read perhaps as punishments for committing sex acts, though it is admittedly difficult to know for sure.[42] But sex was excluded in principle for a

---

[34]Rapp, *BMLB*, 36.
[35]Athanasius, *The Life of Antony and the Letter to Marcellinus*, trans. Robert C. Gregg (New York: Paulist Press, 1980), 34. Rapp likewise speculates that the *Life of Symeon* was written to show that the saint was "equally immune" to opposite-sex and same-sex temptations. Rapp, *BMLB*, 161.
[36]Rapp, *BMLB*, 100.
[37]Ibid., 101.
[38]Ibid., 83.
[39]Ibid., 101. The praising of these relationships contains direct overlap with what would become the ceremonies. Ibid., 132.
[40]Ibid., 138.
[41]Ibid., 139.
[42]Ibid., 139-40.

simple reason. Following Paul, "a monastic pair is to be considered far superior to marriage."[43]

But if the ritual of brotherhood emerged from the "widespread, respected, and respectable" fact of paired monasticism, it did not stop there.[44] Soon the ritual leapt beyond the monastery walls.[45] Slowly, it evolved into what was basically a network strategy, manifesting a desire for spiritual or political advancement. When, for example, in the seventh century the patriarch of Constantinople sought to be united to the holy man Theodore of Sykeon, it was "to be assured of his prayers as an intercessor in this life and in the next."[46] Being united to the holy man in brotherhood assured him the prayer would be offered. The goal was mutual support. As troubling times swept through the empire, "Spiritual kinship offered the possibility of an extension of family relations across the monastic-lay boundary in a way that could be regarded as legitimate because it involved an ecclesiastical ritual."[47] One famous example is a wealthy woman arranging a spiritual brotherhood for her son with a man named Basil when she hears the prophecy that he will become an emperor. Boswell interpreted this as a cover for gay sex.[48] While this cannot be ruled out, the far clearer indiscretion illustrated here is excessive ambition. The plot finally enabled the wealthy widow to be processed to Constantinople when her son attained his high status under Emperor Basil I.[49]

We do, however, have cases where sex does seem to clearly be involved in these rituals, but interestingly it was between a woman and a man. It was evident that brother-making rituals—or sibling-making in this case—were sometimes a cover for adultery and were quickly disciplined. As Rapp puts it, "These condemnations confirm that sexual relations were not expected or intended to follow from the ritual, at least in the understanding of the

---

[43]Ibid., 142.
[44]Ibid., 151. "Paired monasticism was a widespread, respected, and respectable option within the spectrum of monastic living arrangements." Ibid., 157. All three great monastic reform movements in Byzantine history encourage such pairings. Ibid., 177.
[45]Ibid., 171.
[46]Ibid., 189.
[47]Ibid., 193.
[48]Boswell, *SSU*, 231-39.
[49]Rapp, *BMLB*, 201-10.

priests who performed it."[50] When we learn that sibling-making could also happen between Catholics and Greeks, and sometimes with other religions as well, the reason for the crackdown on these rituals is clear. Not because of—as befits the Boswell thesis—a sweeping gust of homophobia but because the ritual threatened to undermine the ties of communities.

But perhaps most troubling for Boswell's attempt to tether brother-making to same-sex erotics is that we actually do have record in Byzantium of two male lovers who were in dialogue with the emperor as to whether their relationship as lovers prohibited their sisters from getting married. The fact that they referred to each other as lovers and not brothers indicated "there was no need to employ brother-making to formalize their relationships."[51]

In sum, brother-making ceremonies emerged from the deep bonds formed by pairs of monks in ancient Christianity. The rituals of bonding then crossed the boundaries of the monasteries, involving lay people, who sometimes exploited the ritual as a means of social advancement. But they could still be used for their original purpose—to seal and ratify a deep Christian friendship or perhaps to heal a rift. And that is how they have continued, albeit rarely, to this day. We can imagine that Boswell, who launched *CSTH* with a meditation on the inevitably provisional nature of scholarship, would have conceded many of these developments.[52]

FIN-DE-SIÈCLE ICONS

Meanwhile, however, something strange was happening to the icon of Sergius and Bacchus that had been used on the cover of Boswell's book. Early public controversy regarding *SSU* appeared in Garry Trudeau's nationally syndicated cartoon *Doonesbury*, where the sagacious progressive tortures the hidebound conservative with the unimpeachable truth of Boswell's thesis, making the conservative who can't handle the truth sick to his stomach. But the history of these ceremonies, as we've seen, is a good bit more complex than a comic strip can convey. The more immediate and pervasive visual response, however, came from the icons.

---

[50]Ibid., 238.

[51]Ibid., 241.

[52]The specific quote is from the great French historian Henri Pirenne, for whom "rapid obsolescence . . . is the very proof of the progress of scholarship." Boswell, *CSTH*, 3.

Take, for example, the contemporary icon painter and Franciscan priest Robert Lentz, who gave us the well-known modern icons of Thomas Merton, Oscar Romero, Dorothy Day, Martin Luther King Jr., and Cesar Chavez. Lentz is not cavalier. "I can't paint heresy, I can't paint falsehood. . . . How do I justify what seems like the good thing to do, because if I can't justify it I'm not just going to do it to make somebody feel good."[53] Many of his icons are very responsible and necessary additions to the canon. His icon of Sergius and Bacchus was painted the same year as Boswell's *Same Sex Unions* was published.[54] The icon itself is actually quite cautious. Echoing the phrase that encapsulates the brother-making ceremonies, Lentz paints not one soul and one body, but "one soul in two bodies." Their bodies are not united in Lentz's icon, nor in the sixth-century original. But if the space separating them conveys any expectations of chastity, that does not appear to be how the icon has been interpreted. The original was processed in the Chicago Gay Pride parade the year of its creation, helping launch Sergius and Bacchus to their status as gay icons today.

Lentz went on to revive the iconography of two other saints that Boswell discussed, Polyeuct and Nearchus. This image first appeared in 1998 at a welcoming ceremony at Chicago's Episcopal Cathedral of St. James with Robert Lentz in attendance.[55] In this icon, however, the embrace between the two saints tightens, with a heart effect conveyed by their merging halos.[56]

But then, the deluge. The readily google-able icons that followed Lentz certainly put the Bacchus in Sergius and Bacchus. Later uses of the theme, inescapably salacious, leave little to the imagination. It is not uncommon to see such icons as portals—not to the prototypes themselves as Byzantine tradition teaches, but to some less savory sites on the internet. How then is

---

[53]Robert Lentz OFM, "Episode 8—Jesus Christ Liberator," YouTube video, 1:01-1:20, March 30, 2015, www.youtube.com/watch?v=9TNhMtnouP0.

[54]The image can be seen on his website, where it is accompanied by Boswell's interpretation of the saints: "Recent attention to early Greek manuscripts has also revealed that they were openly gay men. These manuscripts indicate acceptance of homosexuality by earlier Christians." Robert Lentz OFM, "Sergius and Bacchus," image plus commentary dated 2014, accessed March 3, 2017, http://robertlentz.com/selected-works.

[55]Dennis O'Neill, *Passionate Holiness: Marginalized Christian Devotions for Distinctive Peoples* (Victoria, BC: Trafford Publishing, 2010), 83.

[56]Lentz's "Saints Polyeuct and Nearchus" (1995) icon can be viewed at Flikr.com, "Saints Polyeuct and Nearchus by Robert Lentz," posted by Kittredge Cherry, February 16, 2010, www.flickr.com/photos/jesusinlove/4363823458.

one to respond to this proliferation of images? The saints have emerged as icons for the gay community, which has been unjustly brutalized. But considering what we now know about Boswell's original argument, it is difficult not to sympathize with the Orthodox priest who complains that when he sought icons of his own tradition, unduly erotic images were the first that surfaced on the web.[57]

One way forward perhaps is to set such icons in broad historical relief. Which is to say, this is not the first time that Byzantine images have been so employed. To contextualize these images, it is instructive to look at the use and abuse of the Orthodox visual tradition, not in America at the end of the last millennium but in Vienna a century before. The Austrian painter Gustav Klimt deployed the gold ground of Byzantine mosaics to lend a heavenly aura to the erotic imagery he painted in the city of Sigmund Freud. And though Klimt is known to have a voyeuristic fascination with lesbians, it is his heterosexual affairs that might be the target of traditional Christian concern. After all, as Kyle Harper puts it, the attacks on heterosexual fornication dwarfed any ancient Christian animus toward same-sex acts.[58]

The environment in which Klimt emerged in Vienna is well described in a 1911 comedy by Marco Brocener. "An artist," says one of the characters, "as his long as his creative power is fresh and original, must have no ties, must be free as a bird in the air. He should regard woman only as an episode, as a sweet plaything. Should he marry, he will have a bothersome nuisance in his home, his concentration will lack the inner calm from which great works are born."[59] Such was the Viennese atmosphere, "marked by its blend of intellect and eroticism," in which Klimt emerged.[60] Some feminists hail him for having led these sweet young things "on their path to freedom by lifting the taboo over eroticism,"[61] but a Christian might not agree. Others point

---

[57]Father Edward Pehanich, "A Twisted Tale of Two Saints: Sts Sergius and Baccus," American Carpatho-Russian Orthodox Diocese of the USA, accessed March 3, 2017, www.acrod.org/read ingroom/saints/sergius-bacchus. Father Pehanich's concluding words are pertinent: "While we affirm and uphold the teaching of our Faith and teach the need for repentance, we must never treat those who identify themselves as gay with hatred, contempt, or rejection."
[58]Harper, *From Shame to Sin*, 143.
[59]Tobias G. Natter and Gerbert Frodl, eds., *Klimt's Women* (New Haven: Yale University Press, 2000), 28.
[60]Ibid., 30.
[61]Ibid., 31. See also Jill Lloyd, ed., *Birth of the Modern: Style and Identity in Vienna 1900* (Munich, Germany: Hirmer Verlag, 2011), 137.

out that "Klimt clearly divided women into those he respected, even exalted, and those he slept with."[62] This sounds far too close to the sexual mores of ancient Rome, which Christianity successfully opposed.

The persistence of those Christian mores is why Klimt enjoyed the *succès de scandale* that came from his university paintings, commissioned one hundred years before Lentz's Sergius and Bacchus icons. As J. B. Bullen put it, Klimt chose the most incorporeal style—the Byzantine icon—to couch his message of "salvation through physical coition."[63] Other artists, however, remixed Byzantine art as a summons to traditional faith. Even more so than Vienna, Paris at the end of the nineteenth century was inhabited by the soul of Byzantium.[64] But for Maurice Denis the style did not signify decadence but the "antidote against the poison of naturalism."[65] For Denis, "Byzantine painting is surely the most perfect type of Christian art," and was now the mark of any truly modern art.[66] Byzantine painting was the "magnificence of the immutable," and "an equivalence between the harmony of forms and the logic of Dogma."[67] And so the Byzantine tradition could be distorted to encode new sexual liberties or recast as a call for Christian renewal in the face of decadence.[68]

Perhaps a contemporary corollary to Denis can be found in Mark Dukes's interior painting cycle at San Francisco's St. Gregory of Nyssa Episcopal Church, completed in 2009. Like Robert Lentz, Dukes offers a version of Sergius and Bacchus. But the descriptive phrasing that accompanies the pair is exceedingly responsible and more accurately reflects what we now know about the brother-making ceremonies with which Sergius and Bacchus were associated: "The ancient veneration of these two men offers gay Christians and those who love and support them a ray of hope showing the Church openly honored two people of the same gender in a loving relationship."[69]

[62]Ibid., 133.

[63]J. B. Bullen, *Byzantium Rediscovered* (London; New York: Phaidon, 2003), 51.

[64]Michael Paul Driskel, *Representing Belief: Religion, Art, and Society in Nineteenth-Century France* (University Park, PA: Pennsylvania State University Press, 1992), 231.

[65]Ibid., 228.

[66]Ibid., 236.

[67]Ibid.

[68]See the repeated discussion of Maurice Denis in the excellent study by Jonathan Anderson and William Dyrness, *Modern Art and the Life of a Culture* (Downers Grove, IL: InterVarsity Press, 2016).

[69]"Short Biographies of Some of God's Friends," St. Gregory of Nyssa Episcopal Church, accessed March 3, 2017, www.saintgregorys.org/saints-by-name.html.

While they are not called gay—for the category did not then exist—the saints do indeed offer hope for contemporary Christians who identify as gay. Brother-making was not, as Boswell believed, gay marriage. But it was, we now know, well described as "an open honoring of two people of the same gender in a loving relationship." That is a statement for which Rapp's more exhaustive research gives ample historical precedent. This deployment of the ancient iconographical tradition assists in the delicate task of welcoming Christians who identify as gay while reminding them that to walk the challenging path of celibacy is not to walk alone.

REFRAMING BOSWELL'S JEWISH ANALOGY

The Boswell thesis comprises four points, only two of which have been mentioned thus far. His remaining claims were "that early medieval Christians showed no real animosity toward same-sex eroticism" (thesis 3) and "that it was only in the twelfth and thirteenth centuries that Christian writers formulated a significant hostility toward homosexuality, and then read that hostility back into their scriptures and early tradition" (thesis 4).[70] Whether or not these theses can withstand the scrutiny of new developments in research is beyond the scope of this chapter.[71] But however hostility to same-sex activity is measured, the penalties—the incineration of male prostitutes, for example—testify to the intoxicating combination of Christianity with political power.[72] To state the obvious, we must prefer our society's approach to homosexual practice, or to adultery for that matter (the penalty for which, under Emperor Justinian, was death).[73] And it is here that Boswell can be of special assistance. He was fond of making the connection of gay people to the Jews, an analogy that offers an instructive way forward—albeit in a manner Boswell might not have intended.[74]

---

[70]Kuefler, *Boswell Thesis*, 2.
[71]Kyle Harper would be one place to start. If "slaves [in Greco-Roman culture] were subjected to untrammeled sexual abuse" (*From Shame to Sin*, 26), then Christianity's condemnation of fornication of all kinds was liberating precisely because it applied to slaves as well. To deliberately distort Nietzsche's phrase, Christianity truly offered a slave morality, which is part of what made it revolutionary. When the Christian transvaluation of all values was complete, a slave could even accuse his master of sexual abuse, "signaling a total breakdown of the ancient sexual order" (15).
[72]Harper, *From Shame to Sin*, 153.
[73]Boswell, *CSTH*, 171.
[74]Ibid., 273.

Needless to say, Christian persecution of Jews was horrific as well. But such catastrophic failures are now more visible, causing many to describe our time as one of "dramatic and unprecedented shift in Jewish Christian relations."[75] Accusations of anti-Semitism can now take their place in a wider reexamination of Christianity's complicity in the persecution of Jews. "We show our Christianity," said T. S. Eliot, "in the way in which we are aware of our faults and shortcomings, and the way in which we are sorry for them."[76] Faced with Martin Luther's anti-Semitism, responsible theologians have argued it is "neither in harmony with the core of his theology nor with the stance of the apostle Paul regarding the relationship between Jews and Christians . . . consequently, Luther's attitude to the Jews is against his better judgment."[77] But all of this, for a Christian at least, can be asserted while believing that Jesus is the Messiah whom the Jews were wrong to reject.[78]

It is here that Boswell's Jewish analogy can be newly deployed. The shift that has happened to the acceptance of gay and lesbian persons is better than their rampant persecution in late antiquity, in the Middle Ages, or more recently in the United States. But we can celebrate that achievement while continuing to urge the path of celibacy, which Boswell eloquently described as "not denying sexuality, but dedicating it."[79] Which is to say, the supposed choice between homophobia and an unqualified celebration of homosexual practice is as false a dichotomy as the choice between anti-Semitism and denial that Jesus is the Christ. If "a *Christian* Jesus . . . [is] good news for Judaism and for Jews," then traditional Christian sexual ethics can be good news for the gay community as well.[80]

---

[75]"Dabru Emet: A Jewish Statement on Christians and Christianity," in *Jews and Christians: People of God*, ed. Carl E. Braaten and Robert W. Jenson (Grand Rapids: Eerdmans, 2003), 179ff. The interdenominational signatories are Tikva Frymer-Kensky (University of Chicago), David Novak (University of Toronto), Peter Ochs (University of Virginia), and Michael Singer (University of Notre Dame).

[76]T. S. Eliot, "Sermon Preached in Magdalene College Chapel, 6," cited in Jason Harding, ed., *T. S. Eliot in Context* (Cambridge: Cambridge University Press, 2011), 310.

[77]Eric Gritsch, *Martin Luther's Anti-Semitism: Against His Better Judgment* (Grand Rapids: Eerdmans, 2012), 138.

[78]Such a strategy, moreover, is recommended by Christian and Jews alike. See Peter Ochs, *Another Reformation: Postliberal Christianity and the Jews* (Grand Rapids: Baker Academic, 2011); Jacques Ellul, *An Unjust God? A Christian Theology of Israel in Light of Romans 9-11* (Eugene, OR: Cascade Books, 2012).

[79]John Boswell, "Jews, Gay People, and Bicycle Riders," 1:31:49.

[80]Paul Zahl, *The First Christian: Universal Truth in the Teachings of Jesus* (Grand Rapids: Eerdmans, 2003), 10.

The ancient brother-making ceremonies, moreover, give the church ample precedent for honoring pairs of same-sex Christians who seek to live this struggle *together*. Such ceremonies might afford a daring third way that simultaneously acknowledges the deficit in same-sex friendships in our society without endorsing same-sex marriage. A concluding example from Byzantium illustrates this well—a Sergius and Bacchus–like relationship at its best that is anything but a cover for fornication. It comes from the *Spiritual Meadow* by John Moschus, composed around 600 AD. The story speaks of two brothers pursuing the ascetic life who have sworn never to be separated from each other.[81] As was commonly said in Byzantium, they were to "drive the golden chariot of virtue" together.[82] But when one of them backslides to pursue sexual fulfillment, the bonded friendship is what ultimately brings the wandering partner back. Asked to be released from brotherhood, the wavering partner is denied. The faithful partner even follows his backsliding brother into the city where he stands outside the "den of fornication" while his brother indulges in sin. They worked together as day laborers, but each night the pattern continues, one brother giving himself to the pleasures of the city, while the other repents for his brother's sin. Worn down by his partner's resolve, the erring brother at last repents, and they return to the wilderness *together* to be saved. For a church seeking to illustrate this kind of friendship in their sanctuaries, an icon of Sergius and Bacchus—in its original sixth-century formulation at least—remains an excellent choice. Both saints hold the cross of martyrdom, refusing to succumb to an ancient—or modern—empire's demands.[83]

---

[81]Harper, *From Shame to Sin*, 237.

[82]Rapp, *BMLB*, 173.

[83]The July/August 2013 cover of *Spirituality & Health* issued one such command: "Thou Shalt Have Great Sex." The story's subtitle was "In a world where Judeo-Christian faith no longer writes the rules on intimacy, who will define the new sexual ethics?" Don Lattin, "In Pursuit of Sacred Sex," *Spirituality & Health*, July/August 2013, http://spiritualityhealth.com/articles/pursuit-sacred-sex.

14

What Makes Sex Beautiful?

Marriage, Aesthetics, and the Image of God in Genesis 1–2 and Revelation 21–22

MATT O'REILLY

W HEN IT COMES TO SEX, evangelicals tend to be known for what we are against rather than for what we favor. We are well-known for telling people the sort of sex they are having—or desire to have—is bad. Sadly, we are not generally known for setting forth a theological vision of human sexuality, marriage, and singleness that is positive, constructive, and lovely. I happily affirm that our shared commitment to the sacred union between a man and woman is good and true, but I also fear that we have not always successfully articulated and embodied the beauty of that union. Our reputation is one of critique, not celebration. We seem always on our heels, always playing defense, always deconstructing as we respond to the latest novelty of aberrant sexual practice.

Please do not misunderstand me; we certainly need that sort of work. We need competent and courageous people to expose the problems and dangers of sexual behavior not aligned with God's best. We need pastors, laypersons, and scholars who understand why the alternatives to God's design are harmful and who can engage the arguments with winsome clarity and substance.[1] The deconstructive task is essential. But the deconstructing tool

---

[1]See, e.g., Robert A. J. Gagnon, *The Bible and Homosexual Practice: Texts and Hermeneutics* (Nashville: Abingdon Press, 2002). For an example of the deconstructive task in my own ecclesial

cannot be the only one in our box. In fact, it probably should not be the first tool for which we reach. We must also be about the constructive task of setting forth a positive and beautiful vision of biblical and historic Christian sexuality.[2] Both approaches are necessary.

There are plenty of people in our churches who know instinctively that the many and varied sexualities presently abounding in our culture are inherently problematic. The problem is that we—their pastors—have not given them a robust theology of human sexuality to substantiate the tradition they have inherited. This is not to suggest that no one is writing helpful books about human sexuality; it is to suggest that such material seldom finds its way into the regular teaching ministry of many local churches. And so, without solid constructive and compelling theology, our people are left to be "tossed to and fro and blown about by every wind of doctrine" (Eph 4:14).[3]

At this point in the game, it should be exceedingly clear to us that rational argument alone will not win the day. We can spout off syllogisms with regularity, but we should not—indeed, we cannot—assume that this strategy will be effective to persuade others that our view is true and theirs false, or that our view is good and theirs bad. All of us are likely to understand that such approaches often heighten defensiveness and make persuasion all the less likely. That is where the argument of this paper comes in. In seeking to persuade others of the Christian vision of sexuality, the vision we set forth must be not only true and good but beautiful as well. Or to put it another way, we cannot rely solely on logic and ethics; we must also do aesthetics.

Why aesthetics? The answer is given by Catholic philosopher and theologian Peter Kreeft who has observed that "there is no argument against beauty." Kreeft insists that truth, goodness, and beauty "are the three things

---

context written with charity and excellence, see Bill T. Arnold, *Seeing Black and White in a Gray World: The Need for Theological Reasoning in the Church's Debate over Sexuality* (Franklin, TN: Seedbed Publishing, 2014). For a non-faith-based approach, see Sherif Girgis, Ryan T. Anderson, and Robert P. George, *What Is Marriage? Man and Woman: A Defense* (New York: Encounter Books, 2012); Patrick Lee and Robert P. George, *Conjugal Union: What Marriage Is and Why It Matters* (New York: Cambridge University Press, 2014).

[2]For a recent and accessible book that engages in this constructive task, see Beth Felker Jones, *Faithful: A Theology of Sex* (Grand Rapids: Zondervan, 2015).

[3]All scriptural quotations in this chapter are from the New Revised Standard Version unless otherwise noted.

we all need, and need absolutely, and know we need, and know we need absolutely."[4] If we want to be found persuasive when it comes to the church's millennia-old teaching on marriage and sexuality, we must not only set forth logical and moral arguments; we must also set forth a vision of such stunning beauty that no argument can be raised against it. And in so doing, we will discover the truth of one further point made by Kreeft, namely that "aesthetics proves to be more, not less, adequate than intellectual or moral analogies."[5] Beauty is a delight, brothers and sisters, and because it is a delight, it is also deeply persuasive.

So with the essay before you, I hope to begin constructing a framework for thinking about human sexuality in a way that magnifies the beauty of sex as God intended. We will discover that sexual intimacy expressed in the context of heterosexual covenant monogamy is beautiful and desirable, first because it embodies and amplifies the faithful creational love of the triune God, and second because it embodies and amplifies the new creational love of God by pointing forward to the coming redemption, not only of the human race, but of the cosmos as a whole. To put it another way, sex is beautiful because it is the consummate act of a relationship that uniquely reveals the creative and redemptive love of the triune God. To see that, we need to be thinking about sex in relation to theology proper, origins, and eschatology.

A Theological and Aesthetic Approach

Before jumping into the argument itself, I need to say a few things about my method and presuppositions. We need to consider what it means to take a theological and aesthetic approach to what Scripture says about sex and marriage. First, this project is canonically oriented. That is to say, it aims to provide a framework that accounts for and makes sense of the whole of Christian Scripture.[6] All too often when we talk about sex, we focus on this

---

[4]Peter Kreeft, "Lewis's Philosophy of Truth, Goodness, and Beauty," in *C. S. Lewis as Philosopher: Truth, Goodness, and Beauty*, ed. David J. Baggett, Gary R. Habermas, and Jerry L. Walls (Downers Grove, IL: IVP Academic, 2008), 23.

[5]Ibid., 30.

[6]The importance of canonically oriented interpretation by pastor theologians is highlighted by Kevin J. Vanhoozer, "The Pastor Theologian as Public Theologian," in *Becoming a Pastor Theologian: New Possibilities for Church Leadership*, ed. Todd Wilson and Gerald Hiestand (Downers Grove, IL: InterVarsity Press, 2016), 44; cf. Peter Leithart, "The Pastor Theologian as Biblical Theologian: From the Church for the Church," in *Becoming a Pastor Theologian*, 13-17.

or that verse without seeing each one in light of the bigger canonical picture. My insistence that we need to take the whole of Scripture into account flows out of a deep conviction that all of Scripture should be taken seriously as authoritative for the life of the church and its members. Second, the project is theological and trinitarian. By that I mean that I operate with the conviction that the canon speaks to us about God, and the specific God about whom it speaks is the God revealed in Christ and the Spirit, the God who is triune.[7] So while historical criticism of the Bible is important, it is not the endgame. As a member of the clergy and as a Christian reader of Christian Scripture, I am keenly interested to hear what the triune God has to say through Scripture in order that I may faithfully contribute to ordering the life of the church. In this way, this project is an exercise in reading Scripture for the church.

I have already hinted at the third feature of my approach, namely that this project aims to be particularly attentive to aesthetic dimensions of the texts under consideration. I take it as a foundational presupposition that the triune God is the most beautiful being who ever has or ever will exist. All that is beautiful derives its beauty from him, and nothing that is beautiful is so apart from him. Sadly, though, as Richard Viladesau has argued, "theology has often neglected beauty as an object of inquiry."[8] Hans Urs von Balthasar argues this neglect is due in part to using scientific methods for the work of theology.[9] The result is theology as abstract rationalism that is thoroughly unimaginative and uninspiring. We stand in need of recovering an approach to theology that is inherently poetic and accounts for affective dimensions of experience. We need to do theology in a way that attends to the beautiful.[10] Theological aesthetics offer us a way forward. Viladesau defines "theological aesthetics" as interpreting "the objects of aesthetics—sensation, the beautiful, and art—from the properly theological starting point of religious conversion and in light of theological methods."[11] Reading

---

[7]Allan Coppedge, *The God Who Is Triune: Revisioning the Christian Doctrine of God* (Downers Grove, IL: IVP Academic, 2007), 23-78.

[8]Richard Viladesau, *Theological Aesthetics: God in Imagination, Beauty, and Art* (New York: Oxford University Press, 1999), 12.

[9]Hans Urs von Balthasar, *The Glory of the Lord: A Theological Aesthetics*, ed. Joseph Fessia and John Riches, trans. E. Leiva-Merikakis, vol. 1 (San Francisco: Ignatius Press, 2009), 18.

[10]Viladesau, *Theological Aesthetics*, 12-13.

[11]Ibid., 23.

Scripture through this lens means we will be concerned with a theology of beauty and the relationship of beauty to God. This involves recognizing beauty as a quality of divine revelation and a component of theological judgment.[12] It also means that beauty plays a role in our epistemology. We discover and know truth in relation to beauty.

What follows is meant to be an initial step toward a theological aesthetics of marriage and sexuality. No one can say everything that needs to be said, and a single essay is necessarily limited in terms of what it may endeavor to accomplish. The remainder of our time will be given to considering the opening chapters of Genesis and the closing chapters of Revelation, taking the aesthetic elements of the text as an aspect of scriptural revelation that illumines our understanding of marriage and sexuality. My hope is that attention to these matters will allow us to look at contested issues with fresh eyes.

MARRIAGE AND THE BEAUTY OF GOD'S CREATIVE LOVE

We begin with an observation: the opening chapters of Genesis and the closing chapters of Revelation share three common features. Both are set in a garden. Both employ the imagery of a temple as the place of divine dwelling. Both tell the story of a marriage. In Genesis, the man and the woman are wed in Eden where they dwell in the presence of God. In Revelation, the Lamb is wed to his bride and rules from his garden-throne in the new creation where God is at home. We can call this literary structure a canonical *inclusio* (or, with less technical precision, "the Bible's big bookends").[13] The principle of *inclusio* suggests that when we notice similarity at the beginning and the ending of a work, then we should interpret the material in the middle in light of what we find on either end. And if we take the formation of the canon as the work of providence, then we rightly observe these bookends and raise questions about their relation to the rest of the canon. How does the use of nuptial imagery both in the scriptural account of cosmological origins and in the vision of eschatological consummation inform

---

[12]Ibid., 24.
[13]Cf. N. T. Wright, "From Genesis to Revelation: An Anglican Perspective," in *Not Just Good, but Beautiful: The Complementary Relationship Between Man and Woman*, ed. Steven Lopes and Helen Alvaré (Walden, NY: Plough, 2015), 91.

our interpretation of everything else Scripture says with regard to marriage and sex? That is the question that will focus our reflections throughout the rest of this paper.

The unique significance of human beings in relation to the rest of creation is highlighted by multiple features of the text. First, as the creation narrative unfolds, God recognizes six times that the work of his hand is good (Gen 1:4, 10, 12, 18, 21, 25). In Genesis 1:31, after the creation has been crowned with human life, God sees that the work is not merely good but "*very* good" (emphasis added). The presence of human beings increases the goodness of creation as a whole. Second, we have the somewhat monotonous, though occasionally varied, refrain, "And God said, 'Let there be . . .'" (Gen 1:3, 6, 9, 11, 14, 20, 24), which is disrupted in Genesis 1:26 with the alternative, "Then God said, 'Let us make . . .'" as God reflects on his intention to create human beings. We have repeatedly seen divine action; here we discover a level of divine deliberation not earlier present. This deliberation communicates a sense of divine desire and reveals divine intent. Human beings are to be distinguished from the rest of creation in two ways: (1) they are made in the image of God, which is stated in Genesis 1:26 and reiterated twice in Genesis 1:27; (2) they are intended to have dominion or authority over all creation, which is stated in Genesis 1:26 and reiterated in Genesis 1:28-30. While both of these elements are important, I want to focus primarily on the question of the *imago Dei*.

Viladesau would remind us that "God is knowable through word and image *because* and *insofar as* the human being is itself the 'image' of God."[14] Somehow, human beings are designed by God to bear and communicate God's divine image. They are living icons—works of art, we might say—that reveal something of the character of the Creator to the world. Viladesau understands the concept of the *imago Dei* to mean that humanity stands in relation to God as a mirror, a painting, or a sculpture that functions to represent "the form and being of the original reality."[15] The point is that human life was designed by God to communicate the mysterious beauty of God's own life. The question we are presently concerned with is why Genesis develops this revelatory concept of the *imago Dei* by drawing on nuptial imagery. What

---

[14]Viladesau, *Theological Aesthetics*, 90 (italics original).
[15]Ibid.

light is shed on our theological understanding of marriage and sex when we recognize that the image of God is introduced in a context involving gendered complementarity (Gen 1:27) and procreation (Gen 1:28)?

Genesis 1:26-28 sets forth a complementary equality between the male and the female. Both are made in the image of God, and both are given dominion. There is no hint in these verses that either male or female has a greater share in the image than the other or more authority than the other. As far as Genesis 1 is concerned, both image and authority are shared equally by male and female. And yet that very statement carries with it a very specific element of complementarity. One is female; the other is male. They are distinct. They are not the same. The one is not like the other. That which distinguishes the one from the other is their biological and physiological complementarity, highlighted in the text by the command that is also a blessing: "Be fruitful and multiply" (Gen 1:28). So we might say that the image of God is bestowed on humankind in the context of a heterosexual union of two persons equal in dignity and authority. The image is first presented in the context of a marriage. I suggest that God designed the marriage relationship to uniquely reveal something about himself to the world.

As the story moves from Genesis 1 to Genesis 2, it zooms in from the big picture cosmological narrative to the close-up account of those two human beings—one man and one woman. The nuptial imagery becomes more concrete as the man and the woman are brought together and their new relationship is sealed with a covenant. That, after all, is what we get when Adam says, "This at last is bone of my bones and flesh of my flesh" (Gen 2:23). Similar language appears in 2 Samuel 19:12-13 when King David reassures the elders of Judah and Amasa, the commander of his army, by saying, "You are my bone and my flesh" (cf. 2 Sam 19:13). This is an ancient Near Eastern oath of loyalty, and when Adam speaks similar words to Eve, it is the first marriage vow. Despite the risk of anachronism, I suggest he is saying, "I do."

What we find in Genesis 1 and 2 can thus be described as "heterosexual, covenant monogamy." It is heterosexual because there is one *man* and one *woman*. It is monogamous because there is *one* man and *one* woman. It is covenantal because the man has sworn his loyalty to the woman. It is particularly important that marriage is portrayed this way prior to the transgression committed in Genesis 3. Here is marital love as God intended—prior to any of the degrading and damaging consequences of sin—pristine, innocent, beautiful, and intimately interwoven with God's bestowal of the divine image on the human race. This is where our concern with aesthetics becomes increasingly helpful. I take it as a presupposition that the relationship of eternal self-giving and other-oriented love shared among the persons of the God who is triune is inherently beautiful and most beautiful. There is nothing in existence more magnificent in glory, nothing more inherently attractive, than the love that exists eternally between Father, Son, and Holy Spirit. And that God, for some mysterious reason, has chosen to reveal something unique about that inter-Trinitarian love through human marriage. I argue that marriage, and marriage as the context for sexual intimacy, is beautiful because it has been designed to reveal the beauty of eternal divine triune love. Heterosexual covenant monogamy is beautiful because it embodies and magnifies the image of God.

Let me be clear that I am not suggesting that unmarried persons participate in the *imago Dei* to a lesser extent than married persons. Were more space available, it would be worthwhile to show how singleness uniquely reveals and communicates the character of God, though it reveals something different about the character of God than marriage does, and it reveals it differently than marriage does. Both marriage and singleness have dignified and valid roles to play, and I am convinced that we need desperately to recover a robust theology of Christian singleness and chastity. Far too many people have been sold the lies that they must be married to have a full experience of human life and that if they are not having sex, they are not really living. That is profoundly unhelpful, and it has contributed to the mess in which we find ourselves both culturally and ecclesially.

Returning to the relationship between marriage and the divine image, we can make three observations with regard to how heterosexual covenant monogamy reveals and communicates the beauty of the image of God. First, they say first impressions are most important, and the first time we meet God in the pages of Scripture, we discover that he is the Creator. He speaks and worlds come into existence. He utters a word and the world teems with life and vibrancy. Likewise, when the image of God is bestowed on male and female, they are blessed with the command to "be fruitful and multiply, and fill the earth" (Gen 1:28). They are to be cocreators with the Creator, and that happens with the consummation of their covenantal love. When they have sex, another creature who bears the image of the Creator comes into the world. This is the unique property of a heterosexual relationship, and it uniquely magnifies the beauty of God's creative love, even if only by analogy. Kreeft recognizes this when he writes, "As the Spirit proceeds from Father and Son, children proceed from husband and wife, the holy family on Earth manifesting the holy Trinitarian family of heaven, though very imperfectly and obscurely, through a glass darkly."[16] Unlike God they are not able to create ex nihilo. Nevertheless, they have within themselves the gift from God to create new life. In this way, they magnify the beauty of the One who is the author of life.

Second, the complementary equality of the heterosexual union embodies and magnifies the beauty of trinitarian other-oriented love. Our faith in the God who is triune insists that the eternal Creator exists as a unity of differentiated equals. Father, Son, and Spirit are equal in glory, power, majesty, and deity. Nevertheless, the Father is neither Son nor Spirit; the Son is neither Spirit nor Father; the Spirit is neither Father nor Son. They are one in being; they are distinct in person. Drawing on Karl Rahner, Viledesau recognizes that this other-oriented love is an aspect of the *imago Dei* when he writes, "human knowing and loving, which aim at a unity in difference, are the image of God."[17] Likewise, the union of male and female in marriage involves the union of two distinct persons who participate as equals in the image of God and in authority over creation. They are equal in human dignity, yet in heterosexual covenant monogamy the man loves one who is biologically and physiologically distinct from himself, and the woman loves one who is biologically and physiologically distinct from herself. Beth Felker Jones picks up on the aesthetic element when she writes, "Historic Christianity has assumed that marriage and sex bring together—united in one flesh—two sexually differentiated bodies. The fact of that difference is part of the beauty of marriage."[18] The unqualified giving of oneself to another

---

[16]Kreeft, "Lewis's Philosophy of Truth, Goodness, and Beauty," 25. I do not intend to suggest a one-to-one correlation between persons of the Trinity and persons in a human family; the analogy should not be pressed too far.

[17]Viladesau, *Theological Aesthetics*, 91.

[18]Jones, *Faithful*, 34. For an extended analysis of the historic Christian consensus that sexual differentiation is morally significant, see Christopher C. Roberts, *Creation and Covenant: The Significance of Sexual Difference in the Moral Theology of Marriage* (New York: T&T Clark, 2007).

who is clearly and unmistakably different from oneself is part and parcel to an aesthetic account of sex. Marriage is beautiful because it provides a unique opportunity to give oneself to a complementary equal completely and unreservedly. In this way, it represents and magnifies the wonder and glory of eternal triune love.

Third, the covenantal nature of this relationship reveals the beauty of the faithfulness of God. Scripture employs marital imagery to describe God's covenant faithfulness to his people. Consider as one example among many the words of Hosea 2:19-20, "I will take you for my wife forever; I will take you for my wife in righteousness and in justice, in steadfast love, and in mercy. I will take you for my wife in faithfulness; and you shall know the LORD." When God wants to assure his people that he will not turn from them, he reminds them they are his wife, and he will keep his wedding vow. When Adam says to Eve, "bone of my bones and flesh of my flesh" (Gen 2:23), and when husband and wife say "till death us do part," they are taking upon themselves the privilege and the responsibility of embodying for the church and the world the unconditional and unfailing love of God. Again, Jones helpfully makes the point: "The way Christians do—and don't—have sex is anchored in the deepest truth about reality, and it *witnesses to the reality of a God who loves and is faithful to his people.*"[19] The marriage covenant magnifies the beauty of the faithfulness of God. If you want the world to see the unflinching loyalty of God, then sexual intimacy needs to be expressed within the context of the marriage covenant.

These three observations provide us with a framework for reflecting on marital and sexual ethics. If sexual intimacy in the context of heterosexual covenant monogamy is beautiful because it magnifies the beauty of God's creative, self-giving, and faithful love, then sexual practices that fall outside that context have potential to misrepresent or distort that beauty. Consider, for example, two forms of sex that come outside the bounds of the marriage covenant. Adultery is forbidden by God (Ex 20:14) not merely because it is the breaking of a promise but because the promise that is broken was intended to reveal the perfect righteousness and faithfulness of God. Adultery, therefore, distorts the image of God by making God appear unfaithful. It detracts from

---

[19]Jones, *Faithful*, 17 (italics mine).

the beauty of the image of God in humankind. Premarital sex is problematic not because it involves the breaking of a promise (as in the case of adultery) but because it involves the giving of oneself unreservedly to another before the promise and safeguards of the covenant are in place. Some readers may have experienced, and many of us will have known someone who has experienced, the pain and hurt that comes with sex outside the marriage covenant. Sex is an act of self-giving that involves the deepest vulnerability. When you are naked in front of another person, you are vulnerable. They know you. But the covenant makes that vulnerability safe. The covenant creates a context of trust in which two people can be thoroughly transparent with one another without fear. Not long ago I heard a story in the news of a teenage boy who had secretly videotaped a sexual encounter with a girl from his high school. The next day he posted the video on social media, which resulted in immeasurable pain and embarrassment for the young lady. These sorts of stories are now all too common, and they illustrate the horrific potential for suffering when we give ourselves sexually to someone who has not promised to be faithful to us through sickness and in health, poverty and wealth, till death we do part. That is not to say the covenant removes all potential for violation of trust. It obviously does not. It does, however, create a context of trust and safety that does not otherwise exist. So when we teach our children and our church members not to have sex before they are married, it is not because we are being puritanical. It is because there is danger out there. And the beauty of sex in the context of covenantal trust is worth waiting for.

Our aesthetic approach also provides a framework for considering divorce, a problem that plagues American Christianity and one that many pastors struggle to deal with both from the pulpit and in settings of pastoral counseling. Divorce is problematic because when we break the covenant by ending it prematurely, we distort the beauty of the image of God revealed through marriage. We are in effect saying that our God is not faithful to his promises. While divorce is never desirable, it is sometimes permitted in Scripture (see Mt 19:8). The problem among many evangelicals is that we have looked far too lightly on divorce for convenience's sake and, as a result, have damaged our witness with regard to marriage and sexuality. The world does not take us seriously on matters of sexual ethics because we have been far, far too accepting of divorce.

When we consider the ethics of same-sex practices, we can draw on those aspects of our framework that involve biological and physiological complementarity as a means for revealing the self-giving and other-oriented love of the triune persons. If sexual differentiation as male and female tells us something about the other-oriented love of the Trinity, then abandoning that differentiation in favor of same-sex practices distorts the image of God because it portrays God as giving himself to one like himself rather than to one who is different. When the physiologically differentiated marriage partner is exchanged for one who is physiologically identical, the clarity of other-oriented love is lost and replaced by the picture of a being that gives itself to pursuing one like itself. The image of God that is revealed is not that of the trinitarian God who gives himself in love to the other, but of a god who narcissistically pursues one like himself. Furthermore, if procreation embodies and magnifies the beauty of God's creating love, then same-sex practices, which are inherently incapable of reproduction, fail to portray the life-creating beauty of the Creator God. The same-sex relation is fundamentally unable to participate in the cocreative beauty of the image of God bestowed on humankind.

I hope it is increasingly clear that we need a theology of marriage and sex that accounts for the beauty of the image of God that is bound up with the union of male and female in the covenant of marriage. The question that must be asked is this: To what sort of god does our sexuality point? A self-oriented god? A god who breaks his promise? A god with whom we cannot be safe? Or does our sexuality point to a God who always keeps his promises, no matter how hard and no matter what is required? Does it point to a God who gives himself in love to a true other who is clearly distinct? Do our sexual practices point the world to a God who can always be trusted with our vulnerabilities? What does the way we use our sexuality say about the God we serve?

MARRIAGE AND THE BEAUTY OF GOD'S NEW-CREATIONAL LOVE

Given the importance of nuptial imagery in the creation narrative at the beginning of the canon, similar imagery in the new-creation narrative at the end of the canon should not come as a surprise.[20] John's vision of the

---

[20]Wright, "Genesis to Revelation," 89.

new heaven and the new earth begins in Revelation 21:1-2 with the new Jerusalem being described as "a bride adorned for her husband." As the vision proceeds, John is invited to come and see "the bride, the wife of the Lamb" (Rev 21:9). One of my favorite features of this text comes in the next verse where the image transitions from bride to city, which we might have been expecting given the joining of those two images in Revelation 21:2. The point is that a single image is not enough to communicate the profound and striking reality that John sees and hopes to describe, and so he moves back and forth between images.[21] The bride is the city, and the city is the bride. And the city-bride is almost indescribably beautiful: "It has the glory of God and a radiance like a very rare jewel" (Rev 21:11). Apparently John found it difficult to settle on a single jewel, so he mentions several of them. The city-bride is constructed with a variety of precious stones, with pearls and precious metals. The streets are even made of gold. And as the narrative proceeds, we find that there is no temple in the city. As it turns out, the city itself is a temple shaped like a massive holy of holies. And God dwells there physically manifest in the figure of the Lamb. Folk religion has all too often portrayed this city as a destination, as the place where the saints will dwell in glory. But we must remember that the city is the temple, and the city is the bride, the wife of the Lamb. The Lamb is not betrothed to a city in which his church will dwell. The Lamb will be married to the city that is the bride that is his beloved church. The city is not an image of the final home of the saints. The city is itself an image that portrays the beauty of the church in her eschatological glory.[22] We will not walk on streets of gold; we are the streets of gold. And here's the point: John spares no effort in attempting to describe the indescribable beauty of the eschatologically perfected church, and the language of marriage is at the heart of his account. The church is the bride prepared for her groom who is the Lamb, the Son of God, the Christ, Jesus our Lord. What we find in Revelation 21–22 is a vision of our hope that Christ will take us—his people—to himself perfected in every glory and loveliness, without spot or stain or blemish, radiant in beauty.

---

[21]Cf. Robert M. Mullholland, *Revelation*, Cornerstone Biblical Commentary (Carol Stream, IL: Tyndale House, 2011), 587.
[22]Ibid.

If nuptial imagery is interwoven into the vision of Christ's eschatological union with his church, then what does that do to our understanding of marriage in the present?[23] I suggest that marriage functions as a signpost pointing the world forward to the consummation of God's redemptive purposes. Marriage embodies and magnifies the love of God that is committed to new creation, the redemptive love that Christ has for his church. And our findings in Genesis 1 and 2 resonate with what we find in Revelation 21 and 22. The Lamb and his bride are distinct and complementary. One is redeemer, and the other is the redeemed. The one is not the other, and the two must not be confused. The vision also reinforces the unfailing love of God for his people. He will bring salvation to its consummation. The object of the Lamb's marital love is exclusively his church. She is the one he takes to himself. Once again, then, heterosexual covenant monogamy is the fitting relationship to image the other-oriented, unfailing, and single-hearted love of Christ for his church. And to distort that relationship at any of those points is to distort the new-creational and redemptive love of God in Christ to which the relationship points. If the marriage vow ends in divorce, does it not incorrectly suggest that Christ may not keep his promise to his people? If we are not singly devoted to our spouse, do we not falsely portray Christ as one who would run headlong after other lovers? If there is no clear physiological complementarity to marriage, does it not suggest that Christ might go looking for one like himself rather than the other that is his church? Marriage, and sex within marriage, is beautiful when it points the world forward to the consummation of new creation and to the wedding supper of the Lamb. The question we must ask ourselves in particular—and ask the church in general—is whether our marital and sexual practices point forward to the coming reality of heaven and earth wed together, and to the glory of the beauty of the new creation. Do our marriages embody the beauty of the story told in Revelation 21–22? Do they point the world to the wedding supper of the Lamb?

BUILDING ON THE FRAMEWORK

Given our findings to this point, we return to the overall question governing the essay: What makes sex beautiful? My argument is that sex derives its

---

[23]The contrast between the city-bride and the prostitute in Rev 17:1 may shed further light on our questions, though it is beyond the scope of the present essay.

beauty from the marriage relationship, which is designed by God to uniquely embody and magnify his creative and redemptive love. When sex is celebrated in the context of that relationship and as its consummative act, it magnifies the beauty of the triune God. When it moves beyond the boundaries of that relationship, it begins to misrepresent the beauty of God. These conclusions emerge from our analysis of the opening and closing chapters of the canon, but there remain many passages in between that deal further with marriage and sexuality. The task of interpreting those texts must wait for another day. Nevertheless, it is worth taking a moment to point the way forward. What light would be shed on other biblical texts related to human sexuality by considering them through the framework we have constructed today? Does it help us better interpret difficult texts in the Old Testament? Does it aid us in understanding Jesus' indication that there will be no marriage at the resurrection? Does this approach shed light on Paul's understanding of marriage in relation to Christ's love for the church? I am hopeful that the framework I have offered will help us read these and other texts in a way that celebrates a positive vision of marriage and sex.

As we bring our thoughts together, I want to draw our attention to a distinction made by C. S. Lewis in his essay "Meditation in a Toolshed." Upon entrance into a dim shed, Lewis recounts how he noticed a beam of sunlight shining through a crack in the top of the door. You may have had a similar experience of standing in the dark and looking at a beam of light. You see specks of dust floating about in the light while the room all around is completely dark. At this point, Lewis recognizes that this initial experience involves looking at the light. But then he moved so that the beam fell upon his eyes, and in that moment he saw things altogether differently. "Instantly," he writes, "the whole previous picture vanished. I saw no toolshed and (above all) no beam. Instead I saw, framed in the irregular cranny at the top of the door, green leaves moving on the branches of a tree outside and beyond that, 90 odd million miles away, the sun."[24] He is no longer looking *at* the beam; he is looking *along* it. And he finds that these are two strikingly different experiences. For Lewis, this is a simple example of the difference between a young man looking at a young lady and falling head over heels for her only

---

[24]C. S. Lewis, "Meditation in a Toolshed," in *God in the Dock*, ed. Walter Hooper (Grand Rapids: Eerdmans, 1970), 212.

to have a scientist demystify the experience by pointing to the biological factors and stimuli involved in the whole matter. When we look *at* a thing, we get analysis. When we look *along* it, we discover an aesthetic.

When we look *at* a thing that is designed to be looked *along* toward something else, we can easily lose sight of that first thing's true beauty. I am concerned that this is what we have done with marriage. We have looked straight at marriage and made logical and moral arguments aplenty, but we have forgotten to look along the relationship for the beauty to which it points. We have done the analysis and neglected the aesthetic. We have become so caught up in defending marriage against aberrant alternatives and become so focused on the thing itself that we have forgotten it was designed to point beyond itself to the beauty of the glory of the creative and redemptive love of the God who is triune. We stand at a point where we need desperately to recover the ability to look along. And when we do, we will be more equipped and more able not only to defend but to enjoy and magnify the beauty of marriage and human sexuality as God designed.

List of Contributors

Daniel J. Brendsel (PhD, Wheaton College) is minister of college and 20s life and adult education and director of the Mission Training Academy at Grace Church of DuPage in Warrenville, Illinois. He is coauthor of *An Interpretive Lexicon of New Testament Greek* and author of *"Isaiah Saw His Glory": The Use of Isaiah 52–53 in John 12*.

Denny Burk (PhD, The Southern Baptist Theological Seminary) is professor of biblical studies at Boyce College in Louisville, Kentucky. He serves as associate pastor at Kenwood Baptist Church and as president of the Council on Biblical Manhood & Womanhood. He is the author of *Transforming Homosexuality* (P&R, 2015) and *What Is the Meaning of Sex?* (Crossway, 2013). He writes a daily commentary on theology, politics, and culture at DennyBurk.com.

Gerald Hiestand (PhD candidate in Classical Studies, University of Reading) is senior associate pastor at Calvary Memorial Church in Oak Park, Illinois, and the cofounder and director of the Center for Pastor Theologians. He is the coauthor of *The Pastor Theologian: Resurrecting an Ancient Vision* (Zondervan, 2015) and coeditor of *Becoming a Pastor Theologian: New Possibilities for Church Leadership* (IVP Academic, 2016).

Wesley Hill (PhD, Durham University) is assistant professor of biblical studies at Trinity School for Ministry in Ambridge, Pennsylvania. He is the author of *Washed and Waiting: Reflections on Christian Faithfulness and Homosexuality* (Zondervan, second edition 2016), *Paul and the Trinity: Persons, Relations, and the Pauline Letters* (Eerdmans, 2015), and *Spiritual Friendship: Finding Love in the Church as a Celibate Gay Christian* (Brazos, 2015).

Beth Felker Jones (PhD, Duke University) is professor of theology at Wheaton College in Wheaton, Illinois, where she lives with her husband and four children. She is the author of a number of books, including *Faithful: A Theology of Sex* and *Practicing Chri stian Doctrine: An Introduction to Thinking and Living Theologically*.

Matthew Levering (PhD, Boston College) is James N. and Mary D. Perry Jr. Chair of Theology at Mundelein Seminary. He is the author or editor of over thirty books, including *Biblical Natural Law* and *The Betrayal of Charity*. He is the cofounder of the Chicago Theological Initiative and has been an active participant in Evangelicals and Catholics Together since 2004.

Matthew Mason (PhD candidate in Divinity, University of Aberdeen) is rector of Christ Church Salisbury, UK, and a fellow of the Center for Pastor Theologians. He is the content editor for the *Bulletin of Ecclesial Theology*.

Matthew J. Milliner (PhD, Princeton University) is associate professor of art history at Wheaton College and catechist at All Souls Anglican Church in Wheaton, Illinois.

Richard Mouw (PhD, University of Chicago) is president emeritus of Fuller Theological Seminary, where he presently serves as professor of faith and public life. He is a columnist for Religion News Service and a member of the advisory board of the Center for Pastor Theologians.

Matt O'Reilly (PhD, University of Gloucestershire) is pastor at St. Mark United Methodist Church in Mobile, Alabama, a fellow of the Center for Pastor Theologians, and an adjunct member of the faculties of Asbury Theological Seminary and Wesley Biblical Seminary. He writes regularly at mattoreilly.net.

Amy Peeler (PhD, Princeton Theological Seminary) is associate professor of New Testament at Wheaton College and associate rector at St. Mark's Episcopal Church, Geneva, Illinois. She is author of *"You Are My Son": The Family of God in the Epistle to the Hebrews* (T&T Clark, 2014).

Jeremy Treat (PhD, Wheaton College) is pastor for preaching and vision at Reality LA and adjunct professor of theology at Biola University. He is the author of *The Crucified King: Atonement and Kingdom in Biblical and Systematic Theology* (Zondervan, 2014).

Joel Willitts (PhD, Cambridge University) is professor in the Biblical and Theological Studies Department at North Park University in Chicago, Illinois. In addition to scholarly works on the Jewish context of the New Testament, he writes about the struggle to live an openhearted life as a survivor of childhood sexual trauma on his blog at joelwillitts.com.

Todd Wilson (PhD, Cambridge University) is the senior pastor of Calvary Memorial Church in Oak Park, Illinois, and the cofounder and chairman of the Center for Pastor Theologians. Todd is the author or editor of a number of books, including *Real Christian: Bearing the Marks of Authentic Faith* and *Mere Sexuality: Rediscovering the Christian Vision of Sexuality.*

Name Index

Subject Index

Scripture Index

CENTER FOR
PASTOR THEOLOGIANS

The Center for Pastor Theologians (CPT) is an evangelical organization dedicated to assisting pastors in the study and written production of biblical and theological scholarship for the ecclesial renewal of theology and the theological renewal of the church. The CPT believes that the contemporary bifurcation between the pastoral calling and theological formation has resulted in the loss of a distinctly ecclesial voice in contemporary theology. It seeks to resurrect this voice. Led by the conviction that pastors can—indeed must—once again serve as the church's most important theologians, it is the aim of the CPT to provide a context of theological engagement for those pastors who desire to make ongoing contributions to the wider theological and scholarly community for the renewal of both theology and the church.

Toward this end, the CPT focuses on three key initiatives: our pastor theologian fellowships, our *Bulletin of Ecclesial Theology*, and our annual conference. For more information, visit pastortheologians.com.

Finding the Textbook You Need

The IVP Academic Textbook Selector
is an online tool for instantly finding the IVP books
suitable for over 250 courses across 24 disciplines.

---

ivpacademic.com
